COURAGE, RESISTANCE, AND \

INTER-AMERICA SERIES / EDITED BY HOWARD CAMPBELL, DUNCAN EARLE, AND JOHN PETERSON

In the new "Inter-American" epoch to come, our borderland zones may expand well past the confines of geopolitical lines. Social knowledge of these dynamic interfaces offers rich insights into the pressing and complex issues that affect both the borderlands and beyond. The Inter-America Series comprises a wide interdisciplinary range of cutting-edge books that explicitly or implicitly enlist border issues to discuss larger concepts, perspectives, and theories from the "borderland" vantage and will be appropriate for the classroom, the library, and the wider reading public.

COURAGE, RESISTANCE, AND WOMEN IN CIUDAD JUÁREZ

Challenges to Militarization

BY KATHLEEN STAUDT AND ZULMA Y. MÉNDEZ

UNIVERSITY OF TEXAS PRESS *Austin*

Requests for permission to reproduce material from this work should be sent to:
    Permissions
    University of Texas Press
    P.O. Box 7819
    Austin, TX 78713-7819
    http://utpress.utexas.edu/index.php/rp-form

♾ The paper used in this book meets the minimum requirements
of ANSI/NISO Z39.48-1992 (R1997) (Permanence of Paper).

LIBRARY OF CONGRESS CATALOGING-IN-PUBLICATION DATA

Staudt, Kathleen A.
    Courage, resistance, and women in Ciudad Juárez : challenges to
militarization / by Kathleen Staudt and Zulma Y. Méndez. — First edition.
        pages   cm. — (Inter-America series)
    Includes bibliographical references and index.
    ISBN 978-0-292-76087-5 (cloth : alk. paper) — ISBN 978-0-292-76358-6
(pbk. : alk. paper)
    1. Violence—Mexico—Ciudad Juárez.   2. Social movements—Mexico—Ciudad
Juárez.   3. Women—Political activity—Mexico—Ciudad Juárez.   4. Women—
Violence against—Mexico—Ciudad Juárez.   5. Militarism—Mexico—Ciudad
Juárez.   6. Human rights—Mexico—Ciudad Juárez.   I. Méndez, Zulma Y.
II. Title.
    HN120.C48S73   2015
    305.420972—dc23
                                                                2014017673

doi:10.7560/760875

TO MOSI AND ASHA, SON AND DAUGHTER. — KS
PARA LA RESISTENCIA JUARENSE. — ZYM

PARA QUE LAS PERSONAS Y LAS MUERTES NUNCA
MÁS SEAN UN "DAÑO COLATERAL."
SO THAT PEOPLE'S DEATHS ARE NEVER AGAIN
CALLED "COLLATERAL DAMAGE."

CONTENTS

OUR JOURNEYS TOWARD completion of this book have been long, but exciting and meaningful. We became friends and colleagues back in the 1990s, and our pathways crossed sporadically at various times when we came into constant contact in the EdD program at the University of Texas at El Paso, each of us from a different disciplinary background— political science and education—yet active researchers in interdisciplinary ways and learning from our transnational border: the place and its people. We are fortunate to live and teach here in El Paso now and to draw inspiration from the borderlands community and its receptivity to academics who have one foot in the scholarly world and the other in the world of action. Kathleen (Kathy) arrived at the border in 1977 as someone who specialized in comparative politics, within the political science discipline, with a focus on women and gender. At the University of Wisconsin, where she received her PhD, she was fortunate to enroll in several classes taught by James Scott before he moved to Yale University. At the border, Kathy's research designs have often used a comparative approach, advancing concepts and theory with insights from border space—this "in-between" place, as it has been termed by various border theorists. However, in recent years, her books have aimed to craft border theory out of the hybridized realities of border places, which expand toward mainstream societies with the spread of the less-visible borders of identity and the enforcement of, for example, immigration laws.

Zulma, a *fronteriza*, grew up in Ciudad Juárez but has been a commuter of the Juárez–El Paso border for most of her life. She has taught both at the Universidad Autónoma de Ciudad Juárez and at the University of Texas at El Paso; currently, she teaches at El Colegio de Chihuahua in Ciudad Juárez. As a scholar in the field of education, her work is concerned with questions of policy and curriculum reform. Employing what are known as the "untutored means" of ethnographic approaches to the study of education that she learned from her professors and mentors Reba Page (at the University of California, Riverside) and Alejandro Lugo (formerly at the University of Texas at El Paso, now at the University of Illinois at Urbana-Champaign), Zulma analyzes and writes here on the activism that she has witnessed—and practiced—over the course of her life in various human rights organizations in Ciudad Juárez.

Each of us would like to thank people and organizations that opened doors of insight and participation to us. We also thank the reviewers of this manuscript for their close reading, perceptive insights, and suggestions. Zulma begins.

Subcomandante Marcos of the Ejército Zapatista de Liberación Nacional once said (paraphrasing Heidegger) that when danger arises, what saves also surfaces. During the last years, filled with adversity and challenges for activists and citizens in Ciudad Juárez, my colleagues in Grupo de Articulación Justicia en Juárez and in Movimiento Pacto por la Cultura have been an everlasting source of wisdom, strength, inspiration, and hope. *Gracias, compañeros y compañeras.* Special recognition goes to my dear friends Willivaldo Delgadillo Fabela, Imelda Marrufo Nava, Kerry Doyle, Emilia González Tercero, and Verónica Corchado. In the moments of despair and difficulty, as well as those of sheer happiness, they are what saves.

Much gratitude to my colleagues and students at UTEP's Department of Educational Leadership and Foundations; the years I shared with them were crucial in my growth and learning. I am indebted to the Center for Inter-American and Border Studies, especially to former director María Socorro Tabuenca Córdoba and to Interim Director Sandra Garabano. Their generosity and support facilitated much of my work on this book.

Siempre, in the ups and downs of life, I know I can count on the love and company of my father, Ramón Méndez Chaparro, and the wit and wisdom of my brother, Ramón César Méndez Villanueva. I am forever grateful for their existence. Renato A. Díaz is my best friend and beloved partner. *Gracias por lo compartido.*

Kathy continues, with thanks to Irasema Coronado for her friendship, coauthorships (especially in *Fronteras No Más: Toward Social Justice at the U.S.–Mexico Border* [2002], the first book to focus on cross-border organizing), and leadership in the binational Coalition against Violence toward Women and Families at the U.S.–Mexico Border, in which we both participated. I also appreciate the friendship and scholarly collaboration of Mexican politics specialist Tony Payan, social work academic-activist Mark Lusk, and Gregory Rocha, whose expertise in local politics surpasses all.

I value the experience and training I received from people in the real world of politics, from feminist mentor and President Carter political appointee Arvonne Fraser, augmenting and enriching my political science PhD and introducing me into a coworker relationship with pioneering feminist political scientist Jane Jaquette in the late 1970s, to the various organizers and leaders in the local affiliates of the Industrial Areas Foundation, with its lengthy track record of community organizing and relational work. Thank you Kevin Courtney, Tara Pérez, Arturo Aguila, and Rabbi Larry Bach! Other faith-based leaders "practice what they preach" in social-justice work, besides Rabbi Bach. Among them, I thank the Reverend John Nelsen, Father Pablo Matta, Rubén García, Monsignor/Father Arturo Bañuelas, the Reverend Katie Houts, and Pastor Wayne Kendrick. I was amazed at the El Paso City Council's leadership on the border exercised in 2009 and 2010 and was honored to work with some of its representatives as well as UTEP scholar-leaders in the huge Global Public Policy Forum on the War on Drugs conference in 2009 (http://warondrugsconference.utep.edu); I value the opportunity I had to work with Linda Corchado and the follow-up leadership that historian Oscar Martínez provided to these efforts.

For their journalistic efforts that go above and beyond covering Juárez as a place of doom, I thank Sito Negrón for his coverage of the U.S. drug war and Kent Paterson, of Frontera North-South News, Laura Carlsen, Mexico City–based editor of the Center for International Programs' Americas Program, and even some distant mainstream journalists who kept the tragedy of women's murders alive and visible despite their eclipse by the huge increase in homicide in Ciudad Juárez.

Finally, though, I am grateful for the opportunity for friendship and coauthorship with Zulma Méndez. Zulma brings the nuanced, deep understanding and broker capabilities that so fully enrich this book and its contents. We complement one another in this border space: the largest metropolitan region through which a territorial borderline runs, the epicenter of violence during what many in both countries call the "absurd" drug wars, and now, importantly, the new epicenter of grassroots organizing that inspires mainstream Mexico, transnational activists, and civil-society counterparts on the U.S. side of the border.

As a humble gesture of our gratitude and solidarity for the work that Juarense human rights activists undertake with great risk to their lives, we are donating the royalties that this volume might generate to the Centro de Derechos Humanos Paso del Norte, A.C. Led by Father Oscar Enríquez, and sustained with the unrelenting efforts of nuns and other women who mostly volunteer their time and work, this human rights advocacy center offers its services, free of charge, to those who knock on its door. Illegally raided by federal police officers, who broke in and caused damage to its facilities and computer systems, the center has continued to denounce human rights abuses and took the first documented case of forced disappearance during the presidency of Felipe Calderón (who is now a fellow at Harvard University) to the Inter-American Court of Human Rights.

COURAGE, RESISTANCE, AND WOMEN IN CIUDAD JUÁREZ

INTRODUCTION: CONCEPTUALIZING COURAGE AND RESISTANCE IN A MIRED HUMAN RIGHTS CONTEXT

It is important to document and keep records of violations. We commend you. Also, we invite you to document ways you have resisted . . .
NORA CORTIÑAS, JUROR, PERMANENT PEOPLES' TRIBUNAL, MAY 2012, CIUDAD JUÁREZ

THE MEXICAN AND U.S. drug wars have wreaked havoc on Mexico, where at least 60,000 and as many as 120,000 people have been murdered since 2006 at the hands of organized criminals, drug traffickers, and law enforcement officials in the context of the so-called war on drugs.[1] Both governments have responded with policies that militarize the conflict: Mexico since President Felipe Calderón (2006–2012), with its *guerra contra el narcotrafico*, also known as the *guerra contra las drogas*, and the United States, with its forty-year-old drug war, immigration control, and antiterrorism efforts. Such solutions have aggravated violence in various parts of Mexico, but pressure has been building for social investment, with new casts of political characters and courageous resistance among civil-society activists to militarization despite an atmosphere of fear and intimidation.

In this book, we examine civil-society activism in the borderlands—what some have called *la Resistencia Juarense* (the Juarense Resistance)—in the first decade of the twenty-first century. Ciudad Juárez, its population once hovering at 2 million people and now counted as 1.3 million, according to Mexico's census (INEGI 2010), is part of a transnational metropolitan community that includes El Paso, Texas, with its population of nearly 800,000 people, thereby creating a space historically known as the Paso del Norte region of more than 2 million people. Ciudad Juárez has been the border center point and ground zero for the violence of the drug war, with annual, always-contested murder rates that rose from over 400 in 2007 to approximately 1,600 in 2008, 2,600 in 2009, 3,100 in 2010, and back down to below the 2008 rate in 2011 until murders spread elsewhere, especially to northeastern Mexico, and sloped downward in Ciudad Juárez through 2013 (see chapter 3 for figures).[2] Although there is a long history of mobilization in Ciudad Juárez, the gender-based violence—specifically what in Mexico is called the *feminicidio* ("femicide," a contested term)[3]—that began in the 1990s instigated a vigorous activism that previewed and alerted people to the huge growth in violence that ultimately occurred when officials failed to cleanse law enforcement institutions, which operate with almost-total impunity.

Ciudad Juárez is also Mexico's ground zero center point for organizing and activism against the militarization. The second stage of anti-femicide activism—about which we provide analysis in the following chapter—joined anti-militarization forces to provide a gendered counternarrative to the official narratives during the Calderón administration. Like Juarense activists, we frequently use the term "gender," which highlights the social construction of and visibility of women and men, rather than the burial of women in overall figures or analyses of reality—an analytic burial ground so common for centuries. Javier Sicilia, of the national Movimiento por la Paz con Justicia y Dignidad (Movement for Peace with Justice and Dignity), organized a caravan to the central border region twice, including on his trip from West to East Coast in the United States (as we analyze in chapter 6). Thus, the Paso del Norte region has also become a center space for activism, and increasingly cross-border civil-society activism, with its triumphs and its challenges.

This introductory chapter is divided into several parts. First we propose a reframing of the U.S.–Mexico borderlands with analyses of social movements during this era of personal and electronic networking. Then we provide the focus of the book: everyday organizing at the border as it connects with transnational organizing. After that, we take some time and space to elaborate on our research methods and then on the theoretical impulses that we hope to advance in the book. To close, we provide an outline of chapters.

REFRAMING THE U.S.–MEXICO BORDERLANDS

Historically, the borderlands have been framed in state-centric ways, focusing on the relative ease of trade and/or immigration controls (see

Payan 2006 for periodization). Yet others treat the two sides of the borderline—the borderlands—as interdependent regions (Martínez 1994; Staudt, Fuentes, and Monárrez Fragoso 2010) of hybridity (Anzaldúa 1987; García-Canclini 1995), including hybridized educational practices (Rippberger and Staudt 2003) in a regional zone of "inspection" and control (Lugo 2008), drug wars (Campbell 2009), and cross-border activism (Staudt and Coronado 2002). Some border theorists, increasingly utilizing interdisciplinary and anthropological approaches, ask whether the border region is a hybrid region (Heyman 2012) or a polarized one, with each side treating the "other" side in distancing ways (Vila 2000, 2005; on "othering," see Bhabha 1994). In this book, we consider that theoretical question—hybridized or polarized?—with regard to civil-society activism in the central, iconic border region of Ciudad Juárez–El Paso, the largest transnational metropolitan region in the world. Gloria Anzaldúa and others have written that the border zone of 14 million people in counties and *municipios*, according to the censuses of both countries (Staudt and Coronado 2002: chap. 1), represents a special, hybrid place of both conflicting and blending tendencies, what Susan Rippberger and Staudt call morphing (2003) in the complex political socialization that not only constructs public schools and nationalist identities imposed upon students but also reflects the interdependence of the region (see Heyman 2012 on the theoretical overview).

More recently, journalists and essayists have framed and represented the border as a place of chaos, violence, and mayhem, implying a future of hopelessness (for examples, see, among many, Bowden 1998, 2010; Poppa 2010; Rodríguez 2012; Vulliamy 2010; Washington Valdez 2005) in a "failed state" (Grayson 2009). Gendered social constructions overlay some of the framing. In particular, Rosa-Linda Fregoso uses the word "voyeur" for Charles Bowden, with his "racist and colonialist gaze."[4] Nevertheless, economic boosters, such as the organizers of events like Juárez Competitiva 2011 with transnational business-oriented groups, as we develop in the next chapter, continue to tout the size and competitiveness of the border area for secure global manufacturing investments (but see Lugo 2008 and selections in Staudt, Fuentes, and Monárrez Fragoso 2010). The global neoliberal economic agenda shrouds the transnational border region, as does an increasingly militarized war-on-drugs approach that wreaks havoc on the borderlands (see selections in Payan, Staudt, and Kruszewski 2013).

In our book, we reframe the border and while acknowledging its complexities in the militarization of both Mexican and U.S. govern-

ment policies, focus on civil-society activists who resist this militarization and tenuously (though at times uneasily) weave together anti-
femicide and anti-militarization social forces toward a conglomeration
of peace and justice movements. Activists have fostered not only close
cross-border solidarity in faith-based action and even an electoral campaign, but also distant transnational activism in the Permanent Peoples'
Tribunal, in which moral authorities from around the world held the
Mexican government to account, deliberately launched in Ciudad
Juárez. Civil-society activists do their work through interlocking relationships augmented with Facebook and Twitter in social and electronic networks with multiple names. Egregious cases of violence—
whether those responsible are officials or organized criminals—have
triggered game-changing shifts in perception about state militarization.
By "game changing," we mean dramatic shifts in organizational strategy
that emerge from the public delegitimization of official discourses (further elaborated in chapter 3).[5] Local Juarense activists network with
activists elsewhere, especially in Mexico City, Latin America, and
Europe, but also with activists on the U.S. side of the border, some of
whom work in solidarity with colleagues and others of whom disseminate the doom and gloom of mainstream media–framed messages. Anti-
militarization as well as anti-femicide activists maneuver courageously
in a country dubbed the most dangerous place for journalists and activists. In fact, UNESCO urged Mexico to approve legislation that would
provide protective mechanisms for journalists and human rights activists (UNESCO 2012; also see CPJ 2010). Within the media, however, one
finds both courage and complicity with government and/or organized
crime, whether from threats or rewards. One sometimes hears that parts
of the media can be "extortionists" in their decisions about what to publish and how to frame the stories, as media owners are always careful
of maintaining their highly lucrative contracts for publicity from local,
state, and federal agencies. Our focus in this book, however, is on local
to transnational civil-society organizing activities.

EVERYDAY ORGANIZING AS IT CONNECTS
WITH TRANSNATIONAL FORCES

We begin the book with conceptualizations of civil-society activism.
We view civil society, at its most basic level, as independent of the state
and of the private sphere of familial relationships. Yet we recognize that
conceptions of civil society vary in many nations and even in border-

lands where the state and nation may merge in muddied ways. European border theorists Liam O'Dowd and Bohdana Dimitrovova (2011) note the different Eastern and Western conceptions of civil society that, while viewed in relation to the state, mean different things in states with more or less attention to the "rule of law" and with higher or lower levels of distrust in society and in connection with the state. One thread in our book involves consideration of whether U.S. and Mexican conceptions of civil society at the border are similar or not, given different state structures. Moreover, we consider the tensions that exist when the idealized independence of civil society becomes, in practice, less autonomous, with registration, tax-exempt legal status, and subsidies from government, whether observed in the U.S. women's movement of the 1970s (Staudt 2008: chap. 5), international nongovernmental organizations (Korten 1990; Alvarez 1998), or organizations struggling to decide whether to apply for government grants in the violence of Ciudad Juárez during the Calderón administration (Doyle 2011a).

Our analysis of resistance draws on political anthropologist James Scott's writings about everyday forms of resistance, including artful resistance, and the "hidden and official transcripts" that shape people's lives (1990). By "resistance," we mean conscious actions that challenge, reject, or strategically ignore official discourse and its legitimation discourse. Guided also by Sidney Tarrow's analysis of political opportunity structures (1998), we consider the ever-dynamic and ever-changing opportunities in the contexts of national governments in the borderlands and in the shifting contexts where once-marginalized mothers, feminists, and human rights activists began to interface with anti-militarization activists toward a more gender-balanced struggle to reclaim civil-society space amid an atmosphere of fear and intimidation.

Peace and justice activists do their work using social technology, particularly Facebook, Twitter, and listservs, in addition to traditional face-to-face organizing, activism, marches, and rallies. Strong activist ties, we expect, require *personal* relationships of trust. Long before journalists coined the phrase "Arab Spring," Juarense activists used similar techniques to open up, challenge, and create counternarratives, albeit in a country that calls itself a democracy, unlike the dictatorships that fell during the Arab Spring. We draw also on human rights theorists in international studies (particularly Thomas Risse, Stephen Ropp, and Kathryn Sikkink 1999) who posit the ways that local activists draw on transnational activists and that institutions and the media bring leverage and alliances with media, international institutions, and other governments and thereby create a "boomerang" effect on their national governments (ideally) to negotiate and acquire responsiveness. Yet we know that U.S. drug-war priorities undermine or prolong such negotiations (Staudt, 2014).

In the United States, human rights challenges to officials frequently gain little traction (Soohoo, Albira, and Davis 2007) compared with the hegemonic version of border security that aims to control the border and the flow of drugs and immigrants. Moreover, the exponential growth in alternative media may or may not complement the mainstream media and its decision-maker readers, who presumably operate in the official spheres. For the boomerang effect to occur, media coverage is required, particularly mainstream media coverage, to expand awareness in the wider public and to generate organized constituencies that engage with decision makers to make policy and legal changes, perhaps with a new cast of characters elected to public office.

KEY QUESTIONS

Throughout this book, we ask and explore several key questions:

1. When and how do the hidden and official transcripts become "public," exposing the problematic nature of the so-called war on drugs, with its militarization and violence? What has been the role of women's activism in exposing these transcripts, and how does this form of resistance put women at the forefront, provoking resistance as "game changers" in the adverse context of Ciudad Juárez and overall contemporary activism? What is the role of U.S. and other transnational activists in supporting and extending awareness of women's "public transcripts" and with what import for the attainment of justice?
2. How are coalitions and alliances formed among activists whose agendas have at times clashed? Most particularly, how do the anti-femicide activists come to make alliances with the anti-militarization movement?
3. How do the seemingly disparate agendas of transnational business elites resonate with grassroots activists? Acknowledging diversity among both elites and grassroots people, what sorts of divisions exist within elite and grassroots[6] groups?

Civil-society activism in the borderlands offers the potential to analyze binational and transnational organizations—including the efforts associated with the decision of the Inter-American Court of Human Rights in the Campo Algodonero (cotton field, located in Ciudad Juárez) case that held the Mexican state responsible for three young women's murders and that mandated detailed policy and institutional changes— that operate in very different political opportunity structures of two sovereign governments, Mexico and the United States. We analyze the connections, disconnections, and different strategies that justice activists pursue. We further illustrate our analysis with the use of photographs and other kinds of images, also widely employed by activists to document their actions in this age of widespread access to cell phones, digital cameras, tablets, and laptops.

RESEARCH METHODS

The methodology for this book relies on our participant observation as both scholars and activists, conversations with fellow activists, and the in-depth interpretative analysis involved in ethnography. As Edward Schatz conveys with the subtitle of his book *Political Ethnography: What Immersion Contributes to the Study of Power* (2009), we are immersed in border civil-society institutional spaces. We are scholar-activists who have lived, taught, and worked in the borderlands for a combined total of sixty adult years. In an additional contribution to qualitative analysis, our book discusses the approach to "knowing" that activism brings to analysis. Each substantive chapter in the book uses case-study vignettes from both sides of the U.S.–Mexico border that are vividly and "thickly" portrayed and analyzed, in ethnographic tradition.

The sources for our ethnographic analysis are cases, public performance events, documents, the media in print and electronic form (so important in international human rights theorizing and activism), and public elections. Our vignettes describe the valiant game-changer women and mothers who have defied official transcripts, and we analyze messages in large listservs that offer (sometimes gendered) regular body counts—a type of border activism that feeds the frenzy of militarization by polarizing and reinforcing borderlines for the United States, pointing at the "other" side, where violence and mayhem reign, as the "laboratory of the future" (Bowden 1998).

Moreover, we offer analysis of a primary-election struggle in El Paso between U.S. Democratic Party congressional candidates, representing two contrasting visions of the border: militarization versus trade. Finally, we examine several events that illustrate contemporary civil-society activism: one, focused on transnational court-like tribunals, with global precedents in country-specific locations, and another, a faith-grounded effort toward cross-border solidarity illustrating the changing public face of some segments of the Catholic Church at the border and its display/performance of syncretic indigenous and religious symbols. We analyze the visits of Javier Sicilia and caravan visitors to the central borderlands in 2011 and 2012.

Like the year 2000, the year 2012 was once again a time when simultaneous presidential campaigns occurred in Mexico and the United States for the six-year term and four-year term, respectively. In the concluding chapter, we rethread all the elements of this study and offer a grounded perspective of what the future may bring for the border under President Enrique Peña Nieto. In the first part of his six-year term, we observe continuities with his predecessor amid new, globally framed narratives about Mexico, its trading prospects, and its middle-class consumer population that is growing (O'Neill 2012) but still small, given official poverty figures that show a poverty rate of nearly half (O'Neill 2012: chap. 5 footnotes).

In our hope for a post-conflict future in our binational metropolitan region, we seek to document gendered resistance to violence and militarization. We also analyze how this resistance has intervened in and interfaced with femicide deniers' discourse, thus reexposing this form of violence against women at a critical time in Ciudad Juárez when its incidence has escalated fivefold (albeit when homicide has increased over tenfold). We highlight women's and men's agency, and describe and analyze the performances of masculinity in militarization (on gendered resistance, also see Marchand and Runyan 2011).

In his book, taking cues from Michel Foucault on power and resistance, James Scott eloquently analyzes domination and resistance (1990). Like Scott, we note the activists' creative and clever performance and linguistic arts (see their gendered forms in chapters 3 and 4), sometimes emergent during election season as people mock the candidates and elections with new words like *candigato*.[7] He highlights the often "hidden" transcripts. We compare the range of not-so-hidden transcripts in the forms of resistance that vary from standard social-movement organizing to social-networking technology among Facebook "friends" and *tuiteros*, who tweet with widely available cell phones.[8]

Methodologically, we draw both on our participant observation of most of the rallies and marches described herein as well as planning and collaborative efforts and on analysis of some of the content and discourse in technological communications, from electronic communications and Facebook. We are interested in the spread of ideas and action. In political movements and campaigns, the few who attend meetings can become the "messengers." As active, long-term inhabitants and citizens of the borderlands, profoundly engaged in border community life, we view ourselves as *nodos* (nodes) who join deep knowledge about context with brokering and connecting roles in various networks. Together, as noted earlier, we have lived at the border, taught courses on the border and its ethnography, and researched at the border for more than sixty years. Scholar Sergio Aguayo, of El Colegio de México, has discussed "a mutual distrust between activists and academics," yet he belongs to both camps because, as he says, "they are two different kinds of knowledge that have to be fused to bring about change" (quoted in Lloyd 2005: A27). In the United States as well, tensions exist between scholarly activists and movement activists, between theory and action. As David Croteau discusses, "Academia can become a velvet cage," containing obstacles to making relevant and meaningful contributions to action (2005: 20). We wholeheartedly agree and endeavor toward a hybrid practice.

Our participant observation takes place in the binational border community of loosely organized human rights–movement activism. Méndez is a *fronteriza* from Ciudad Juárez and a lifelong resident of the borderlands. She draws on her activism and work with various grassroots organizations, including Movimiento Pacto por la Cultura (Cultural Pact Movement) and the coalition of organizations known as Grupo de Articulación Justicia en Juárez (Articulation of Groups for Justice in Juárez), as well as her collaboration with other local human rights groups and coalitions such as Red Mesa de Mujeres de Ciudad Juárez (Roundtable Network of Women in Ciudad Juárez), to begin to explore and render an admittedly incomplete history of activism and resistance in her community.

It was especially during the last four years of Felipe Calderón's presidential mandate that an observably increased police state coincided with the establishment of terror in the streets. Activists and citizens resisted and mobilized, despite and amidst the daily displays of brutal violence, including beheadings, public executions, corpses dumped on the streets, extortion, the apparition of mantas with threatening messages, disappearances of people, escalating murder rates, and the constant violation of human rights by the local police, the federal police, and the Mexican army. In this volatile and complex landscape, Méndez—like other activists, scholars, and journalists—tried to document.

Staudt draws on participant observation in local politics, in past and current activism with human rights and faith-based social-justice non-governmental organizations and the Coalition against Violence toward Women and Families at the U.S.–Mexico Border, and in the dramatic activism of first-stage anti-femicide movements (2008). She was the co-ordinator of the campus-community binational conference in 2009, the Global Public Policy Forum on the War on Drugs, that brought academics, officials, and advocates together for a huge, first-ever effort to connect the havoc of Mexico's drug war to those seeking alternatives to the U.S. drug war (http://warondrugsconference.utep.edu), and she participated in follow-up activities thereafter. Staudt values the aspects of this book that unpack further the first stage of anti-femicide activism through 2004, transitioning to its second stage of alliances against all forms of violence and militarization, and linking the mobilizations to anti-militarization peace and justice movements.

Moreover, we both—in different capacities—have participated in planning and implementing various solidarity events, among them one on January 29, 2011, "A Bi-national Day of Action," which brought together activists at the border wall/fence in Anapra, Chihuahua, and Sunland Park, New Mexico; a follow-up ¡BASTA! Border Activism Summit for Teaching and Action in mid-October 2011; preparation for both the Permanent Peoples' Tribunal in Ciudad Juárez, May 2012, and poet and pacifist Javier Sicilia's Caravana del Consuelo (Consolation Caravan) to the borderlands in June 2011 and his subsequent U.S. Caravan for Peace, which stopped in El Paso in August 2012 and acquired support from the El Paso City Council (albeit only symbolically, with a resolution) in a central, engaged dialogue rather than the alternative, a sometimes marginalized enclave engagement, as in other U.S. cities.

Anthropologist Ruth Behar has written incisively about the "central dilemma of all efforts at witnessing," including research. In exploring this dilemma she asks about the "limits" of "respect, piety, pathos" that one should consider in deciding to record or not to record. Yet, in the end the question poignantly lingers: If horror cannot be stopped, "shouldn't you at least document it?" (Behar 1996: 2). Individually and together, we agonized over these dilemmas regularly. As organizers and activists, in our personal and academic lives, we have witnessed—from varying perspectives and angles—the "horrors" of the long-term violence in Ciudad Juárez, the early femicide in the 1990s and the current murders and violence of the contemporary era. However, like the citizens of the borderlands, we sought to move beyond victimization and confront and contest the identities that apocalyptic journalism attributes to *fronterizos* and *fronterizas*. That is why we are inspired by the work of Pilar Riaño-Alcalá, *Dwellers of Memory* (2006). We set out to document and narrate—as the horror continues—the valiant activism and resistance of people at the borderlands that has as a backdrop one of the darkest ongoing chapters in Mexico's history, and in particular, one of the most fatidic episodes in the life of these borderlands: what some analysts call "the *sexenio de la muerte*" (the six-year [presidential] term of death) (Osorno 2011).

Impelled—not unlike other human rights activists in the region—by an "urge to remember" (Barsalou and Baxter 2007: 1), our aim is twofold: to document and to intervene. We document to memorialize the victims of violence; and we document as a way of intervening and shedding light on the unrelenting work of the "surviving community" (14). Thus, our chapter's epigraph from Argentinian Nora Cortiñas, cofounder of Las Madres de la Plaza de Mayo in Buenos Aires, offers inspiration to us and, we hope, to readers. Ironically or not, her presence at the 2012 Permanent Peoples' Tribunal establishes threaded connections to the mothers in Argentina who challenged disappearances and military, state-sanctioned terrorism in the late 1970s dirty war (see Winn 2006: chap. 7). As Barsalou and Baxter remind us, memorials to "the righteous" present communities with the possibility of "celebrat[ing] courageous people and positive values that existed even during the worst times" (2007: 6).

Our book threads itself to multiple forms of knowledge, as we relay below. We link the work to transnational activism and Mexican politics, especially focusing on women and gender. First, however, we couch the discussion with the rationale for focusing on women and gender. We follow that with a review of related literature.

WHY WOMEN'S STUDIES? WHY GENDER STUDIES?

Some may wonder why our book focuses on women, gender, and gendered relations between men and women. We both bring a feminist perspective to our research, that is, a researchable attention to historic and comparative hierarchies in societies in which men dominate women, and methodologically, an appreciation for the value of various vantage points in social reality. We are also keenly aware of how, in the academic world before 1970, few scholarly works included women or focused on gender. For example, when Staudt first began to do research on the unequal distribution of policy benefits to women and to men in the mid-1970s, she was taking a risk in the discipline of political science, which had theretofore primarily focused on men as elected leaders in political and economic systems that, historically, men had designed and gained privilege from, a constructed reality that varies by class, ethnicity, and nationality.

Academic attention changed markedly beginning in the 1970s, with the rise of public opinion polls that often showed differences between women and men, highlighted feminist and women's political movements, and institutionalized the gendered disaggregation of data in many governmental agencies and international bodies, such as the United Nations Development Programme's annual *Human Development Report*. The highlights of gendered difference reveal a more comprehensive reality, while gender "mainstreaming" sometimes renders women invisible (once again, as in centuries of academic analysis or in violence statistics, which once normalized violence against women, especially in their homes).

Besides that academic research, women's and gender studies programs have gained relatively secure places in higher education since the 1970s. Permanent courses in the university curriculum specialize on women and gender or violence against women. Peer-reviewed journals like *Violence Against Women* or the journal *Men and Masculinities* offer space for highly specialized research. And many nongovernmental organizations focus on violence against women in North America and countries all over the world. Indeed, violence against women is the one issue that seems common to women worldwide, regardless of nationality, class, and ethnicity.

In this study, we describe how the visibility of women's murders in early 1990s Ciudad Juárez gave rise to feminist and human rights movements that were born in the city and then spread across national borders and onto other continents. Homicide occurred in the city, but men's murders did not exhibit a sexualized component of rape and other brutalities that were identified in women's murders, so feminist scholars in Mexico named the murders *feminicidio*, from earlier scholarly work on femicide. This focus on women did not mean that homicide was irrelevant. Rather, homicide was and continues to be tragic and hardly attended to, given the numbing perpetuation of police impunity, or the lack of investigation or prosecution of crimes. Far more men than women were murdered between 1990 and 2010 in both Mexico and the United States. An influential U.S. border listserv moderator, Molly Molloy, raises the question repeatedly, why continue the focus on women, for they are only 10 to 20 percent of the murdered? The question has the possible effects of minimalizing and marginalizing women's murders, just as happened before the 1960s–1970s women's movement, when U.S. police had impunity on assaults, rapes, and domestic violence murders. We analyze that U.S. social media activism in chapter 4. At a 2012 International Studies Association panel, most feminists in the audience underwent shock when it was suggested that women mute their voices on violence against women to sharpen the single focus on demilitarization (Staudt observation April 2012). Violence against women and militarization are inextricably linked, we believe, as did others in that panel audience and as did the feminists who documented, denounced, and condemned militarization during the last Encuentro Feminista Latinoamericano y del Caribe (Latin American and Caribbean Feminist Meeting), held in Bogotá, Colombia, in 2011. We document these connections in great analytic detail in this book.

In a study of civil-society activism at the border, one cannot fail to notice that women leaders, mothers, and family members of female murder victims have often provided the rallying cry to mobilize social movements, organize groups, and build alliances against public policies that perpetuate police impunity and militarization strategies that do little to end drug and gun smuggling across borders. This book identifies and analyzes deeply and thickly moments and events where women leaders became what we call "game changers"—and by their actions placing their lives in great risk—in countering the dominant official narratives that muted personal, human tragedies or the murder counts reported in some media. The eventual conjunction of the anti-femicide and anti-militarization forces, we argue, offers compelling transformations that are well worth understanding and perhaps modeling in other parts of North America and the world.

This book is certainly not the first to focus on women and gender in times of political crisis and political transition. In Latin America during the 1970s, especially under the authoritarian military dictatorships of Chile and Argentina, women entered the public streets and protested. Among the more visible protesters, we note the Madres de la Plaza de Mayo, in Argentina, who hung signs and pictures of their disappeared

Cross with a sign reading "Ni una más" (Not one more) and nails commemorating femicide victims in Ciudad Juárez at the international port of entry to the United States. Photo by Renato Díaz.

and murdered adult children in weekly gatherings—a movement immortalized in Lourdes Portillo's documentary *Las Madres: The Mothers of the Plaza de Mayo* (1986; also see Winn 2006). At the time, women seemed to have protection in their social construction as "mothers" in a respected, sacred sphere during the brutal dictatorship. Had men circled the plaza with those names and pictures, perhaps the military regime would have murdered them with impunity. But are protections still in place? The protection racket called the state may no longer protect women activists.

Moreover, the victimization of women and children seems to generate special attention, even public rage, for reasons that may be linked to stereotypes about their weakness, their enclosure, their traditional covering with modest clothing, their segregation, or, historically and comparatively, their seclusion in private places, such as purdah (even if such places offer little or no legal protection from violence and harm). The private/public divide, corresponding to female and male space, has been historical reality and comparative practice in many societies. The so-called protections, or pretense of protections, may no longer hold for women who "invade" public space, integrate the workplace, and/or defy traditional norms. If and when violence against women occurs, it may appear more shocking to the public than violence against men, given the socially construed precepts described above. Such different perceptions are neither fair nor equal, but they do give rise to social movements with a creative deployment of symbols and performativity to frame and highlight their agendas.

In Ciudad Juárez, women active in human rights movements are increasingly concerned about their safety and that of other mothers and families who demand justice. They have reason to be concerned, for as the cases of Josefina Reyes Salazar and Marisela Escobedo illustrate, women activists in Mexico—as the United Nations sustains—are often stigmatized and criminalized; they become vulnerable targets in the current context of militarization.

RELATED BODIES OF KNOWLEDGE: TRANSNATIONAL ACTIVISM, WOMEN, AND MEXICAN POLITICS

Analysts of transnational social movements have heretofore focused on established, well-endowed organizations (Keck and Sikkink 1998), antiglobalization movements (Eschle and Maiguashca 2005), contentious politics around the North American Free Trade Agreement (Ayres and Macdonald 2009), and democratic globalization (Smith 2008) as they interfaced with the World Social Forums of 2003 (Eschle and Mai-guashca 2010; see selections in Jaquette 2009). None of these glob-alization books deal with militarization or connect *the global to the local* in transnational organizing *in specific places*, such as the Perma-nent Peoples' Tribunal, which we analyze in chapter 5. Our book fills a vacuum in that regard.

Our book also addresses a void in Mexican and border politics. Ana-lysts of Mexican politics have heretofore focused primarily on political elites in the twentieth century; see Roderic Camp's many books, in-cluding one that shows the continuous, overwhelmingly male, middle- and upper-class social origins of Mexican leadership (2010: 76, 107). In his mammoth *Oxford Handbook of Mexican Politics* (2012), Camp as-sembles thirty-one chapters, but none of them focus on border poli-tics and grassroots-movement activism save one, by Shannon Mattiace, on nationally known indigenous and environmental nongovernmental organizations. Basically, the literature obsessively focuses on *electoral* politics, as does Dresser (2012), as opposed to civil-society activism— the shift that we make and emphasize in this book. Moreover, beyond journalistic accounts, we have yet to see analysis of the impact of social networking and electronic activism on electoral politics. Yet, from the ground, we hear and observe how technology can modernize corrup-tion or disseminate information about candidates. For example, wide-spread cell phone–camera use has made it possible for people to provide *pruebas* (proofs) that they voted for the party of the presidential candi-date offering vouchers and has aided people in documenting a number of illegal actions to co-opt voters or buy their votes in favor of the Par-tido Revolucionario Institucional (PRI) during the 2012 presidential election. For another example, YouTube videos show violence against women in President Enrique Peña Nieto's state when he was governor and in his personal life, not that it made much difference in the elec-toral outcome and the alleged corruption associated with his election.

Our book also speaks to analysis of women and gender in civil-society activism in politics. Women's community and electoral activism has been covered well in Victoria Rodríguez's edited collection *Women's Participation in Mexican Political Life* (1998), as it has also in her fine analysis covering a full and broad range of women and Mexican poli-tics (2003). Adriana Ortiz-Ortega and Mercedes Barquet analyze "gen-dering transitions to democracy" in Mexico and in particular, "women's ability to reconstitute politics" (2010: 108), though they focus on state and national levels, rather than on civil society, as we do. Staudt and Irasema Coronado provide analysis of some of the first comparative cross-border activism in multiple policy arenas in their 2002 book *Fronteras no Más*. In her 2008 work *Violence and Activism at the U.S.–Mexico Border*, Staudt examines first-stage anti-femicide feminist and human rights activism, well before the exponential increase in violence and militarization and the growing conjuncture of what we call activism against all forms of violence in the peace and justice movement of the contemporary era that we analyze in this book. Martha Estela Pérez García (2005 and 2011) chronicles Juarense anti-femicide activism. Julia Monárrez Fragoso, the premier scholar of *feminicidio*, maintains a database (1998–) of sexualized murders at El Colegio de la Frontera Norte (COLEF) (see, for example, 2009). Jane Jaquette's edited collection *Feminist Agendas and Democracy in Latin America* (2009) contains fine chapters on the new era of organizing after feminist policy achievements, albeit achievements hardly implemented, but most chapters focus on South America. Rosa-Linda Fregoso and Cynthia Bejarano (2010) focus on what they call "feminicide" in the Western hemisphere with academic chapters and testimonies. The scholarly analysis of electronic social activism is in its infancy (but see Karpf 2012 on the United States).

THEORETICAL IMPULSES

Below we introduce the main theorist on whom we draw for this book and whose ideas we advance with border and gender perspectives in the analysis and conclusions. Our theoretical emphases in this book draw on bottom-up, grassroots perspectives, and on social networking at multiple levels and in multiple spaces.

READING JAMES SCOTT WITH A BORDER GENDER LENS

Some analyses assess border space in top-down, deterministic ways. Drawing on James Scott's concepts, we avoid "seeing like a state" (his 1998 book title) or even social scientifically reifying statist gazes. Rather, we argue that bottom-up, or grounded, grassroots perspectives reveal important insights about the totality of the population in the Paso del Norte region, which consists of two nation-states, the United States and Mexico; three states, Texas, New Mexico, and Chihuahua; and several local governments, county and city in the United States and municipal in Mexico.

Scott, a political scientist, developed the concept of "hidden transcripts" on the "performative aspects of power" (Sivaramakrishnan 2005: 324, 326) that in a collection of six articles in a twenty-year retrospective in *American Anthropologist* on his work was argued to have "entered fully and immediately into the anthropological lexicon destined for immortality" (Greenhouse 2005: 356). In *The Moral Economy of the Peasant* (1976), Scott challenged rational-actor, academic-centered interpretations with a phenomenological approach that reintroduced normative language used by those who are governed to counter those who govern.

Although our work focuses on urban dwellers, not peasants, we draw on Scott's insights, as have others, for their far-reaching capacity to open lines of inquiry into early twenty-first-century power relations in a North American border region. It seemed especially appropriate that we—Staudt a political scientist and Méndez an ethnographer—would draw on Scott's work, given his intellectual growth in both political science and anthropology.

Scott, who began his interpretive writing during the Vietnam War, countered the hegemony of modernization and its encapsulation of agricultural societies, offering the "alternative" economy of peasant societies. Just as he addressed normative concepts, we elevate people's voices in civil society who call for justice, claiming the right to live with security and dignity. In Ciudad Juárez, feminists and mothers called for justice for the murders of girls and women beginning in the 1990s amid police impunity and continued calling for it with the surge in the murders of men a decade into the twenty-first century. Such language of justice was used by Javier Sicilia and the Movimiento por la Paz con Justicia y Dignidad, beginning in 2011. Scott's fieldwork began in Southeast Asia and specifically in Malaysia, where he contrasted the discrepant discourses between elites and the peasant majority in the context of unequal power relations. In *Weapons of the Weak* (1977), he analyzed peasant voices and actions; in his 1990 book, he called this "fugitive political conduct" (xii) of subordinate groups. In so doing, he brought welcome expansion to the theretofore narrow and specialized political science focus on elections, voting, lobbying, and elite political behavior. Peasant voices appeared contradictory at times and in specific contexts, such as in the face of authority, where humble and deferential voices of compliance and acquiescence coexisted with actions of non-compliance, sabotage, gossip, and resistance.

Scott artfully wrote *Domination and the Arts of Resistance* (1990) to provide a sweeping historical and contemporary analysis of these themes in comparative and international perspectives. He incorporated literary works, memoirs, and even the narratives of people deemed "slaves" into the book. He analyzed many instances of individual and collective resistance that, when accumulating and widening over time, nudge at and finally augment the decay and crumpling of seemingly powerful elites and political-economic regimes encased in dominant public ideological transcripts. Scott also said that "the notion of a hidden transcript helps us understand those rare moments of political electricity when, often for the first time in memory, the hidden transcript is spoken directly and publicly in the teeth of power" (1990: xiii). In this book, we offer vignettes of such politically electric moments.

Although Scott says the public transcript term is a "shorthand way of describing the open interaction between subordinates and those who dominate" (1990: 2), his perspective draws enough on Antonio Gramsci for him to acknowledge that official public transcripts provide "convincing evidence for the hegemony of dominant values, for the hegemony of dominant discourse" (1990: 4). The dominant speak to, at, and about subordinates.

At the U.S.–Mexico border, some subordinates internalize this ideology. Yet at borders, we must ask who or what is the hegemonic force, given that there are two nation-states in which global economic forces shape a landscape of transnational manufacturing operations, its workforce, and the everyday life of its residents. In Ciudad Juárez, there is real fear in a city where murder rates increased nearly tenfold from 2007 to 2010, involving not only organized criminals but also federal, state, and municipal police, against whom many human rights claims have been filed.

Scott, one of many who analyze discourse critically, gives us language to contrast and analyze the context of power relations in Ciudad Juárez. These power relations are rendered complex by the presence of global manufacturing capital (Fuentes and Peña 2010), national military and police forces in what is a federal system of government with state and municipal control, transnational criminal networks, and the always-hovering U.S. presence, sometimes called the "Colossus of the North" (Winn 2006). Chapter 2 sets the context with the interplay of activism and official discourses. Global manufacturers' organizations reimagine the city as one of the most economically competitive worldwide (as the "Juárez Competitiva" conference emphasized), for foreign investment and for profitable business, given low labor and transportation costs to the United States. Chapter 5 examines competing

Young men and women carry a sign with the words "Alto a la impunidad/Fuera soldados de la ciudad" (Stop impunity/Soldiers out of the city) with emblematic anti-femicide "Ni una más," showing the convergence of two movements (against militarization and violence against women). Photo by Zulma Y. Méndez.

discourses about the border—one that it is to be controlled through militarization and the other that it can be managed with efficient binational trade—among Democrats in the primary election for one of the few genuinely "border" seats in the U.S. Congress, the Sixteenth Congressional District of Texas.[9]

Our analysis is gendered in the sense that it uses the social construction and lenses of men and women in the multiple layering of relationships among people. In Scott's work on the (backstage) drama of linguistic performance, he notes the "hyper-polite forms" of respectful address (1990: 30). Women, central to the way civil society is organized in Juárez, whether as leaders, mothers, or victims, might use "hyper-polite forms" of language. Hyper-polite language uses, so ritualized in neocolonial Mexican traditions, were deliberately transgressed in risky acts of defiance and resistance. In chapter 3, we describe several gendered examples of courageous acts that not only insult, but do so in emasculating ways. Such gender defiance became coupled with murderous consequences when Marisela Escobedo was assassinated after her persistently public demands for justice over her daughter Rubí's murder, with the killer gone free (at least for a few years, until allegedly killed by organized criminals).

SOCIAL NETWORKING

In this book, our attention is also devoted to civil-society organization and its cross-border activities and impacts. Some Juárez-based networks and organizations target their media messaging and dramatic resistance rallies to transnational audiences, as well as to the Mexican state and national representatives, though with uneven results. Occasionally, activists' media messaging can backfire, as happened with Javier Sicilia's press conference in El Paso during his first caravan to the border. Yet this approach was precisely the one used by anti-femicide activists of the 1990s and a few years after—an approach that generated some symbolic changes in legislation, but hardly dented the U.S.-Mexican hegemonic ideology that maintains and prioritizes a militarized response in its longest "war," the war on drugs.

At the border, a vacuum exists in binational political institutions with policy-making authority, representatives of border spatial con-

No Más Sangre's "No more blood" signs at a demonstration in Villas de Salvárcar during Javier Sicilia's Caravana del Consuelo in 2011. Photo by Renato Díaz.

A man holds a sign at the Marcha contra la Violencia (March against Violence) in Juárez on December 6, 2009, that reads in part "A dignified life is the right of all humans. In Mexico millions live excluded from development and without the real possibility of achieving it . . ." Photo by Renato Díaz.

stituencies, and accountability to border residents. Ultimately, as we argue in our conclusion, local and national civil society will, we hope, propel the demand for those political institutions.

A special focus in this book is an analysis of social-networking technology. Our evidence shows that while technology provides for speed and growth potential in movements that challenge militarization and promote more inclusive gender justice, technology also exposes activists to risks from government surveillance, hijacked agendas, and potential agents provocateurs. In 2002, Staudt and Coronado analyzed the opportunities for and obstacles to cross-border activism around the environment, labor unions, business, and human rights, using the benefits and drawbacks of the prevalent "personalism" for ties that bind people together. At the time, electronic communication was in its infancy, as was social networking through Facebook and other means. Several years later, Staudt (2008) discussed accountability problems plus the national and class biases that emerged sporadically in the first stage of the anti-femicide/anti-VAW (Violence against Women) mobilizations. The contributions of website designers, graphic artists, and musicians—augmented through technological means—facilitated a wider scope and spread of awareness among new audiences, especially those who did not usually identify with political activism. At that time, websites, fund-raising, and information and misinformation campaigns enhanced but also complicated the efforts of those "close to the ground" in the region (Staudt 2008: chap. 4).

Currently, activists in Mexico widely employ digital technology and social networks, especially e-mail, Facebook, and Twitter, to mobilize people and communicate their perspectives. This is true for groups and activists in Juárez whose legitimate concerns with reprisal for their activities have found that the use of digital media offers an efficient way to denounce human rights abuses, to enhance the organization of rallies and marches, and to disseminate information. In preparing the research design for this book, we pondered the task of creating an inventory for all the anti-femicide and anti-militarization Facebook pages in the region: the "likes," the "shares," the "friending" (or "unfriending"), but determined that such a project would be breathtaking in scope and ultimately too ambitious for an area with new dynamics in shifting contexts that would be imperfectly tapped electronically. With e-mail monikers that disguise names, our ability to trace friends, foes, government intelligence agents, and voyeurs in social networks would be nearly impossible.

OUTLINE OF CHAPTERS

In chapter 2, "Historicizing and Contextualizing the Place: Three Historic Junctures," we examine the Paso del Norte metropolitan region as a global manufacturing site, a gateway for drug shipping, and the location of extensive local, binational, and transnational human rights and feminist organizing from the 1990s onward, including the anti-militarization resistance. The chapter sets the stage for our analysis of President Calderón's militarized drug war—a war that meshed with the lengthy war on drugs in the United States, which has the world's largest drug-consuming population.

In chapter 3, "From Fear and Intimidation to Game-Changing Activism," we focus on three case-study public vignettes that highlight women whose no-longer-hidden resistance transformed many Juarenses' and Mexicans' responses to the president's militarized war: (1) Luz María Dávila, whose sons were killed in the Villas de Salvárcar massacre in 2010 and who challenged President Calderón at a high-visibility public event when he was announcing the Todos Somos Juárez program, (2) Marisela Escobedo, who was assassinated after her many protests about the injustices associated with her daughter's killer gone free, and (3) the activists who protested the way the government responded to some mandates by the Inter-American Court of Human Rights, including the construction of a public memorial for the victims of the Campo Algodonero murders.

Chapter 4, "'Fed Up' with Militarization and Murders, via Social Media," analyzes the reach and power of social media (Facebook, Twitter, YouTube, e-mail) in several case-study vignettes, including one in which thousands of people "friended" "Harto de la Violencia" (fed up with violence) on Facebook. Moreover, we discuss Facebook followings, Facebook exchanges, and Twitter tweets in a false-alarm massacre that generated attention from the media and officials at the municipal and state levels. The chapter also examines large electronic listservs on the U.S. side that regularly report (sometimes gendered) body counts, publicizing skyrocketing murder rates among men, sustaining the violent border narrative, and periodically undermining Juarense feminist activists. Despite the speed and scope of dissemination, such listservs also pose risks to activists for surveillance and backlash. We also analyze what we call other "e-actions," such as the protests against U.S. cosmetics and clothing manufacturers who aimed to commercialize the murders in Juárez.

In chapter 5, "Toward Transnational Solidarity: Contesting the Border Narrative in a U.S. Congressional Race, Tribunals, and Faith-Based Activism," we examine the ways solidarity events moved outward and upward among activists and electoral competitors representing divergent border agendas. The agendas reflect the Democratic Party primary contest between the two main U.S. congressional candidates: a long-term incumbent, who was a former border patrol sector chief and partial architect of the border-security apparatus, and his challenger, who focused on trade and employment issues.

In chapter 6, "South-to-North Solidarity: Sicilia and Peace and Justice Movements at the Border," we describe and analyze two caravan visits that Javier Sicilia and *caravaneros* and *caravaneras* made to the region in 2011 and 2012. Sicilia's early ambivalence about an all-out critique of militarization contributed to some polarization among activists. However, his 2012 U.S. Caravan for Peace, around which many U.S. organizations partnered in states from the West to the East Coast, generated rallies and press coverage, most of it alternative and Spanish except for places like El Paso, where Sicilia engaged local officials on the city council and obtained consensus support (with one abstention), after some posturing over gun-control policies.

The final chapter, "Conclusion: Reflections on the Possibilities of Post-Conflict Peace and Justice," revisits the key questions of the research on new alliances among activists and on feminist agendas in making formerly "hidden transcripts" public, the electoral regime where policy decisions are made, and the transnational elite, some organizations of which challenge militarization and seek more economic interdependence on their terms—terms not necessarily conducive to economic justice. We tie together the theoretical impulses of this book and hope to advance them with this analysis and its spatial location in the transnational borderlands. In the 2012 Mexican presidential election, the PRI triumphed, albeit with challenges from youth movements and charges of national Televisa media complicity. And Ciudad Juárez's murder rates have declined, the causes and consequences of which decline we unpack. We close with considerations of the effects that the border movement activists, the caravan, and Javier Sicilia might have for demilitarization, peace, and justice, including gender justice.

CHAPTER TWO

HISTORICIZING AND CONTEXTUALIZING
THE PLACE: THREE HISTORIC JUNCTURES

My first struggle was on women's labor rights, then against
feminicidio, *and now against militarization.*
CIPRIANA JURADO, PANELIST, VOICE OF THE VOICELESS CONFERENCE,
APRIL 28, 2012, EL PASO

IN MANY WAYS, the struggles of Cipriana Jurado parallel the history
of social justice–oriented civil-society activism in Ciudad Juárez. A
migrant to Ciudad Juárez, Jurado worked in its export-processing factory (maquiladora) sector and later became a labor-rights activist. In
the mid-1990s, she participated in the struggle against femicide/*feminicidio* and subsequently denounced and mobilized against President
Felipe Calderón's strategy of militarization since 2007 in Mexico and
especially 2008 in Ciudad Juárez—a strategy that has been in place for
more than five years and has resulted in approximately 10,000 murders
in a city of 1.3 million people.

A general climate of fear and an unprecedented exodus of people
have been observed in Mexico, and most particularly in Ciudad Juárez.
For instance, the International Displacement Monitoring Centre—
citing researchers at the Universidad Autónoma de Ciudad Juárez—
documented 220,000 people "who had left their place of residence" in
Ciudad Juárez as a result of "the violence of drug cartels and the government's military response" in 2011 (IDMC 2011: 1). Among the thousands of people leaving the city was Cipriana Jurado, whose exodus
was related to a documented climate of persecution against activists
in Mexico, but especially in Juárez. Forced to leave, Jurado was granted
asylum in 2010 by the U.S. government. She is one of the rare successful political-asylum cases, considering that the success rate for
Mexico (the nation with the second-largest number of asylum appli-

cants to the United States, after China) was 2 percent in 2007, but after that declined to a mere 1 percent, according to U.S. Department of Justice figures (2012).

Cipriana Jurado's Mexico, like many countries in the mid-twentieth-century Americas, pursued import-substitution industrialization economic strategies. In fact, after its revolution in 1910, Mexico grew rapidly under a nationally oriented industrialized economy concentrated in particular urban regions, where it expanded, spurring a variety of labor struggles. But world economic systems rapidly changed in the last quarter of the twentieth century, with the adoption of national and international policies facilitating export production to take advantage of low-cost labor, the General Agreement on Tariffs and Trade, and free-trade agreements, including the 1994 North American Free Trade Agreement (NAFTA), among others. This process is part of globalization, defined as "an uneven process whereby the barriers of time and space are reduced, new social relations between distant people are fostered and new centres of authority are created" (O'Brien and Williams 2007, cited in Hobden 2011: 72).

Paradoxically, the compression of time and space experienced with globalization was not circumscribed exclusively to economic productivity. Time and space compression is visible and present in the spread of the Internet, social-media activism, and electronic networking as means to denounce, resist, and organize against the effects of economic restructuration: death, femicide, homicide, militarism, and displacement. As this chapter and book illustrate, narratives and images of Ciudad Juárez—whether as maquiladora capital of the Americas, as hopeless and macabre iconic city of violence, or as epicenter of resistance and struggle—also spread with speed.

Globalization shapes the borderlands and everyday lived reality of its residents and workers. As globalization deepened, foreign direct investment (FDI) expanded, with the conjuncture of binational policies that stimulate the United States' and other countries' FDI at Mexico's northern border, particularly in the central Paso del Norte and western Pacific regions, namely, Ciudad Juárez and Tijuana. This expansion took place with the recruitment in the 1960s and 1970s of female export-processing factory workers, many of whom migrated northward from Mexico's north-central states. Close to the United States and thus having low-cost transportation advantages, yet far from U.S. minimum or average wages, maquiladora workers earned approximately US$3–4 daily, which reduced labor costs for global manufacturers.

Surprisingly, the daily minimum wage has changed little over the decades. Given Mexico's *peso* devaluations, legal minimum wages remain similar in dollar terms. As was the case at the inception of manufacturing production in the U.S.–Mexico borderlands, women and gender are central to the most recent history of civil-society activism in the region.

We contend that just as globalization stimulated legal trade in export-processing production, it also stimulated illegal trade in drugs and guns, along with civil-society activism against unfair labor practices, violence against women, and militarized drug wars. One difference between then and now is the use of high-speed Internet technology for media coverage and exposure of human rights abuses and, following that, coalitions among local and global activists and organizations whose particular agendas and perspectives do not always coincide. Just as globalization compresses time and space in economic sectors, it also compresses time and space among activists in a globalized-local world. Each era is associated with cross-border/transnational elements that wax and wane with varying degrees of solidarity, sensitivity, and support.

Our chapter identifies three historic junctures that have impacted border activism: export-processing industrialization, gendered border violence, and anti-militarization alliances. In addition, we explore and discuss how each of the junctures shapes public policies and discourse, or "official transcripts." But most particularly, we investigate how these, in turn, shape the work of activists.

FIRST LAYER: EXPORT-PROCESSING INDUSTRIALIZATION

Though historians may balk, we begin this chapter in the 1960s as both Mexico's Border Industrialization Program and the United States government's tariff incentives stimulated low-cost assembly-line production in northern Mexico (for earlier historical treatment of the region, see Lugo 2008: chap. 2; Martínez 1978; Staudt 1998: chap. 3). During the next two decades of export-oriented industrialization, young women—about 80 percent of the workforce—constituted the vast majority of globalized assembly-line workers. Their presence spawned a voluminous body of academic research and equally significant activism (Fernández-Kelly 1983; Lugo 2008; Tiano 1994). Lorraine Gray immortalized the working conditions and management discourse in her

A "Reacciona y Acciona" (React and Act) banner, showing participation of managers and workers, at the Marcha contra la Violencia (March against Violence) in Juárez on December 6, 2009. Photo by Renato Díaz.

documentary comparing Mexico and the Philippines titled *The Global Assembly Line* (1986). By the 1990s, the industrial complex had diversified in both product lines and gender balance (Lugo 2008), with the earlier feminization leading to marginalization (Murphy Aguilar and Tiano 2011). Most assembly-line workers earned the minimum wage in Mexico.

Mexican labor unions, historically, have been closely tied to the dominant political party, the Partido Revolucionario Institucional (PRI) (Middlebrook 1995). Moreover, a strong tradition of company unions called "ghost unions" also exists, though independent unions like the Frente Auténtico del Trabajo (Authentic Labor Front) also operate in cross-border solidarity with the U.S. United Electrical Workers Union (La Botz 2012; Staudt and Coronado 2002: chap. 5). Despite the usually critical treatment of union affiliation, David Fairris conducted empirical analysis of union and non-union workers with wage data and found overall benefits to unionized workers (2006).

Although independent research on maquiladoras has diminished recently, Alejandro Lugo's work is noteworthy for its insightful analysis of gender constructions at a time when the industry recruited a more gender-balanced workforce, beginning in the late 1980s and thereafter, with the arrival of automotive industries "running away from strong labor unions in the American Midwest" (2008: 74, 78). Like María Patricia Fernández-Kelly earlier, Lugo conducted ethnographic research, and he worked in several plants, where he analyzed struggles among workers and marked disciplinary practices (Lugo 2008: 89; also see Mikker Palafox 2010), especially associated with reinforcing masculinities through the use of tropes to tease and shame men to work harder. Like most plants, one in which he worked had a union affiliated with the Confederación de Trabajadores Mexicanos (Mexican Workers' Confederation), an arm of the PRI (Lugo 2008: 157). In rich analysis of the constant shortage of chairs in the sewing factory where he worked, Lugo thickly describes the uselessness of union delegates, their unavailability to workers, and their tendency to blame individual workers or blacklist them for any complaints. One worker relayed how union delegates listened mainly to company personnel and middle management; also, she said, "we haven't had a union meeting in a year" (2008: 176–180).

Despite the insightful scholarship on life inside manufacturing plants at the borderlands, less is known about the independent workers' organizations spurred by the unequal labor exchange that characterizes maquiladoras in Ciudad Juárez, some of which include the Centro de Orientación de la Mujer Obrera (COMO) (Woman Workers' Orientation Center), the Centro de Estudios y Taller Laboral, A.C. (CETLAC) (Labor and Workshop Studies Center), and the Centro de Investigación y Solidaridad Obrera (CISO) (Center for Research in Workers' Solidarity Center) (De la O Martínez 2008). COMO provided long-term training for ex-maquiladora workers with a curriculum that aimed to increase consciousness of the global economy (Peña 1997; Staudt 1987). In fact, though, Gay Young's empirical comparison in the 1980s showed that the workers' strike experiences fostered greater political awareness than COMO's training course (1987). Many women would learn from experience about protesting, coalescing, and making a spectacle of government impunity in the antiviolence organizing that followed.

Given the heavy presence and organization of global manufacturing capital (Fuentes and Peña 2010; see below), power relations between workers and management have changed little. Because worker-management industrial relations continued to fester, some manufacturing plants moved operations abroad, particularly to China, coinciding with the downturn in the U.S. economy during the middle of the 2000–2010 period. The departure of manufacturing plants made more evident the absence of a national industry and the city's weak economic base. A collective idea persisted among the city's economic and political elites that reified the maquiladora model as a necessary evil. Thus, when some plants announced their return to Juárez at the end of the decade, the local newspapers portrayed a sense of relief at having them back.

OFFICIAL DISCOURSES ABOUT FOREIGN BUSINESS GROWTH

In stark language, sociologist-scholar Julia Monárrez Fragoso (2010a) analyzes the juxtaposition of El Paso and Ciudad Juárez as two cities, two worlds apart as well as the business elite's image of the cities versus the realities of everyday violence, crime, and murder, which were only aggravated after President Calderón created the military Joint Operation Chihuahua in 2008. Monárrez discusses the industrial elite's celebration of Ciudad Juárez as the "world capital of export-processing factories," complete with pictures of smiling young women workers on billboards in the city.

The export-processing sector of more than 300 maquiladoras, many of which subcontract with U.S. firms, suffered a setback after the 2008 U.S. recession, causing some worker layoffs. Yet increased foreign investment and expansion occurred, despite the violence, the federal police presence, and the military occupation of the city beginning in March 2008, after which murders skyrocketed, to peak at over 3,000 in 2010. In the year after June 2009, approximately 24,000 manufacturing jobs were added, and tractor-trailer traffic in El Paso's busy ports of entry, valued at $42 billion in trade, increased by 22 percent (Aguilar 2010). According to José Armendáriz Bailon, chairman of the Asociación de Maquiladoras, A.C. (AMAC), in Juárez, the export-processing factories employ about 187,000 workers, and "business is doing quite well" given the competitively priced wages that now hover near or below China's factory workers' wages (Arsenault 2011). The *Economist*'s upbeat "Special Report: Mexico" shows China's manufacturing wage increasing by over 500 percent since 2000, but Mexico's manufacturing wage increasing by less than 50 percent, thereby nearly equalizing labor costs to foreign investors (*Economist* 2012d: 5). In Ciudad Juárez, the foreign export-processing factories, albeit secured with costly private security systems and government forces, seem to float in a different world from the ordinary streets.

Meanwhile, the regional binational official transcripts, including those of the business community, pretend that all is normal and celebrate new foreign investments in the city's industrial sector, where approximately 20,000 more maquiladora jobs have been added each year since 2009. Paradoxically, economic expansion occurs, with protection from private security systems, thereby continuing to take advantage of the low labor costs and transportation assets.

CRACKS AND FISSURES IN BORDER OFFICIAL TRANSCRIPTS?

To border people, a near-incestuous relationship often seems to exist between government and the business elites, all of whom spend considerable resources to cleanse the image of the city or, via militarized parlance, to clean up crime. In the binational border region, the wealthy business class is well organized and funded. The Paso del Norte Group (PdNG), a binational organization with over three hundred well-connected members in business and government, was a sponsored, nomination-only, annual-fee and entrance-fee organization that merged with the Borderplex Alliance, a binational group. In 2010, with U.S. government funding, PdNG organized a "community development" meeting in Ciudad Juárez with registered civil associations for social service projects. On the Mexico side, Juárez Competitiva was an image-changing event that sought to promote more foreign investment and tourism in Ciudad Juárez. In October 2011, the Juárez Competitiva operation organized a costly two-week conference complete with high-profile musicians and expensive speakers like former mayor Rudolph Giuliani of New York City and former head of the Soviet Union Mikhail Gorbachev (Martínez-Cabrera 2011). The event aimed to cleanse the city's image for both English- and Spanish-language audiences. Both cities at the border also have their various chambers of commerce and industry, the members of which are well connected and subsidized through government "partnerships" under the shroud of military and federal law enforcement agencies. Remarkably similar efforts to cleanse Ciudad Juárez's name occurred at the height of first-stage anti-femicide activism (Staudt 2008: chap. 4).

Yet signs of division exist within the official transcripts, going back decades, as we discuss below. As far back as 1983–1986, competition occurred between the PRI and the Partido Acción Nacional (PAN) over the municipal presidency (mayoralty) of Juárez, as happened elsewhere in northern Mexico with concerns about the lack of transparency and accountability within the dominant PRI (Rodríguez and Ward 1994). Multiple newspapers compete in Juárez, among them *Norte de Ciudad Juárez* and *Diario de Juárez*, which cover and critique state and local government differently. In 1999, Plan Estratégico de Juárez was formed, seeking to generate residents' input in survey-based community planning (modeled after Bilbao, Spain). Albeit a high-fee civil association, it insistently calls for more transparent and honest government. Some prominent leaders affiliated with the organization invited the left-of-center Partido de la Revolución Democrática (PRD) presidential candidate (in 2006 and 2012) Andrés Manuel López Obrador to the city—a city with historically limited support for the PRD, but one in the throes of alternating PRI- and PAN-dominated municipal and state governments. Important for this study on antiviolence coalitions, Plan Juárez (as its English-language website is named) leaders collaborated with Grupo de Articulación Justicia en Juárez (discussed in the "third layer" section below), the Permanent Peoples' Tribunal (discussed in chapter 5), and the organizers of the 2009 Global Public Policy Forum on the War on Drugs at the University of Texas at El Paso, bringing former mayor Sergio Fajardo of Medellín, Colombia, to the drug-war conference, where he emphasized social and economic investment over militarization to restore city security. Moreover, the business-governmental elite in northern Mexico has often contested the ways that Mexico City generates revenue, without comparable return or compensation for the challenges of governing a border city and ports of entry (Staudt 1998: chap. 3).

These fissures became more prominent with the upsurge in violence, in 2008, as Juarenses fled the city. The exodus consisted not only of economically marginal residents, but also of wealthy people who closed their Juárez businesses, set up businesses in El Paso or elsewhere, and moved their families to safer, more secure locations. The network La Red is a Juárez business group based in El Paso with monthly meetings and a public voice. Even former municipal president José Reyes Ferriz, mayor of the city during its most tumultuous times (see his picture in chapter 5), lived with his family in El Paso while he governed Ciudad Juárez, although he was mocked by the public and media for doing so.

These fissures suggest that parts of the elite are fed up with the government's inability to provide security for its population and businesses. Small businesses struggle to survive with the chronic extortion. Even professionals cannot do their work, as the doctors' strike in 2010 illustrated, with 4,000–5,000 medical personnel in white coats making a very public statement about their government (Paterson 2010c). Impunity in law enforcement and the lack of a system of rule by law take their toll on many people, from low to high income, from businesspeople to workers. As Rubén García of Annunciation House (see chapter 5) stated publicly at the Voice of the Voiceless event in 2012, "People who seek refuge are complaining not about the cartels; they are complaining about the police" (Staudt and Méndez observation).

SECOND LAYER: GENDERED BORDER VIOLENCE

Two stages of networking against violence toward women produced extensive coalition building, political strategizing, and interacting with flawed government institutions. The first stage began in the 1990s and continued through 2004 as feminists and mothers seeking justice for their murdered daughters became a social movement that mobilized various groups and inspired organizing models for the subsequent development of coalition building around anti-militarization efforts. Activists networked across borders and created both a national and an international presence. These street protests peaked in 2004, after numerous but ineffective government commissions did not appease activists or solve problems. Thereafter, preparations began for legal action against the Mexican state at the Inter-American Court of Human Rights in the inter-American system (i.e., the case of *González et al. v. Mexico*, also known as the Campo Algodonero case), moving toward the peak of the second stage, 2010–2012.

FIRST-STAGE ACTIVISM: WHEN THE HIDDEN BECAME PUBLIC

From 1993 onward, shocking news coverage of woman-killing began to be reported. Victims, usually young and poor, were being found in the desert periphery surrounding Ciudad Juárez. Many had been brutalized before death, apparently raped and tortured, with breasts cut off, carvings on their backs, or burned to death. Initially, local and state authorities attempted to construe such deaths as isolated events that had happened to women whose reputations they questioned by publicly stating that they frequented places they should not have, were out late at night, or lacked adequate parental supervision. However,

Esther Chávez Cano, a well-known feminist and longtime women's rights activist and editorialist for *Diario de Juárez*, had begun to document each death by collecting and keeping clippings in a cardboard box for every single murder as it was documented by local newspapers, starting in 1993 (see a list in Chávez Cano 2002; also read her memoir, published after her passing, 2010). Chávez Cano's database alerted the public to the sexualized brutality and the emerging patterns that some of the killings exhibited.

At the Universidad Autónoma de Ciudad Juárez (UACJ) and other research centers, such as El Colegio de la Frontera Norte–Ciudad Juárez, feminists and scholars interested in gender issues engaged with the activists' claims and data. It was at the end of the 1990s that Julia Monárrez's work, drawing from Jane Caputi and Diana Russell (1992), provided local activists and scholars with a vocabulary with which to name the atrocious killings as *feminicidio* (but see chapter 1, note 3, on the contentious definitions). Naming the problem of women's killings in Juárez was critical for raising awareness in the community, but also for critiquing local and state authorities in Juárez and Chihuahua regarding the nature of such violence. Thus, *feminicidio* began to be understood as the extreme act of violence against women, on a continuum of violent actions exercised by men, that is a result of their gender (Monárrez and Fuentes 2004).

Initially, the Coordinadora en Pro de los Derechos de las Mujeres (CPDM) (Coordination for Women's Rights) was the central body; its most visible figure was Esther Chávez Cano. Martha Estela Pérez García (2005) identifies the antiviolence activism as beginning with the CPDM's formation in 1994. The CPDM consisted of fourteen organizations (Pérez García 2005: 231) of three types: place-based, issue-based, and identity-based, each with diverse organizing experiences and bases of support in community development and social work (such as Organización Popular Independiente [Independent Popular Organization]), labor (such as COMO and CETLAC), and religion (Tonantzin, founded by nuns), and including veteran human rights groups such as Comité Independiente de Derechos Humanos de Chihuahua (Chihuahua Independent Committee for Human Rights), founded in the 1970s as a result of the "dirty war" against students and urban guerrillas. Specifically women's organizations included Mujeres por Juárez (Women for Juárez); Centro para el Desarrollo Integral de la Mujer, A.C. (CEDIMAC) (Integral Women's Development Center); 8 de marzo (March 8), a feminist group that had a history of advocacy for reproductive-rights policy and pro-choice perspectives; the Comité de Lucha contra la Violencia (Committee for the Struggle against Violence); Red Mesa de Mujeres de Ciudad Juárez (Roundtable Network of Women in Ciudad Juárez); and Voces sin Eco (Voices without Echo).

Among the vast and varied organizations, mostly grassroots, that formed the CPDM, only Voces sin Eco, founded in 1998, was organized by family members of victims of femicide. Voces sin Eco's founders, Guillermina González and Paula Flores, were the sister and mother of Sagrario González, a young maquiladora worker and victim of femicide. The organization brought together those mothers who, in collective action, found a certain solace and consolation (what poet and pacifist Javier Sicilia [2011] calls *primera justicia*, or "first justice"), plus the strength and knowledge to demand justice. From the beginning, Voces sin Eco claimed its autonomy based on other nonvictim organizations in the community (Pérez García 2005). As such, its members procured their own resources by selling secondhand clothes so that they could work full-time to make the problem of femicide visible and demand justice. The pink crosses that identify femicide—at least in Latin America, the United States, and parts of Europe—are attributed to Sagrario González's sister and mother. Devout Catholics and at one time active participants in their parish, they along with other members of Voces sin Eco would use the proceeds of their secondhand sales to buy the pink and black paint with which they marked the wooden electrical poles of the city that had witnessed—but would now memorialize—the brutal killings of its daughters.

In response to femicide during the mid-1990s, local and then gradually national, binational, and international civil-society activism emerged. In Juárez, women's strategies unearthed the hidden and made violence visible along with demands for justice. Pérez García (2005) calls this unprecedented in the contemporary history of the city. That is, though the city had experienced a long history of struggles and organized movements, it wasn't until the mid-1990s that women led a struggle that directly involved women's rights and issues. Others would learn from their triumphs and failures.

OFFICIAL DISCOURSE: SUPERFICIAL RESPONSES In the late 1990s and into the new millennium, local authorities continued to negate and ignore the problem of femicide as a "myth" (Godínez Leal 2007). Municipal and state officials blamed the victims for their presence on the streets or their clothing choices. Officials also issued patronizing advertising campaigns, calling on women to avoid risks and on men to "protect" women (Tabuenca Córdova 2010). The government established several special commissioners and investigative groups over the years. For instance, in 1996 Chihuahua's PAN governor, Francisco Barrio Terrazas, inaugurated the Unidad Especializada en Delitos Sexuales y contra la Familia (Specialized Unit for Sex Crimes and against the Family) as well as the Fiscalía Especial para la Investigación de Homicidios de Mujeres, Desaparecidas y Atención a Víctimas (Special Prosecutor for the Investigation of Women's Homicides, Disappeared, and Attention to Victims), both of which activists monitored. However, none controlled enough resources or had enough authority to change law enforcement institutions or to facilitate social investments in education and the economy (Ravelo Blancas, cited in Godínez Leal 2007; also see Morfín 2004 and what Staudt called "bureaucratic decorations" [2008: chap. 5]).

The murders, at least a third of which were sexualized killings, occurred with little to no official investigation and perhaps in complicity with local and state police. The lack of investigation and prosecution has long been common in Mexico (Zepeda Lecuona 2002; selections in Cornelius and Shirk 2007), and that deficiency in the rule of law continues to this day. Both government and scholarly sources acknowledge that after crime and criminal capture, virtually no investigation and prosecution occur. A Tecnológico de Monterrey study found that 98.5 percent of illicit activity remains in impunity, and the rest of all those charged with crimes are tried (El Informador 2010).

If the CPDM's relations with Governor Barrio's state authorities were uneasy during the middle and late 1990s, its relations with the entering PRI governor, Patricio Martínez García, during his term (1998–2004) were confrontational. Martínez García refused to recognize responsibility for the escalating femicide, putting blame on his predecessor for his inability to stop it. Also, he deferred responsibility to the federal government and what he viewed as its inability to stop drug trafficking and provide the necessary appropriations to face the problem. He and his cabinet viewed femicide as related to drugs and addiction and women's night life, which put them at risk and in contact with "drunks" (Pérez García 2005: 153). Meanwhile, the usual lack of investigation and prosecution prevailed.

The confrontations and bad press, which according to Pérez García (2005) were instigated by the state government, propagated demoralization in many of the activists. In addition, different goals and strategies existed among antiviolence activists, many of whom actively cultivated fund-raising efforts or sought political office, and some mothers dared to ask, "Who profits from our pain?" A former community activist and founder of Mujeres por Juárez, Victoria Caraveo Vallina, was appointed to head the government agency Instituto Chihuahuense de la Mujer under Governor Martínez García. A member of a wealthy and politically prominent family, Caraveo Vallina's polemical statements—once in office—questioning the veracity of activists' statements and local groups' statistics on femicide exacerbated the already complicated interlocution between the state government and the local activist groups. Furthermore, divisiveness occurred between those in Caraveo Vallina's organization (Mujeres por Juárez) and the rest of the CPDM with regard to access to resources and governmental services, as a few mothers of femicide victims or missing daughters (whom Caraveo Vallina referred to as "mis madres" [*my* mothers]) followed her lead with patronage-like promises to get resources for houses, counseling, and other assistance (these and other details in Staudt 2008 and Pérez García 2005). Paradoxically, while Caraveo Vallina turned into a gatekeeper and filtered which cases would receive governmental attention and which would not, city elites openly criticized activists as greedy opportunists who profited from victims of femicide. It was as if officials articulated a denial of violence against women by sidetracking debates over numeric counts.

Perhaps it was the CPDM members' lack of a well-designed media strategy to effectively respond to the malicious attacks by the local and state government that made them the targets of government-instigated attacks that placed blame on them for the bad image portrayed of the city, one that it was said could possibly deter foreign investment. The many external pressures, and also the internal disputes among members of the CPDM, debilitated the movement. Yet, despite the ruptures that anti-femicide activism had experienced and the unrelenting governmental "smear campaign[s]" against individual and civil-society groups (Amnesty International 2003: 60), by the end of the 1990s, many of the CPDM's member organizations had gained invaluable experience in mobilizing, in establishing and enhancing their networks, and in delineating a clear direction for their movement—now conceived beyond the CPDM.

[Activists' incessant work of public denunciation placed femicide in the collective consciousness and made a spectacle of the state's ineffectiveness.] Newspapers in Ciudad Juárez contained extensive coverage of femicide even though its representation in print was often questioned by activists, who decried such work as sensationalist, and as revictimizing women. One of the first U.S. writers to bring the killings to an English-language audience was Charles Bowden, in collaboration with photojournalist Julián Cardona. Their work documented and portrayed the mummified female bodies in the desert to a large U.S. audience (1996). However, filmmakers Lourdes Portillo, in *Señorita extraviada* (2001), and Rafael Bonilla, in *La batalla de las cruces* (2005), brought agency to the victimhood characterization with their documentation of the struggles of activists and mothers seeking justice for their murdered daughters. Their films were shown to wide audiences in the United States and Mexico, in both Spanish- and English-language versions.

TRANSITIONS TO SECOND-STAGE ANTIVIOLENCE ACTIVISM

The 2001 discovery of eight young women's bodies brazenly dumped in Campo Algodonero (cotton field) inside Juárez during the pre-2005 stage of activism would galvanize mobilizations onto the streets on both sides of the border, provoke official backlash strategies of divide and rule, and ultimately focus activists on quieter strategies, such as pursuing legal action to gain justice. As the formerly hidden violence against women became public elsewhere in the state of Chihuahua and in Mexico generally, various congressional and federal agencies' actions multiplied the attention being given to a woman's right to live a life free from violence (as stated in the title of a 2007 law, Ley General de Acceso de las Mujeres a Una Vida Libre de Violencia, passed in the Mexico Cámara de Diputados) (Red Mesa de Mujeres de Ciudad Juárez and CLADEM 2012).

Several international agencies, including the Convention on the Elimination of All Forms of Discrimination against Women and the UN High Commission for Human Rights, issued various landmark reports in 2005 and 2006. Most important was the 2005 Inter-American Court of Human Rights' admittance of the cases of three Campo Algodonero femicide victims: Esmeralda Herrera Monreal, Claudia Ivette González, and Laura Berenice Ramos Monárrez (Red Mesa de Mujeres de Ciudad Juárez and CLADEM 2012).

Visibility for the anti-femicide movement grew on a global scale. Besides the activities of border organizations and university conferences in Mexico and the United States (Universidad Nacional Autónoma de México, University of California at Los Angeles, and Arizona State University), Eve Ensler's play *The Vagina Monologues*—performed world-wide—added a new monologue in 2003 about a murdered maquiladora worker. The Mexico Solidarity Network organized caravans to cross the United States, raising funds in cities and on campuses, and spreading awareness about femicide and the exploitative economy (Mueller, Hansen, and Qualtire 2009), an effective, personalized mass-mobilization strategy that would be renewed in 2011–2012 with Javier Sicilia's caravans (see chapter 6).

The shift from first- to second-stage antiviolence organizing also illustrates the shift in political context, most notably the political op-portunity structure (Tarrow 1998). Given growing elite hostility and inaction, the opportunity structure changed. In the second stage of anti-femicide activism, in 2005 and thereafter, targeted feminist legal activism emerged among activists in Ciudad Juárez in its shifting po-litical opportunity structure. However, this occurred amid some ten-sion and division; the decrease in marching and protesting was some-times viewed as indifference. As Melissa Wright quoted Esther Chávez Cano from her interview with her, "The silence terrifies me. . . . No one is protesting. . . . There are no press conferences. No marches. It's like we're back in 1993" (Wright 2010: 211). Wright goes on to discuss the fragmentation among activists, who were going in different direc-tions. Why the internal fissures?, Wright asks, and quotes sociologist Rosalba Robles, who lamented, "The in-fighting makes all of this so hard" (Wright 2010: 213). By 2008, though, once military occupation began, with the associated escalating violence, a climate of fear reigned in the city, generating differences over strategies and diminished oppor-tunities to engage with government among significant alliances (Doyle 2011a). Yet the pathway was carved: using dramatic activism to make a spectacle of the state was a strategy that would reemerge in 2010 and thereafter.

The changing political opportunity structure also produced a shift in organizational alliances and priority positions. Leaders in a key col-laborative alliance, Movimiento Pacto por la Cultura (Cultural Pact Movement), founded in the early 1990s as an umbrella to focus on cul-ture and the arts—a political-engagement approach common in the Americas (Winn 2006: chap. 11), reinvigorated itself and reorganized its priorities around violence and its reduction, highlighting femicide, vio-lence against women, and gender injustices. Its members were women (including Méndez) and men who were committed to ending violence

Movimiento Pacto por la Cultura activists march for peace. Photo by Renato Díaz.

against women (Doyle 2011a: 38) and some feminist men who had learned much from the near decade of women's organizing. Although not connected to movements in Chile and Argentina during the repression there in the 1970s and 1980s, conjunctures occurred between women and men over connecting violence in Argentine and Chilean society and violence in the home with calls for "democracy" in both (Winn 2006: chap. 6). Mothers and other women organizing for human rights in Chile (*por la vida*, as they called it) became famous for their human rights demands about human lives heard worldwide.

In Juárez, the Pacto developed a three-page position paper in 2004. In its preliminary statement, a major consideration was the "más urgentes que enfrentar—como es el caso de la violencia" (urgency in facing issues—such as the violence) and the development of diverse social capital for the synergy it offers (Pacto por la Cultura en Juárez 2004). Although alignments differed, signatories with overlapping memberships in various organizations wove together commitments to organize around the most urgent of problems: the violence that both women and men had a stake in reducing. In 2010, Pacto joined an even

Soldiers on duty during the Marcha del Coraje, Dolor y Desagravio, which took place in February 2010 in response to the Villas de Salvárcar massacre. The soldier on the right takes photos of marchers. Photo by Renato Díaz.

larger coalition with a wider set of partners, Grupo de Articulación Justicia en Juárez, discussed in the following section, on the third layer of activism against militarization.

In sum, the second-stage women's activism strategy for organizing and mobilizing put less emphasis on marches and rallies and more on public discussion forums, litigation, political work, and work related to culture and the arts through the formation of women's collectives. Women leaders became part of other organizations, including the coalition of groups affiliated with the Red Mesa de Mujeres. Overlapping members and the learning that occurs as people share precedents and strategies helped to provide a broader base of power from which to challenge and resist the militarization that aggravated rather than solved or reduced violence in Juárez from 2008 onward.

THIRD LAYER: ANTI-MILITARIZATION ALLIANCES

The U.S.–Mexico border has long been a place of low-intensity conflict (Dunn 1996), analyzed since the 1980s and joined subsequently in U.S. "wars" on drugs, terrorism, and immigration (Payan 2006) with enforcement from triangular linkages among bureaucratic agencies, politicians, and corporate contractors who contribute to political campaigns in the "Border Security Industrial Complex" (Staudt, Payan, and Dunn 2009). U.S. military bases and air spaces cloud the Southwest, as an Air National Guard air traffic–control map illuminates (www.seeandavoid .org). Another map, titled "El Paso, Ciudad Juárez, Southern New Mexico: An Exceptional Test Bed for Homeland Security Technologies," drawn for a transnational business audience by the El Paso Regional Economic Development Corporation (REDCO, integrated with the Paso del Norte Group, but then eliminated in 2013), shows four international ports of entry, with about three-fourths of the image at their north and northeast dominated by large shapes showing Fort Bliss (a U.S. army base), White Sands Missile Range, and Holloman Air Force Base. Beneath the image, the text's headline touts the "robust presence of state, local, and federal partners," listing the following entities as "border security assets": the Joint Task Force North (Department of Defense), the El Paso Intelligence Center (part of the federal Drug Enforcement Agency), and the Border Patrol Field Intelligence Center, plus a sentence on U.S. Customs and Border Protection (Department of Homeland Security) and the Federal Bureau of Investigation, which "provide frontline defense against transnational threats and protect the American public against terrorists and instruments of terror."

The global regime of free trade, symbolized in North America as NAFTA, and the continuing porousness of the border during the 1990s meant that northward migrants crossed successfully and obtained jobs in the United States. However, the tragedy of the attacks on September 11, 2001, hardened the border and U.S. border enforcement. Soon after 9/11, President Bush's Executive Order 13228 equated immigration with terrorism (analyzed fully in Staudt 2009 and 2011). And the ongoing drug trade led to the expansion from the one-sided, U.S. militarization of the border to a two-sided, binational militarization soon after President Calderón took office in 2006. The collaboration expanded under the 2008 U.S. Mérida Initiative, a technical and hardware assistance program with $1.6 billion in funding appropriated through 2013 (United States Department of State). Well before this new collaboration, the United States had helped to foster the prohibitionist drug-control regime worldwide (Global Commission on Drug Policy 2011).

President Calderón, elected in 2006 for the six-year, constitutionally mandated one-term, no-immediate-succession presidency of Mexico, launched his version of a war on drugs and on organized crime. Such

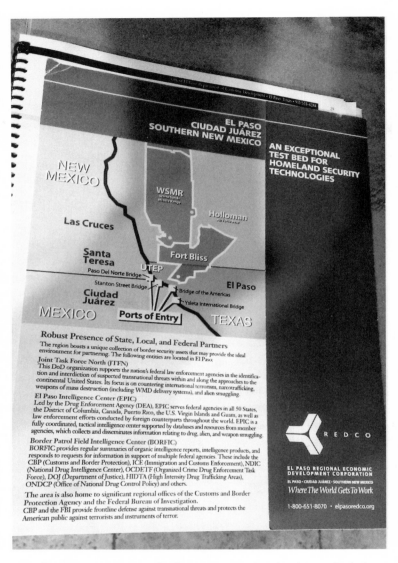

Map illustrating economic and military connection at the El Paso–Ciudad Juárez border. Reprinted from a REDCO flyer.

a war was admittedly a challenge since complicity had historically been woven between cartels and officials at federal, state, and municipal levels (Payan, Staudt, and Kruszewski 2013). With support from Mexico's Congress, Calderón channeled precious budgetary resources away from economic and social development to law enforcement in order to bring competing drug cartels under control. At the outset, in 2007–2008, the competition between the Juárez and Sinaloa cartels, fighting over market space and gateway regions, was particularly brutal in northern Mexico and in Ciudad Juárez specifically.

Government agencies in Mexico and their U.S. counterparts portray the war on drugs and organized crime as one that President Calderón has been gradually winning through the capture of major drug lords and their public display at press conferences. Officials often instantly refer to murders as being "executions" among criminals and thus presume guilt and complicity on the part of the victims, even though most crimes go without investigation or prosecution. Until January 2010, four years into his six-year term, the president had never visited Ciudad Juárez, the murder capital of Mexico and of the world, a city that Interior Secretary Alejandro Poiré of Mexico declared to have suffered the worst of the violence (*Economist* 2012d: 9).

While there is no doubt that the cartels and their affiliated gangs use brutal methods, official forces have also murdered and plundered (Human Rights Watch 2011) in a problematic law enforcement context wherein little to no investigation is conducted. At least 60,000 (but as many as 120,000) people have been murdered since 2007 in Mexico (Human Rights Watch 2011), at least 10,000 of them in Ciudad Juárez alone.

REVISITING MILITARIZATION WITH A HYPERMASCULINIZED AND GENDERED LENS

Héctor Padilla Delgado is one of the few academic analysts to connect violence, militarization, and gender in the "new" disorder of Ciudad Juárez (2011). He (and we) emphasizes "new" because historically, the city—though called a "city of vice" (Vila 2000)—was a relatively peaceful place compared to the contemporary period. Even the 1911 Battle of Juárez during the Mexican Revolution reported fewer casualties than those in Juárez in 2008 and annually for several years thereafter.

Padilla calls militarization, with its threats and counterthreats, the "maquinaria del miedo" (machinery of fear) where "la fuerza habla" (force talks) (2009: 309). At the peak of military occupation, military vehicles patrolled the city, with officers clothed in uniforms and masks and carrying huge assault weapons. Checkpoints had been set up around the city and at the center, like the Green Zone in Baghdad. Organized criminals not only killed individuals execution style, but also massacred groups of people (such as the teens at a birthday party in Villas de Salvárcar, covered in the next chapter), tortured victims to convey messages through the display of mutilated dead bodies in public "performances" (see Domínguez-Ruvalcaba and Corona 2010), and communicated fear through social media and YouTube. Indeed, with the vast increases in the grisly murders of men in brutal, public style, the atmosphere became reminiscent of the early years of femicide, causing any who had doubted the number of women's murders to rethink their position that activists exaggerated the problem. We consider femicide to have been a *preview* for the subsequent violence, making the horrors believable to more people.

Border scholars like Pablo Vila and Alejandro Lugo construct "masculinity performances" in northern Mexico that counter U.S. masculinity, suggesting a polarized approach, partly to reinforce national identity (Staudt 2008: 48). However, the construction of masculinity via militarization is a binational display of hybridity in the transnational practice of masculinities among those who occupy aggressive institutions of control. Padilla goes one step further in conceptualizing the "machismo-autoritarismo" of the generals turned preventive police, public security agents, and police chiefs (2011: 316). In Ciudad Juárez, the most recent personification of authoritarian hypermasculinity, from 2011 to 2013, was Police Chief Julián Leyzaola, already known for his human rights abuses and use of torture to "cleanse" Tijuana and its police force (Finnegan 2010).

The federal police demonstrate brutality equal to that of the local police force under Leyzaola. At the Primer Foro contra la Militarización y la Violencia (First Forum against Militarization and Violence), October 29–31, 2010, at the Universidad Autónoma de Ciudad Juárez, organized by the Frente Plural Ciudadano (Plural Citizens' Front), a young sociology student named José Darío Alvarez was shot and gravely wounded by a federal police officer. This was a "shoot to kill": the officer positioned his gun, aimed, and shot José Darío through his back, and the bullet exited through his torso, exposing some intestines, all while march participants, including José Darío, made it inside the univer-

Student protesters carry a "Prohibido olvidar" (Forgetting is forbidden) banner commemorating the near-fatal shooting of student José Darío Alvarez by federal police. Photo by Renato Díaz.

sity, where the *foro* was to take place. The attempted murder lives on in protest images.

Amid this massive carnage, what some have coined an "undeclared civil war," the murders of women continue and have increased by almost five times (Monárrez Fragoso 1998–). Men's murders, however, have increased by nearly ten times. Other horrors also occur, obscured by militarization and war: forced disappearances, kidnappings, routine extortions, and human trafficking. Militarization and the war have almost rendered women's murders invisible and erased the insights that gendered lenses once brought (though see chapter 5). Authorities instantly attribute murders to cartel vendettas, but women's groups have been able to regenerate some of the public attention that had faded as a result of the backlash and resentment against the high-visibility organizing through 2004 and from "femicide deniers" (see chapter 4). The overall carnage made femicide believable, and once anti-militarization forces surfaced, a joint forum for antiviolence networking became more visible in a conjuncture of second-stage anti-femicide and anti-militarization activism.

GRUPO DE ARTICULACIÓN: SYNERGIES FROM
JOINT ACTIVISM AGAINST VIOLENCE

Grupo de Articulación Justicia en Juárez (Articulation of Groups for
Justice in Juárez), founded in 2010 at the peak of the drug war, consists
of established and newer *asociaciones civiles* (civil associations) and
grassroots organizations (with a decidedly human rights agenda) that
had informally operated as a network at various historical moments
in the city. The organizations in Grupo de Articulación formalized ties
in a founding document where they identify an unprecedented human
rights crisis defined by police impunity, violence, and militarization
that call for concerted action. They also stress a commitment to strategically working together during the "city's emergency" and in light of
the increasing risk faced by human rights activists across the nation resulting from the state's public attack on their activism.

Organizations in Grupo de Articulación include those of both older
and newer vintage. Among those with a long history of two decades
or more in the community, we identify Comunidades Eclesiales de
Base (Eclesiastic Base Communities), Comisión de Solidaridad y Defensa de los Derechos Humanos (Solidarity and Defense Commission
for Human Rights), and Organización Popular Independiente (Independent Popular Organization). Those of more recent vintage, but with
seasoned members, include Centro de Mujeres Tonantzin (Tonantzin
Women's Center), Centro de Derechos Humanos Paso del Norte (Paso
del Norte Center for Human Rights), Casa Amiga (Friendship House),
Movimiento Pacto por la Cultura, Red Mesa de Mujeres, Plan Estratégico de Juárez, Comité Médico Ciudadano (Citizens' Medical Committee), Mujeres de Pacto (Women's Pact), Consejo Ciudadano por el
Desarrollo Social, A.C. (Citizens' Council for Social Development), and
Colectiva Arte Comunidad y Equidad, A.C. (Art Community and Eq-
uity Collective). Together, they accumulate a wealth of experience, and
their members are well known and respected activists in the city.

In the last three years, Grupo de Articulación has displayed its strong
connections and collaborative work with three of the most visible and
significant social movements in Mexico: Javier Sicilia's Movimiento
por la Paz con Justicia y Dignidad (Movement for Peace with Justice and
Dignity), No Más Sangre (No More Blood), and the Permanent Peoples'
Tribunal. These connections and work are evident in the prominent
role Grupo de Articulación played in the organization of activities and
mobilizations in the city, including the Caravana del Consuelo, led by

Javier Sicilia to Ciudad Juárez; the participation of an important number of activists from Grupo de Articulación in the Un Minuto por No Más Sangre open-mike event held June 6, 2011, in Mexico City with high-profile artists, journalists, and scholars, from all walks of life, speaking for one minute over a twenty-four-hour period for "no more blood"; and the Permanent Peoples' Tribunal, held in Ciudad Juárez, which hosted more than 250 participants from communities across Mexico. Grupo networks multiple bases with diverse agendas, such as feminists, cultural rights activists, human rights advocates, and church-based community organizers, among others.

OFFICIAL DISCOURSE: BINATIONAL COLLABORATION PURPORTEDLY INTACT

Official transcripts, emanating from seemingly strong leaders and institutions, illustrate continuity over time and across borders. The transcripts are disseminated through diverse print and electronic media in both Mexico and the United States; social media both counter and reinforce these dominant perspectives. The Calderón administration's public stance bears a striking resemblance to that of the United States under both Republican (Bush) and Democratic (Obama) presidents in their official binational cooperation from capital cities to the border.

The United States portrays Mexico as a strong ally that is conducting its own war on drugs, like the drug war the United States has pursued for over forty years. There has been murky public and not-so-public support for the multiple and fragmented U.S. bureaucratic agencies that have operated for decades under multiple presidents. Such support increased with the 2008 announcement of the three-year Mérida Initiative, with a budget of over $1 billion, under the outgoing Bush administration. The program has been maintained under the Obama administration (United States Department of State). Some dents in the narrative occurred with Secretary of State Hillary Clinton's acknowledgment, on a visit to Monterrey, Mexico, on March 26, 2009, that profitable U.S. drug demand drives the ruthless supplier and shipping cartels (United States Department of State 2009).

CRACKS IN THE BINATIONAL DIVIDE   U.S. Department of State cable traffic through WikiLeaks revealed the façade of official transcripts when formerly secret comments offered more realistic assessments of Mexico's flawed war on drugs, broadcast worldwide. WikiLeaks also demonstrated the extent to which U.S. agendas and personnel penetrated the inner sanctum of a once-nationalist Mexico that prides itself on sovereignty. Indeed, as early as late 2006, before Calderón took power as president after a flawed, close election, readers of WikiLeaks reported on the U.S. Embassy's secret report "Strengthening Calderón's Weak Hand," in which a cable announced, "We will begin vigorous transition planning across the board with the Calderón team" (Petrich Moreno 2012).

According to *La Jornada* journalist Blanche Petrich Moreno (2012), WikiLeaks disseminated cables initially to Spain's *El País* in late 2010, and very soon thereafter, to other newspapers, with *La Jornada* the first recipient in Latin America. After a WikiLeaks team spent a month reviewing the nearly 8,000 pages of cable traffic between the U.S. Embassy in Mexico and the State Department sent over two decades, they published revelations and uploaded documents. The titles of more than 100 published articles reveal insights: for example, "The Army Is Comfortable Letting the Cartels Fight Each Other." Most important about the sum total was the "unprecedented cooperation between American and Mexican officers" and the "level of US influence and involvement in Mexico's counter-narcotics and security policies." Curiously, Petrich Moreno notes, little debate occurred in other Mexican media about "the ongoing role of the United States in our sovereign affairs." Her note leads to inferences that mainstream Mexican media stifled or silenced the debate.

While some Mexican print and electronic media outlets valiantly cover crime and drug wars, despite the assassination of sixty-six journalists in Mexico from 2000 to 2011 and the disappearance of twelve between 2005 and 2010 (United Nations 2011; CPJ 2010), other media outlets take orders from cartels about what to print. Such is the case in northeastern Mexico, where major print media report no crime, but delegate such risky activity to media on the U.S. side of the border and/ or to Mexico-based social media (some of which are under threat, as the beheadings and grisly and intimidating public displays of 2011 chillingly communicated) (Correa-Cabrera and Nava 2013). In Ciudad Juárez, reporter Armando Rodríguez and photographer Luis Carlos Santiago Orozco were assassinated in 2008 and 2010, respectively. Both worked for the major newspaper *Diario de Juárez*, which adopted a policy in 2008 of continuing to report crime, military, and federal police news, but without bylines, as collective solidarity in the face of the threat and to reduce risks to individual journalists.

In the United States, more cracks in the public transcript could be heard, with voices such as Senator Patrick Leahy, a Democrat from Vermont, calling for 15 percent of funding to be held back should human rights abuses be documented (Seelke and Finklea 2013). Wiki-Leaks, of course, widened fissures with its realistic and embarrassing language in quotations of U.S. officials about Calderón's war on drugs. The BBC quoted one U.S. cable description of security institutions as being "locked in a zero-sum competition in which one agency's success is viewed as another's failure, [and in which] information is closely guarded and joint operations are all but unheard of" (BBC 2010).

The costs of militarization inhibit public investment in social, economic, and health sectors of the city. Moreover, punitive drug-law enforcement policies detract from spending on drug prevention and treatment. As the next chapter analyzes, a massacre of teens at a birthday party in the neighborhood Villas de Salvárcar triggered a change in people's perceptions and fostered, finally, a federal response when President Calderón visited the city after the massacre not just once or twice, but three times, and announced with great fanfare the multi-agency, multilevel public-investment plan called Todos Somos Juárez.

Leaders in the third layer of activism, cynical about official discourses and leveraging the cracks in that discourse, demonstrate the power of multiple and overlapping synergies that have developed among anti-violence activists, whether they focus on women, men and women, or militarization. Grupo de Articulación provided a wide umbrella under which leaders could cohere and strategize to organize momentous actions. Personal, face-to-face organizing multiplies deep relationships, ideas, and strategies in exponential ways. Social media quickly disseminated ideas as well as tensions. By 2010, the stage was set to generate fruitful alliances among different kinds of activists in Ciudad Juárez and eventually the rest of the country that produced a coherence we demonstrate in subsequent chapters.

REFLECTIONS: TOWARD THE BODY OF THIS BOOK

In this chapter, we threaded the activism in Ciudad Juárez from labor struggles to anti-femicide in its first and second stages. Activists challenged injustice with their counternarratives, with occasional but meager victories, many of them the formation of commissions and the passage of laws and policies, albeit unenforced. Although low-intensity conflict had been simmering at the border for decades, with the outbreak of cartel and military violence in 2008 and onward, the government pursued a militarization strategy and a promise of security and cleaner law enforcement institutions. These promises have yet to be fulfilled.

Yet underneath the façade of official pretense in discourses from the United States and Mexico, a façade cracked by WikiLeaks and other reality checks, through 2009 one found a relatively fearful public, one that initially tolerated or accepted some of the discourse (Monárrez Fragoso 2010a: 30) but gradually diversified and shifted its perspective (Díaz 2012) with three momentous events in 2010 and 2011 that we discuss in subsequent chapters. Perhaps this was not coincidental, given the pioneering and courageous feminists, mothers, and human rights leaders and activists surrounding the anti-femicide struggle of a decade past who joined collaborative organizations like Movimiento Pacto por la Cultura—women's voices and women leaders who once again galvanized change, just as they had in the antiviolence activism of a decade earlier. We note below how some of their discourse was gendered, adding nuance to the often hidden-within-hidden discourses of the wider public: whether speaking as women or as mothers who challenged the gender hierarchy and legitimacy of rulers' inability to "protect" or respect the rule of law in the protection racket called the state.

CHAPTER THREE

FROM FEAR AND INTIMIDATION TO
GAME-CHANGING ACTIVISM

To publicly say one's word is to stand up and say, "I, us, WE ARE, and we denounce and demand." (Méndez translation)
DICTAMEN, TRIBUNAL PERMANENTE DE LOS PUEBLOS, CAPÍTULO MÉXICO, MAY 2011 (P. 24)

IN THIS CHAPTER, we develop alternative perspectives of Ciudad Juárez, Mexico's fifth-largest city, located at the northern border of Mexico and long viewed as the infamous site of *feminicidio* and as the disputed territory of drug cartels. In response to organized crime, both the Mexican and U.S. governments have militarized their sides of the border, with Mexico's military and federal police presence diminished in the post-Calderón era. Along with those two massive, masked, and heavily armed forces, the municipal police force also operates with a militarized logic, as it did under the command of Lt. Col. Julián Leyzaola, an official on leave from the Mexican army who was police chief from 2011 to 2013. Together, the constant surveillance, display of sophisticated weaponry, and numerous checkpoints across the city of these three entities gave Juárez the atmosphere of an occupied warzone territory.

Urban aesthetics of warfare, coupled with former president Calderón's belligerent narrative attempting to legitimize his war against drugs and drug cartels, often obscure Juarenses' courageous collective activism and everyday individual resistance to militarization in what Salvador Salazar Gutiérrez and Martha Curiel García (2012) term the *ciudad abatida* (abated city). In addition, journalistic—and academic—accounts about Ciudad Juárez center their attention on documenting and analyzing the systemic violence that is present in the city. However, an emphasis on body counts and narratives of gore, while morbidly seductive, makes invisible the activism and resistance that is of focus in this book.

Drawing on the work of political anthropologist James Scott and his conceptual analysis of "everyday forms of resistance," we analyze the creative and extensive human rights and justice activism in the city, along with the everyday insistence of residents on claiming a normal life, utilizing public space, celebrating life and being alive, and shaping their and their city's future. This chapter also documents the centrality of Juarenses' activism for the rest of Mexico and Latin America, for their organizing and mobilizing efforts are viewed as an inspiration and a model for justice activists across Mexico, Central America, and South America. Yet, while individual resistance and activism have not demilitarized the city entirely or eradicated femicide and disappearances of women, these acts represent a form of power that—reinforced by activists' visible collective activities—challenges the dominant perspective of the city and positively shapes its future viability.

We guide our analysis of the borderlands with the work of political anthropologist James Scott. Scott's conceptions about "public transcripts" and "hidden transcripts" proved useful in our examination of the context of power relations in Ciudad Juárez. The body of this chapter centers on the documentation and analysis of resistance: when the hidden becomes public. The acts of resistance we analyze are gendered, involving women and men and their challenges to the hypermasculinity that prevails in militarized contexts. We render resistance in the form of three game-changing[1] vignettes that describe courageous actions that generated national and international press coverage. We recognize resistance as game changing because the actions that signified it created an inflection point from what had been observed to be pervasively construed as common knowledge or true about what was happening in Ciudad Juárez. Perhaps not coincidentally, given the pioneering and courageous activism of feminists, mothers, and human rights activists surrounding the anti-femicide struggle of the 1990s, women leaders and violence against women once again led to change, just as they had earlier.

Below we describe three game-changing acts of formerly hidden individual resistance that became public and collective in their performance and consequences. We refer to them as game changing given that these acts of resistance inexorably dismantled and publicly delegitimized an insidious discourse that had been prevalent during the first years of the so-called drug war, when troops were deployed and a police state was established to purportedly put an end to what authorities officially recognized as drug-cartel violence. Moreover, the moments of resistance are game changing as they galvanized dissent that had previously remained isolated. Together, the acts of resistance we describe changed how Ciudad Juárez was viewed: by its residents, by the state, and by those in the international environment through third-party media coverage and interpretations of militarization.

VILLAS DE SALVÁRCAR

An example of what Scott (1990) refers to as public transcript, or discourse that casts light on subordinates' formerly contained voices in the presence of authority or the dominant, is Luz María Dávila's interpellation of President Felipe Calderón as a result of a massacre in Villas de Salvárcar, a working-class neighborhood amidst a large industrial park southeast of Juárez. This maquiladora worker's forceful intervention, in February of 2010 in Ciudad Juárez, made public the long-hidden transcript of Juarenses denouncing Calderón's war on drugs as a failed strategy that was becoming increasingly costly for their border community.

According to Father Oscar Enríquez in a speech at the ¡BASTA! Border Activism Summit for Teaching and Action conference about the always-contested numeric details, in 2010 Juárez reported 3,111 murders; in 2009, there were 2,685 killings; and in 2008, there were 1,608 (Enríquez 2011). Through those years of escalating violence, official authorities' discourse insidiously attributed people's murders to the victims' hypothetical—but never proved—connection with the world of drug trafficking, cartels, and gangs. However, it took just a simple few words from Luz María Dávila, a resident of Villas de Salvárcar and the mother of two young men, seventeen-year-old José Luis Piña Dávila and nineteen-year-old Marcos Piña Dávila, killed at Villas de Salvárcar, to irrevocably put in question Calderón's strategy of militarization as a viable means to eradicate drug trafficking. This strategy of challenging official discourse was also one that had been supported by Juarense entrepreneurs and local elites.

Villas de Salvárcar, or Villas, as residents refer to it, experienced the killing of fifteen people at a party on January 30, 2010. The majority of those killed were students in their teenage years and residents of the neighborhood who were attending the birthday celebration of another adolescent. Those who witnessed the event told authorities, the press, and everyone who listened that three groups of armed men traveling in three vehicles descended upon those who were inside the house where the celebration was taking place and opened fire on them. Then they went back to their cars and slowly drove away.

In a matter of hours, the Villas massacre made local, national, and international news. Pressed by national and international public opinion in the media and on social networks, President Calderón was forced to make a statement about the massacre. In Japan, while attending a series of official meetings with dignitaries from that country, President Calderón was quick to attribute the events in Juárez to gang-related activity. Understandably, the parents and families of youngsters whose lives were taken were outraged by the disrespectful and inaccurate presidential pronouncement.

As days passed, and more details of the horrifying crime were made public, opinion in Juárez grew increasingly critical. Villas residents all spoke about their dead. Through the local newspaper, people came to know the students—not the "gang members" that the president claimed had been killed. Those killed were mostly high school students, some of them athletes. Marcos and José Luis, the sons of Luz María Dávila, who lived a few houses from the crime scene, were students. One was a freshman in the local college; the other attended high school.

Villas de Salvárcar parents' outrage spread through the community and caused a public uproar. Thus, within a few days of the massacre, and in response to social discontent, an announcement was made about a presidential visit to the city. It was expected that President Calderón would launch a series of measures to respond to the social crisis that the city was facing. Instead, what was launched turned out to be a *social welfare* and polemical program called Todos Somos Juárez (We're All Juárez) that quickly came under fire since it was constituted by a series of actions that had been determined without input from local organizations or authorities. And though certain local sectors of the population had been invited to the launching of the program, many claimed that Todos Somos Juárez was carelessly designed and put in place merely as a strategy of appeasement, one that strengthened the already privileged while providing little acknowledgment of gendered dimensions of violence, rather than redistributing resources to spread opportunities to more people in the city. In fact, more recently, critics and journalists like Marcela Turati (2012) have documented numerous irregularities with regard to funding allocation, transparency, and accountability in Todos Somos Juárez. Along with community organizations that included human rights groups and activists, members of the entrepreneurial elite and chambers of commerce were invited to attend the meeting to launch the program, which was led by President Calderón. Almost all the members of Calderón's cabinet were present, as well as his secretary of the Interior;[2] members of his security cabinet; the then governor of the state of Chihuahua, José Reyes Baeza; and the then municipal president (mayor) of Juárez, José Reyes Ferriz.

Like most high-profile social and political events in the city, the summit took place at Cibeles, the exclusive convention center in Juárez. That morning, however, Cibeles looked different. Hundreds and hundreds of federal and municipal police, as well as members of the Estado Mayor Presidencial, the elite police force in charge of the president's security, surrounded the center and controlled all traffic. Uninvited activists and organizers, students, teachers, university professors (including Méndez), and family members who had lost a loved one in Calderón's war gathered outside of Cibeles and denounced the criminalization of social life. In contrast to the welcoming mood inside Cibeles's facilities, where government officials, entrepreneurs, and other high-ranking guests shook hands and enthusiastically greeted each other, the main avenue and the smaller streets around the convention center witnessed the presence of angry and somber faces. Signs in hand, people shouted against the police and military presence, which signals the criminalization of social life. They also repudiated Calderón and called him an "assassin." Chants by activists could be heard: "Juárez, Juárez no es cuartel, fuera ejército de él" (Juárez, Juárez is not a barracks, the military must go). Young students, walking defiantly toward the lineup of federal police officers sheltered behind huge plastic shields, would shout: "A estudiar, a aprender, para chota nunca ser" (Let's study, let's learn, so we should never become cops).

Notwithstanding the volatile environment that at many moments threatened to escalate into confrontations with the police, no one was injured or detained. Instead, protesters only experienced what became known as "encapsulation," a widely used strategy of the military and police to neutralize social protest in which officers with shields form barriers around protesters to limit their movements. By encapsulating them, the police literally cornered and kept protesters out of the president's and other high-ranking politicians' motorcades' sight. The "encapsulation" outside the convention center lasted for more than six hours, and during that time, protesters chatted, attempted to convince

Federal police "encapsulate" protesters during President Felipe Calderón's visit to the city to launch Todos Somos Juárez in 2010. Photo by Zulma Y. Méndez.

police that they, the officers, were also part of "the oppressed," improvised chants, and spoke to the media and messengers from authorities and nongovernmental organizations who were inside the convention center who could get near but not across the human barrier created by the police.

Inside Cibeles, Felipe Calderón talked about his government's commitment to transform the city through Todos Somos Juárez and invited the audience to lead the change via work groups or *mesas* that would carry out the plan to, in the view of government officials, reconstruct the city. Not included in the list of distinguished guests, but helped by human rights activists and members of nongovernmental organizations that had been invited to meet with the president, Luz María Dávila was able to sneak into the meeting, with its promises and commitments abounding. A few minutes into the proceedings, the mayor and the governor had spoken about their own efforts to uplift the city and the state when Luz María interjected. Making her way to the front of the room, without a microphone but with a firm voice that could be heard by the approximately six hundred people in attendance, she said:

I am sorry, Mr. President, but I cannot say you are welcome because in my eyes you are not. I want justice. My sons were youngsters that were attending a [birthday] party. I want you to retract what you said. You said that they were gangsters. Lies. My two sons studied and worked. They were not on the streets. They were my only children and I don't have them anymore. I now want justice. You always talk and do nothing. I want you to put yourself in my place and feel what I am feeling right now. (Dávila 2010; Méndez translation)

As she spoke, the room was mostly silent, though a few murmurs and even scornful laughter could be heard, making more evident the discomfort that her words were eliciting from local, state, and federal authorities present. She called the president's words "lies" in an interaction of usually polite language between subordinates and those in authority. But Luz María was determined to say what many had been unable or unwilling to express: "Here, in this city, in the last two years,

Students and activists "encapsulated" and shouting, "Don't detain us, but arrest the inhabitants of that house as they are the criminals, not us." The building in the background is owned by the prominent Zaragoza family. Photo by Zulma Y. Méndez.

Luz María Dávila, *left*, with Zulma Y. Méndez in front of a picture of Marcos, the younger of her two sons murdered during the Villas de Salvárcar massacre, at the welcoming of Javier Sicilia's Caravana del Consuelo. Photo by Renato Díaz.

murders have taken place. A lot has been taking place and no one does anything. I just want justice, not just for my kids but for everyone." Then, admonishing the president, who had just uttered, "Yes, of course," in response to her demand for justice, she said, "Don't tell me 'of course'; do something. If it had been your kid who was murdered, you would look under rocks for the assassins. But because I don't have the means, I can't look." Turning to the municipal president and the governor, who sat next to the president, she said, "Ferriz and Baeza always say the same thing, but they do not do anything, Mr. President. I don't get justice, I have my two children who were killed, and I want you to put yourself in my place." Ending her interjection, she burst into tears and the audience applauded.

As Luz María made the hidden transcript public, Villas de Salvárcar became an emblematic symbol and representation of the horrifying levels of violence and the ineptitude and dereliction of duty of local, state, and federal authorities. It evinced the high price the community and its members were paying for a war that purportedly targeted cartels but in reality had taken the lives of thousands in the city who had died unarmed, young, and poor, but also whose deaths almost always remained in absolute impunity. These deaths at best were recognized by Mexico's president as "collateral damage" in a war that people did not want and had not asked for.

Luz María's clarity as an interpellator guided activists' work. Inspired by her courage, groups in Juárez expressed their solidarity and saw in her presence and action a galvanizing force that brought together activists and organizers against militarization who subsequently formed two important political groups: the Frente Plural Ciudadano (Plural Citizens' Front) and later the Grupo de Articulación Justicia en Juárez.

By speaking truth to power, Luz María Dávila embodied the "moral reserve" of the city, whose citizens—who continued to be criminalized by the state—restored their dignity and their right to protest and resist. Her words and presence inspired an entire nation, and in 2011, Javier Sicilia, as well as other leaders of important social movements in the country, made contact with her to participate in the Caravana del Consuelo (Consolation Caravan). Luz María is still employed as a worker in a manufacturing plant and continues to be seen as a referent in one of the most dramatic chapters in Mexico's social history. After her intervention at Cibeles, the notion that the thousands of people killed in President Calderón's drug war were members of cartels or linked to the drug business was forever dismantled.

MARISELA ESCOBEDO ORTIZ: CONTINUING FEMICIDE WITH IMPUNITY IN CHIHUAHUA

During the 1990s and early 2000s, Ciudad Juárez became infamous for *feminicidio* (femicide) when, over the course of a decade (1993–2003), mothers and activists counted 370 girls and women who had been murdered, approximately a third of the bodies found dumped in the desert periphery after rape, torture, and mutilation. Municipal and state police carried out little investigation and prosecution, perhaps because of complicity with the crimes. In one brazen example, eight bodies were left inside the city, in a cotton field known as Campo Algodonero, in 2001. There was typical inaction from the state at all levels, but three of these victims' cases were tried successfully against the Mexican state (the national government being responsible under international law) at the Inter-American Court of Human Rights, the preparation for which gave rise to another stage of activism in 2005 and thereafter, backed by the legitimacy of a respected international body (see below).

Yet at all levels, government not only failed to prioritize the murders of women, but also protected murderers and struck out against activists who were calling attention to the continuing femicide and impunity. In her grief and anger about impunity and injustice, Marisela Escobedo Ortiz, mother of murder victim Rubí Frayre Escobedo, made the hidden transcript public in a two-year process that embarrassed Chihuahua governor César Duarte and law enforcement officials in the state of Chihuahua and that culminated in her assassination.

Marisela Escobedo's seventeen-year-old daughter, Rubí, was married to Sergio Barraza Bocanegra, an abusive man in a state that hardly takes its laws against domestic violence seriously. Barraza confessed to killing Rubí in June 2009 and led police to a place where pigs are "farmed" and subsequently slaughtered (*marranera*), where her burned remains were left in parts after he had dismembered her. In the state's unusual move to prosecute a woman killer, Barraza was tried in a court of three judges, but was released for what the judges considered a lack of evidence. Like many, Marisela was shocked at the decision and vowed to appeal and to continue protesting the injustice. She did this for over a year.

By the time Sergio Barraza was released, Rubí's case and Marisela's struggle to bring her daughter's aggressor to justice were widely known. Marisela, unclothed but wrapped in a vinyl banner with Rubí's picture imprinted on it and pushing a stroller with her granddaughter (Rubí's daughter) riding in it, walked to various government offices to demand justice. Often covered by the local press, her walks for justice were made familiar to newspaper readers. She was supported by various anti-femicide activists and by the impetus of social pressure gained through her mobilizing efforts. In another unusual move, the state penalized the judges who dismissed the case and agreed to retry it, but law enforcement officials claimed they could not find Barraza.

Marisela, with her son Juan Manuel Frayre Escobedo and a few close friends (public presentations and Staudt interview with Juan Manuel Frayre Escobedo, September 29, 2011), located Barraza, then living with another woman in the state of Zacatecas. Sharing the results of her own investigation, Marisela reported Barraza's location to the authorities in Chihuahua and Zacatecas, who did nothing. Despite the lack of action or response from authorities, she sought a meeting with former president Felipe Calderón. But in Mexico City, Calderón refused to meet with her.

Unrelenting, Marisela continued her protests at the governor's palace in the city of Chihuahua. From Marisela's perspective, the governor's inaction signaled his complicity—a complicity that later her

Marchers carry a poster during the Caravana del Consuelo showing Marisela Escobedo Ortiz protesting police impunity and the murder of her daughter Rubí Frayre Escobedo. Photo by Renato Díaz.

son Juan Manuel, Rubí's sibling, attributed to the fact that Barraza was a member of and received protection from a criminal group known as "the Zetas" (Dávila 2012 [no relation to Luz María Dávila]). The Zetas are a drug cartel in northeastern Mexico with a particularly ruthless reputation that are commonly known to do contract work with state officials.

A week before her assassination, Marisela confronted the governor "in his face." In a less-than-polite and emasculating way, she said to him in front of others, "You should be ashamed that a woman like me is doing your work." On December 16, 2010, she was killed outside the governor's palace, her death captured on palace videotape for the world to see. In the video, viewers can see that the streets, normally bustling with police and security guards, have been cleared. A gunman (*sicario*) emerges, pulls out his weapon, chases Marisela across the street, and shoots her dead. Thus, in Marisela's son's eyes, "this was a State crime" (quoted in Dávila 2012).

The video of Marisela's assassination has been played and replayed on YouTube on Spanish and English URLs, connecting transnational and international viewers with the murder. Of the multiple videos on YouTube, the one with the largest number of views (nearly 400,000) is the Spanish "Capta cámara ataque a Marisela Escobedo," by *Reforma* (www.reforma.com), a major news source. The number of English-language viewers of this video is also large, especially when one considers that it was shown on primetime television in the United States. NBC (National Broadcasting Company), one of the three main U.S. commercial broadcast television networks in the United States, broadcast an entire hour-long show on the assassination on *Dateline*, a primetime television series, including the video of the killing (NBC 2011).

Marisela and Rubí, like the surviving members of their family, have not received justice. In a surprising turn of events, in November of 2012 the then fugitive Sergio Barraza was reportedly found dead in the state of Zacatecas, where Marisela always contended that he was hiding. Apparently, he, along with other individuals that were purportedly members of the Zetas, died in a cross fire with the military (CNN Mexico 2012). Prior to finding Barraza's corpse, authorities presented Enrique Jiménez Zavala as the murderer of Marisela Escobedo. Immediately, anti-femicide activists reacted in support of Juan Manuel Frayre, who maintains, as an eyewitness, that it was Sergio Barraza's sibling, not Jiménez, who killed his mother outside of the governor's palace (Dávila 2012).

In Marisela Escobedo's long journey toward justice, the way in which the state colluded with criminal groups seemed to be uncovered and shifted from being hidden into the realm of public knowledge. After Marisela's assassination at the doorstep of the governor's palace in the capital city of Chihuahua, the collusion of the state and government officials in the protection of criminal groups could be more clearly seen. Marisela had denounced the impunity with which women were killed and criminals were protected during the terms of both Governor José Reyes Baeza, when Rubí was killed, and Governor César Duarte, though Duarte continuously denied it and simulated otherwise. Thus, while in the Campo Algodonero case the Mexican state—in a sort of abstract way—was found responsible for the deaths of the young women whose corpses were found, Marisela's case identified individual agents of the state as responsible for Rubí's murder and for the impunity of officials in crimes against other women in the federal entity of Chihuahua, where Juárez is also embedded.

Revealing publicly the hidden discourse of disdain toward femicide and gender violence has been critical for activists, both anti-femicide and anti-militarization groups. Many of them, in fact, refuse to sit and dialogue with Governor Duarte to demand justice. Other groups have decided to only "accompany" mothers who still believe that the governor must respond and be held accountable for their daughters' femicides or, in other instances, their disappearances. The hidden transcripts, once made public, problematized and had consequences for Juarense activism.

MEMORIALIZATION AND CAMPO ALGODONERO

Paradoxically, a year prior to Marisela Escobedo's femicide, the tenacity and hard work of women's groups—identified with scorn by the local media and authorities as "feminists"—reached a historical triumph. Years of negligence by Mexican authorities at all levels led parents and activists to take their case to the Inter-American Court of Human Rights in Chile. In December 2009, the court ruled against the Mexican state for the femicide of three young women, Claudia Ivette González, Laura Berenice Ramos Monárrez, and Esmeralda Herrera Monreal.

The bodies of these young women, along with five other corpses of young women, had been dumped in Campo Algodonero, located right across from the Asociación de Maquiladoras headquarters in Ciudad Juárez in 2001. Mothers, feminists, and human rights activists had been protesting the sexualized murders of women since 1993, with limited response from law enforcement and the state. Before the cotton field discovery, single bodies had been discovered in the desert periphery. The casual disposal of eight tortured bodies inside the city became a shocking turning point in escalating the activism and galvanizing binational and transnational anti-femicide solidarity (see Staudt 2008: chap. 4). In 2003, Amnesty International adopted anti-femicide as one of its major causes, issued a monograph with global reach titled *Intolerable Killings: Report of Ten Years of Abductions and Murders of Women in Ciudad Juárez and Chihuahua*, and interacted with officials at national and local levels to try to reduce the threat to women.

The court's decision in *González et al. v. Mexico*, or the Campo Algodonero case, included important features to procure justice for the crimes against the three young victims of femicide. It also mandated a series of measures to prevent and eradicate femicide. The mandates were to be implemented in the short term and obligated the Mexican state to do the following (from Red Mesa de Mujeres de Ciudad Juárez and CLADEM 2012):

1. To reopen the investigations into the disappearance, torture, and murder of the three young women in the case
2. To conduct an investigation of the actions of the public servants responsible for maintaining these crimes in impunity and of those who threatened the Monárrez and Herrera families when they sought answers and justice
3. To publish on local and federal governments' website portals the court's decision in its entirety
4. To create a website with information about every woman and girl who has disappeared since 1993 in the state of Chihuahua
5. To create a national data bank of genetic and forensic information [to determine the identity of bodies through the use of DNA and tissue samples, thereby giving closure to families of missing persons]
6. To indemnify the victims' families
7. To organize a public event where authorities would recognize and apologize for their responsibility for the femicides committed in Ciudad Juárez
8. To build a memorial for Laura Berenice, Esmeralda, Claudia Ivette, and all the victims of femicide
9. To standardize investigation protocols as they pertain to femicide, disappearance, and sexual violence
10. To redesign the Alba Protocol, a protocol for the *immediate* search for missing women and girls, to extend it beyond the downtown area
11. To establish a training program for public servants and an educational program for the general public

With direct implications for local, state, and national authorities in Mexico, the Campo Algodonero sentence also had international resonance as it set an important precedent for other Latin American countries where femicide has been escalating. Notwithstanding, the legal provisions established by the court did not afford Rubí Frayre Escobedo the justice she deserved after she became a victim of femicide, nor Marisela Escobedo, when she was killed demanding justice for Rubí.

Femicide and impunity, as Marisela Escobedo's case illustrates, are still constants. In fact, femicide has continued to increase in recent years, albeit alongside much larger increases in the murders of men. According to Julia Monárrez Fragoso (1998–), from 1993 to mid-December of 2011, 1,340 women were killed. Of those, 500 were killed from 1993 to 2007. From 2007—the year President Calderón deployed troops and announced his war on drugs—to mid-December of 2011, 840 women were killed. The annual statistics thus show an increase in femicide of 500 percent. The increase has gone almost unnoticed by many, except for women's groups, which unrelentingly document and denounce femicide and violence against women as well as the noncompliance of local, state, and federal authorities with the international court's ruling. Moreover, when girls and women disappear—perhaps murdered, perhaps living elsewhere—the total numbers are difficult to count with credibility.

In addition to the legal provisions, the human rights court mandated a series of acts of vindication that the Mexican state had to observe as a means of symbolically repairing the damage infringed upon the three families in the case whose daughters were found in Campo Algodonero. Two of the acts were the construction of a memorial to victims and a public and formal apology to victims' families by official members of the Mexican state. During the presentation of the memorial, women's groups and the families of Claudia Ivette, Laura Berenice, and Esmeralda made public the formerly hidden script that denounced the Mexican state's "actions to simulate compliance with the Campo Algodonero sentence" (CEDIMAC 2011).

It was on November 7, 2011, almost two years after the ruling by the Inter-American Court of Human Rights, that Mexican officials publicly announced the inauguration of the memorial and their intention of "offering public apologies" as well as an "acknowledgment of their responsibility" (CEDIMAC 2011). The federal government's announcement was met with skepticism from women's organizations and from the parents of Esmeralda. The skepticism was related to two issues: the memorial was not yet finished and the federal government had refused to incorporate in it—as was the wish of the families of Claudia Ivette, Laura Berenice, and Esmeralda—the names of all victims of femicide since 1993. In addition, women's groups and families of the femicide victims lamented that only lower-level representation from the federal government was in attendance at the announcement: Vice Secretary of the Interior Felipe Zamora, as opposed to the president or the then

Members of Red Mesa de Mujeres at the memorial to Campo Algodonero victims, *Rosa del Desierto* (desert flower), a bronze sculpture by Chilean artist and Ciudad Juárez resident Verónica Leitón. Photo by Imelda Marrufo Nava.

secretary of the Interior Alejandro Poiré. The governor of Chihuahua was also absent for part of the event, as he fled after mothers shouted at him, another example of gendered language defiance.

Yet, despite the discontent, the inauguration of the memorial proceeded. However, it proceeded without the presence of the families of the three young victims of femicide in the Campo Algodonero case or representatives of most women's groups. Their absence at what should have been a historical event was widely documented by local, national, and international press. Louder than words, the silence of their absence spoke to question Mexico's slow and incomplete compliance and what they saw as simulation with respect to the mandate of an international court.

The few members of women's groups who attended, including some associated with Red Mesa de Mujeres, contributed too to exhibit the hidden script that had long denounced the Mexican state's failure to follow through on the human rights court's mandates. During the event with the vice secretary of the Interior, they publicly supported the outcry by organized parents whose daughters had disappeared: "Ni olvido, ni perdón" (Not forgotten, not forgiven). These outcries made international and national news, thus exhibiting governmental presence and their rhetoric about their compliance as an act of simulation, not one sanctioned by the victims' families and women's groups.

ANALYSIS AND CONCLUSIONS

In this chapter, we have analyzed transformative moments of resistance that challenged the public and official transcripts and revealed courage and resistance among Juarenses. In publicly challenging the regime, Juarenses made visible what had been hidden. The game changers exercised voice and agency to interrogate commonsensical understandings of social reality and how militarization, femicide, and impunity are not only pernicious but fostered by the state. Utilizing public space and challenging officials at all levels, from the president to the governor and municipal officials, these brave women contributed to resignify and dignify life in Juárez.

In these moments of resistance, when the hidden became public, women confronted the hypermasculine political-military regime that ostensibly protects women, children, and men. Yet the regime not only failed to protect and secure civil society, it also maligned the reputations of all those murdered, without proper investigation or prosecution.

Prior to these women's challenges, many Juarenses had lived in fear, either accepting the official transcripts or questioning them only in hidden and quiet ways. Luz María challenged the president in an open and public way, shockingly reinterpreting his easy presumption of guilt about the children massacred at Villas de Salvárcar. In his face and in front of many cameras, she called Calderón's words "lies." In so doing, she shifted the hyper-polite forms that citizens generally use for the president and his actions into the realities of life in Ciudad Juárez: naming the official excuses and explanations as lies, thereby cracking the official public transcript.

Marisela Escobedo, outraged with the injustice the so-called criminal justice system levied against the confessed murderer of her daughter Rubí, became a thorn in the side of law enforcement officials in the state and in the face of the governor. Daily, she protested outside the governor's palace and shamed him with her remarks about his incompetence and that of his administration—a shame with class and gendered elements, from a woman to a man of authority, and from an ordinary person who, with her family, was able to locate the killer, unlike the governor's highly specialized law enforcement experts. Marisela paid the ultimate price for this challenge: assassination.

In our final vignette, we discussed the persistence of the mothers and women's groups in highlighting state inaction in addressing the murders of women. Despite nearly two decades of high-visibility organizing, expert testimony to the Inter-American Court of Human Rights, and the court's judgment against Mexico and its mandates for change, the Mexican government continues to ignore the murders of women. The war on drugs and organized crime, despite its own flaws, abuses, and human rights failings, takes precedence.

Activists used the opportunity of the mandated public commemoration to highlight continuing state intransigence on femicide, and they did so with courage and risk. The mothers of the three murdered young women named in the court decision, plus a broad coalition of women's groups, pressed for a public list of *all* the femicide victims. Utilizing a variety of tactics, some boycotted the commemoration event, while others publicly protested at the event. They vowed to remember and not to forgive in full public view and with public voice. The activism surrounding the public commemoration was widely reported in local, national, and international media, thereby shaming the Mexican government once again. Shall we question international relations theorists like Thomas Risse, Stephen Ropp, and Kathryn Sikkink (1999) on the shaming process or credit the growing resistance of critical masses of issue-based organizations and coalitions? Ultimately, the two reinforce one another.

As we noted earlier, human rights theorists in international relations have posed a set of linkages that local activists use with intransigent governments that abuse human rights. Local activists develop ties with transnational and international organizations, such as United Nations agencies, Amnesty International, and Human Rights Watch. These international organizations press not only the intransigent state, but also other governments in order to exert multiple forms of pressure on abusive states, thereby shaming them into change. International relations theorists have called this the "boomerang" effect (Risse, Ropp, and Sikkink 1999). Such strategies have been effective in addressing political repression in other governments. Moreover, Olga Aiken Araluce has documented some change within Mexico's federal attorney general's office in the adoption of new procedures that incorporate international norms on gender-based murders (2009).

Nevertheless, in Ciudad Juárez, despite multiple boomerangs and escalating forms of shaming the Mexican state over its impunity regarding the murders of women—most notably the Inter-American Court of Human Rights and its mandates to the government—women and men continue to be murdered and to disappear. Activists and individuals have exercised courage and resilience for more than two decades over the murders of women. Initially, the state hardly pretended to consider femicide a public security problem worthy of attention, much less a priority. However, two decades of activism have produced ugly, embarrassing visibility about the Mexican state's neglect of violence against women and the consequences of its inaction (see Staudt 2008), most recently in the international court decision and its mandates to the state, which have been only selectively followed. Still, violence against women prevails unabated. The state is busy fighting militarized wars on drugs and organized crime, in league with the U.S. drug war and with U.S. support under the Mérida Initiative, to establish publicly scripted security, which is really insecurity. Moments of resistance among the formerly hidden voices now reveal this insecurity in individual and collective ways, as we have analyzed.

Despite the pessimism expressed above about the failures of international human rights theory to predict more success in Mexico over reducing violence against women, we retain a realistic sense of guarded optimism about change for several reasons. First, hidden transcripts are surfacing and resistance is emerging from ordinary people. People resist with a variety of tools, including the tried and tested public protests and the new forms: social media, including YouTube videos. Second, feminist activists and women's groups have built coalitions with other organizations to infuse and broaden the critical agenda to include everyday violence and femicide. Finally, elsewhere in Mexico, voices are challenging the public transcripts. One of these voices comes from poet Javier Sicilia, whom *Time* magazine named one of the 2011 "persons of the year" in its focus on protesters from the Arab Spring, the Occupy movement, and elsewhere. Below, we return momentarily to Luz María Dávila, whose action predated that of Sicilia. Women have often been the most hidden among those who break through hidden transcripts.

Luz María Dávila's intervention was the first to publicly interrogate the official governmental rhetoric supported by economic elites and conservative sectors of the middle class with regard to the nature of Calderón's war. That is, she questioned and put on its head the view that this was a war where the casualties were drug lords or cartel members exclusively. Luz María's testimony dismantled the notion that militarization and maintenance of the police state in Juárez were occurring to safeguard the city. Her intervention generated wider public criticism and support from grassroots organizations that had previously been ambivalent about demanding that the military and the federal police leave the streets of Juárez.

Luz María's intervention aimed at reclaiming justice had other effects, too. It tainted the already fragile credibility of President Calderón and his initiatives, including Todos Somos Juárez, which fell into oblivion—without any significant evidence of its impact in the city—once he left office. In 2012, soon after President Enrique Peña Nieto took office, he suggested that Todos Somos Juárez would continue, but groups in Juárez and other critics responded publicly that initiatives without local input were doomed to fail. As we write, a year after Peña Nieto took office, no attempt has been made to continue it.

The importance of Luz María Dávila's intervention is comparable to that of poet and journalist Javier Sicilia. The poet, whose son Juan Francisco Sicilia was killed in March 2011, is a prominent writer. When his son was found dead in Cuernavaca, Morelos, Mexico, the poet came out publicly and demanded a stop to the violence generated by the war on drugs. Claiming that "estamos hasta la madre,"[3] he founded one of the most important citizens' movements in contemporary Mexico, initially demanding that the federal government and specifically President Calderón revise the official security strategy. Subsequently, in June 2011, Sicilia's Movimiento por la Paz con Justicia y Dignidad (Movement for Peace with Justice and Dignity) took the form of a caravan and traveled to the border cities of Juárez and El Paso. Making its way through various states where families of victims would come out to share their stories of loss and grief, his caravan was baptized as the Caravana del Consuelo. The caravan, on its way to Juárez, unearthed formerly faceless and voiceless victims and revealed the dimensions of the tragedy (see chapter 6). Nationally and internationally, people began to understand the magnitude of the crisis that the country is enduring.

In the *Time* article naming him one of many protester persons of the year, Sicilia described one of his most gratifying moments. Like those we have analyzed in this chapter, it involved a woman, a mother by the name of María Elena Herrera, who spoke with the president about her four sons, abducted by gangsters. According to Sicilia, "[T]he President hugged her and I could see he was shaken by her experience. I saw his recognition that the victims are human beings and not statistics. I saw his face of pain and in that moment the President himself became more humanized to me" (*Time* 2011). Like Sicilia, and like many of the people prominent in two decades of feminist activism against femicide, we insist on personalizing the victims and the leaders with their names, rather than exclusively focusing on murder counts, as many do—even social-justice activists.

While impunity still reigns with a strong but weakening public transcript, people from "below" are cracking those transcripts with moments of resistance, formerly hidden but now more public. Women in Mexico, as spokespersons, activists, and femicide victims, break the façade established in hypermasculine regimes that pretend to protect people through militarization and what activists see as the criminalization of social life. Though their resistance and actions are unique and creative, they share much with those of other women in social movements such as the Madres de la Plaza de Mayo in Argentina who have made visible oppressive states that misuse their power and use it against their own citizens.

CHAPTER FOUR

"FED UP" WITH MILITARIZATION AND MURDERS, VIA SOCIAL MEDIA

sólo son mujeres
una nota roja
viento pasajero
que a nadie le importa.
(they're just women
a newspaper police report
wind passing
that nobody cares for.) (Méndez translation)
ARMINÉ ARJONA (STABILE 2010)

IN THIS CHAPTER, we continue our analysis of activism and resistance in the U.S.–Mexico borderlands by employing theoretical and conceptual constructs associated with transnational activism and resistance to government militarization with a "gender lens." Thus, the analysis focuses on the gendered reemergence of more inclusive and comprehensive civil-society activism, centered strongly in Ciudad Juárez and narrated with several cases/vignettes of activism in 2010–2011, along with their muddied complexities, including resistance to the acknowledgment of femicide among not only elites but also some U.S. media activists.

Drawing from both our participant observation of the rallies and marches, and our analysis of social media including electronic communications such as e-mail, YouTube, Facebook, Twitter, and listservs, we focus on the spread of ideas and action. Setting our gaze on social-networking technology allows us to describe how its uses provide for high-speed potential for growth in movements that challenge militarization and promote more inclusive gender justice while at the same time exposing activists to risks. Moreover, building from chapter 3, we show how women and feminist activists interface with and intervene in the emergent peace and justice movements that utilize the technology of small and large listservs, Facebook, and e-mail.

When Staudt and Irasema Coronado (2002) analyzed the opportunities and obstacles in cross-border activism on issues involving the environment, labor unions, business, and human rights, they focused on personal ties that bind people together. At that time, social media were in their infancy, though website designers, graphic artists, and musicians were using technological means to facilitate awareness among wider audiences. Currently, most activists in Mexico employ digital technology and the social networks, especially Facebook and Twitter, to mobilize participants and to communicate their perspectives. This is true for groups and activists in Juárez with legitimate concerns with reprisal for their public activities; they have found in the use of digital media an efficient way to denounce human rights abuses, to enhance the organization of rallies and marches, and to disseminate information. The rest of this chapter describes civil-society activism and resistance to militarization at the border, including its binational solidarity networks, from close and personal to distant and electronically virtual.

In the following sections, we document the ways in which the social networks, mainly Facebook, were employed to organize and maintain mobilization and resistance in Ciudad Juárez, especially during the years of Calderón's drug war. Our portrayal shows how social networks served to keep organizing alive and redefined the ways in which people participated in activism. What follows are discussions of various instances that capture this promising but often unexplored means for organizing, communicating, and resisting.

FACEBOOK AND THE MARCH OF COURAGE

The deployment of troops and their overwhelming presence on the streets of Ciudad Juárez as part of Joint Operation Chihuahua in the early part of 2008 had a double effect. Launched by Genero García Luna, secretary of public security, the operation served to convey the idea that finally governmental action was being taken to mitigate the unprecedented violence that the city was experiencing. Simultaneously and paradoxically, it produced a sense of fear in people as a palpable surveillance apparatus went into action utilizing round-the-clock checkpoints around the city, patrols of heavily armed and masked soldiers and federal police agents, and searches without judicial warrants of all homes in entire neighborhoods to purportedly locate (and sometimes confiscate) weapons that Mexican law prohibits.

Intimidation was not only the result of military and federal police operations under Calderón's so-called war against drug cartels, although fear was ever present as continuous police and military raids escalated human rights violations. But also people were fearful because of a large increase in criminal activity. In most cases, victims did not make official reports of crime to law enforcement, perhaps as a result of the documented fear of the police, police ineffectiveness, and overall perception of police complicity with criminals (Staudt 2008: chap. 5).

Though crime and human rights violations remain for the most part unreported even in 2013, in 2008, the year troops were deployed, a total of 1,608 homicides were registered in the city of Juárez, compared to the 469 in 2007, according to Víctor Quintana (2012). In 2009, the number of homicides in the state increased to 3,249 (Quintana 2012). Of those, 2,685 occurred in Juárez (Enríquez 2011). That number was surpassed in 2010, when 5,212 homicides were documented in the state (Quintana 2012), and Juárez reached an all-time high of 3,111 murders (Enríquez 2011).

Femicide, too, showed a considerable increase in the state. For instance, between the years 1993 and 2007, a range of 19 to 37 femicides occurred annually (Quintana 2012). In 2007, the year prior to the start of Joint Operation Chihuahua and the subsequent militarization and deployment of federal police officers, 25 femicides were recorded (Quintana 2012). In 2008, with the *operativo*, there were 87 documented in the state, 164 in 2009, 304 in 2010 (Enríquez 2011; Quintana 2012), and 282 in 2011 (Quintana 2012).

Other modalities of criminal activity in the state of Chihuahua showed an increase in 2008, with Joint Operation Chihuahua in place. For instance, car theft escalated (from 9,490 in 2007 to 30,757 in 2010). Kidnappings also increased (from 21 in 2007 to 132 in 2010). Homicide rates of youth between 15 and 29 years of age went up (from 201 in 2007 to 1,647 in 2009) (Enríquez 2011; Quintana 2011). In addition to the criminal activity documented, human rights groups received threats to their organizations and members, including activists like Father Oscar Enríquez, director of the Paso del Norte Human Rights Committee; Norma Ledezma, founder and coordinator of Justicia para Nuestras Hijas (Justice for Our Daughters) and mother of Paloma Escobar Ledezma, a femicide victim; Norma Andrade and Marisela Ortiz from Nuestras Hijas de Regreso a Casa (Daughters Back Home); and Cipriana

Jurado Herrera of the Centro de Investigación y Solidaridad Obrera (Center for Research in Workers' Solidarity Center), now in asylum in the United States. The threats occurred in a high-risk environment to activists. In fact, according to the United Nations (2010), in Mexico, human rights activism as well as journalism are considered high-risk activities—so much so that the UN has issued a series of recommendations toward the establishment of policy and protocols for the security of people in these activities.

The UN High Commissioner for Human Rights reports that Mexico's human rights defenders—and particularly women activists—suffer "stigmatization" (2010: 12), confront legal actions and are often penalized by the state, become the potential targets of paramilitary and nonstate actors, and their activities and integrity are unprotected or safeguarded by lax state laws that do not require investigation or punishment for violations against them.

In Juárez, José Darío Alvarez, a nineteen-year-old sociology student participating in an anti-militarization march in 2010, was seriously wounded by a federal police officer, and survived. Though photos, testimonies, and videos show that he was shot as he marched, already inside the local university campus where a series of panels to discuss militarization were to occur, he was stigmatized initially through official rhetoric that attempted to present him as a vandal.

Other human rights defenders from Juárez who did not survive aggressions include Josefina Reyes (killed in 2010), Marisela Escobedo (killed in 2010), and Susana Chávez (killed in 2011). The three women were also stigmatized. In the cases of Reyes and Escobedo, local and state authorities attempted to link them to drug cartels. Those links were never proved and no concrete evidence was ever presented. In the case of Chávez, attempts were made to discredit her by suggesting that she was drinking with her aggressors. Moreover, in the cases of Reyes and Escobedo, their public quest for justice also made them targets of nonstate actors; and despite the fact that they reported to authorities their vulnerability and threats, protection was never afforded. To this day, the murder of Josefina Reyes remains unpunished. Marisela Escobedo's murder underwent trial and José "El Wicked" Jiménez Zavala was convicted, though family members maintain that he is a scapegoat (Méndez interview, December 16, 2012).

Thus, notwithstanding the city's strong tradition of mobilization, in Juárez, the volatile context played a role in transforming activism and mobilization. Once-frequent marches and rallies conspicuously diminished between 2005 and 2009. However, efforts to organize, like the march organized by the Comité Médico Ciudadano demanding a halt to violence, or the one organized after the 2009 assassination of Dr. Manuel Arroyo Galván, a professor of sociology and an activist at the Universidad Autónoma de Ciudad Juárez (UACJ), interrupted the "disbandment," as that period of time is commonly described by activists.[1]

It wasn't until the Marcha del Coraje, Dolor, y Desagravio (March of Courage, Pain, and Vindication) took place in February 2010 in response to the January 30 Villas de Salvárcar massacre that the use of social networks to organize mobilizations was inaugurated in Juárez. The march was spontaneously organized within fifteen days of the incident where fifteen people, mostly adolescents, were killed by gunmen who targeted their victims as they attended the birthday party of one of the youngsters.

"Harto de la Violencia" (Fed Up with Violence) was the alias used by one Facebook user as he introduced himself to others on the social network in February 2010. His alias appeared to resonate with the collective mood at that time. Soon he had friended thousands of Facebook users in Juárez (including Méndez), in other parts of the country, and abroad. An employee of the university library in Juárez, Harto openly admitted not having experience in activism. However, he seemed to connect with others who, like him, had never mobilized before but were "fed up."[2]

In the next few days people visited Harto's Facebook wall. In a matter of days, he became a popular name in the social networks. His popularity was aided by a newspaper story in *Diario de Juárez*, a daily Juárez newspaper, that recounted the unique way in which people—mostly young folks using Facebook—were attempting to organize because they were outraged by the events in Villas de Salvárcar and the response by President Calderón who, from Japan, had quickly dismissed the tragedy as a dispute between gang members.

Finally, via Facebook, a meeting date was scheduled and an open invitation was sent to those who wanted to do something about the violence in the city. Uncertain about the number of people who would actually show up, it was decided that the meeting would be held at the cafeteria of the Centro Cultural Paso del Norte. That option seemed feasible as the cafeteria was situated adjacent to a large outdoor area that could be used if the cafeteria turned out to be too small for the number of people attending. It was important for people to meet, face to face, to begin developing relationships of trust. Contacted via a Facebook invitation, Méndez was at that initial meeting and more thereafter.

The cafeteria space turned out to be insufficient, so the meeting was held outdoors. Sitting on the concrete in a circle, some veteran activists were there, but for the most part there were not-so-familiar faces. Those in attendance, however, were decidedly young. Quickly, the participants, led by some recognizable veteran activists, agreed to carry out the meeting in an organized and efficient way. Introductions were short but warm as each participant offered his or her time and energy in the endeavor that the group decided to take on.

The meeting quickly turned into a brainstorming session that lasted a little more than three hours. Participants proposed and discussed long- and short-term plans and actions. In the long term, some participants suggested the formation of a coalition to demand an end to the violence and militarization. In the short term, participants wanted to take on an action that responded in a timely manner to the events in Villas de Salvárcar.

A march was decided on and the large group divided into small committees to tackle the work. The committees defined the general details. For instance, it was agreed that the march had to serve as a means to express people's outrage for the brutal killing of the mostly young students. Consensus was also reached on the need to convey people's solidarity with families in Villas. And, finally, participants at the meeting agreed that the march would be an act of vindication for the families and citizens of a city increasingly devastated by a war that they did not want or seek out.

Follow-up activities and decisions would be made in subsequent committee meetings and through Facebook via the discussion forum that was available on an older interface of the social network. The Facebook account the group was using, though belonging to and administered by Harto, allowed others to respond to people's queries regarding the upcoming meetings and march. Most importantly, it allowed the use of multimedia to invite participation (see one example of a video invitation that circulated through Facebook: http://resistechihuahua .blogspot.com/2010/02/sos-juarez-marcha-de-coraje-dolor-y.html). Thus, after years of scattered efforts to organize some response to the violence in Juárez, the Marcha del Coraje, Dolor, y Desagravio congregated an animated crowd of about 3,000 people whose chanting included "No que no? Sí que sí, ya volvimos a salir!" (roughly translated as "What'd I tell you? What'd we say? We're back out in the light of day!")

in clear defiance of the display of force that the military and police showed on an everyday basis and that had initially intimidated and kept many out of the streets (for images and a short video of the march, see http://www.youtube.com/watch?v=zKJmUjORtDY).

Indeed, the march of courage, as activists commonly refer to it, was important in that it marked a new era of mobilization, this time decidedly against militarization. It also brought together veteran activists and young activists, as well as established and new organizations. It was in this confluence of generations of activists that agendas began to connect, new alliances began to form, and new actors began to carry out the will of what can be recognized as the emergence of *la Resistencia Juarense*, or the Juarense Resistance, a term initially used by Julián Cardona, a well-known freelance photojournalist and writer whose lens has captured some of the marches and mobilizing efforts of recent years.

MARISELA ESCOBEDO AND MEMORIALIZING IN THE AGE OF FACEBOOK

The massacre at Villas de Salvárcar was still fresh in people's collective memory when news of Marisela Escobedo's homicide spread on a cold December day of 2010 (see chapter 3). Reports that this woman, in her fifties, had been gunned down at the governor's palace doorstep in the city of Chihuahua made their way around the social networks. In a matter of minutes, images of Marisela's unrelenting (but often lonesome) struggle to bring her daughter's partner and self-confessed murderer, Sergio Barraza Bocanegra, to justice populated Facebook.

Announcements of plans to gather by a statue of Benito Juárez, a well-known Juarense landmark located at the entrance to the urban area of the city, quickly circulated on Facebook. People, especially activists, wanted to be there to receive and pay their respects to Marisela's casket when it arrived in Juárez—from the city of Chihuahua—for the funeral service. Despite the short notice, around one hundred people congregated. And when the small caravan with Marisela's body was in sight, attendees, mostly in silence, stood on both sides of the street to allow for the vehicles to make their slow entrance into the city. Many were crying and hugging each other. Marisela was everyone's loss. As the vehicles approached the crowd, they stopped for a few seconds and then drove slowly through as people movingly chanted: "Marisela vive,

vive, vive. La lucha sigue, sigue, sigue" (Marisela lives, lives, lives. The struggle continues, continues, continues) (Méndez observations).

On the days following the death of Marisela, modest memorials on Facebook profiles recuperated the various moments of her struggle for a conviction and for an end to impunity and femicide. Alas, like most mothers of femicide victims, Marisela did not maintain a Facebook account. In fact, there are no records of Marisela's use of social networks to seek support for her cause. However, after her assassination, much of Marisela's two-year fight in the search for justice was widely portrayed and memorialized by activists and others around the world who did use Facebook and the social networks (see international symbolic acts of protest: http://www.metatube.com/en/videos/45234/Protesta-mundial -asesinato-Marisela-Escobedo). Red Mesa de Mujeres de Ciudad Juárez led a march, the Segunda Jornada por la Justicia (Second March for Justice), that was supported by diverse anti-militarization groups in Juárez. The women covered their faces during the march as a way to denounce the dangers they incurred in protesting (see http://www.youtube.com /watch?v=PKez3YKTevU&feature=related). The burka-like coverings conveyed not only a gendered message but also one that acknowledged the need for cover in light of suspected reprisal from authorities who had proven, with Marisela's homicide, that no one could be trusted. In addition, human rights organizations and activists read Marisela's murder as a strong message regarding the risks they undertook if they insisted on continuing their quest for justice and mobilization.

Tributes on Facebook and in other social networks were made by users who were touched and inspired by Marisela's persistence in denouncing the powerful local, state, and federal governments that she had challenged for their inaction. These tributes memorialized Marisela and served various other important purposes: (1) to commemorate her struggle against femicide, (2) to demand justice for her daughter Rubí Frayre Escobedo, (3) to demand justice for Marisela's own femicide, and (4) to denounce and remind Facebook users and other viewers of the troubled state and federal judiciary systems, both incapable of procuring justice. One TV news broadcast, on Canal 44 (based in Juárez), powerfully rendered many of the memorable moments in Marisela's struggle.

The Facebook tributes reveal the creative and incisive ways in which Marisela mobilized. Though she knew some members of and was supported by but held no formal membership in any of the existing groups

Women with burkas march in the Segunda Jornada por la Justicia (Second March for Justice) in January 2011, after the killing of Marisela Escobedo, when the hidden discourse became public. Photo by Renato Díaz.

denouncing femicide, she was often, as seen on videos and other visual documents, surrounded by groups who became activists along with her: her family members and close friends who accompanied her during her protests. Employing an element of performativity, she named and defied frontally the corrupt, misogynous, classist, and sexist order. Perhaps it was the radicalness in her discourse that made her, and her surviving family, the targets of such extreme aggression. It was the extreme aggression that led Marisela's adult children to flee the country. Yet, even in exile, Marisela's oldest son, Juan Manuel, reported to police in El Paso that he had been harassed and had his life threatened by his sister's aggressor's family. In particular, he named Sergio Barraza Bocanegra's brother as the individual who had chased him around the aisles of a Walmart (all caught on the store's security video) in the United States and had threatened to kill his family if he continued on his quest for justice. This occurred prior to Sergio Barraza's murder in the state of Zacatecas.

MOTHERS WITH DISAPPEARED DAUGHTERS: TOWARD GENDERED PRAXIS

On the days after the march to protest the May 29, 2009, homicide of Universidad Autónoma de Ciudad Juárez (UACJ) sociology professor Dr. Manuel Arroyo Galván, a series of meetings were held at the university campus. Those meetings, in late May and early June of 2009, coincided with the first months in the disappearance of Mónica Janeth Alanís Esparza. Her unrelenting parents, Olga Esparza and Ricardo Alanís, standing amidst a small crowd that was strategizing ways to demand a transparent investigation into the death of Arroyo Galván, called attention to the tragedy they were experiencing. It was on this occasion that Méndez first met them.

Mónica Janeth, an eighteen-year-old business administration major at UACJ, had gone to the campus one afternoon in late March 2009. She never returned to the home where she and her parents lived. Used to keeping in touch with her daughter, Olga always explains, when giving testimony, she was worried when Mónica did not respond to calls made to her cell phone. Once Olga returned home and noticed that Mónica was not at home or with her boyfriend, both parents feared that something terrible could have happened.

Troubled, Olga and Ricardo reported the disappearance to local police. However, because Mónica had last been seen with her girlfriend near the bus station in the southeast part of the city, the Alba Protocol (a security mechanism mandating the immediate search by all police corporations for missing girls only in the downtown area of the city) was not activated. Since then, Olga and Ricardo have carried out their own investigations. Leads have taken them to Mexico City and various parts of Ciudad Juárez, but with no success.

Amidst the tragedy of their daughter's disappearance, both found the strength to create two grassroots organizations. The first one they named Comité de Madres y Familiares con Hijas Desaparecidas, or Mothers and Relatives of Disappeared Daughters Committee. More recently, they founded a new organization called Familiares Unidos con Hijas Desaparecidas, which derives from Comité de Madres, which still exists. With a strong group of mothers and other family members of disappeared women, Olga and Ricardo accompanied and supported the search for their and other mothers' daughters. Gradually, they have secured the support of more established women's groups such as Red Mesa de Mujeres, have been heard by various United Nations' missions and work groups, and have had a strong presence in various mobilizations in the city, including a highly visible participation during poet Javier Sicilia's caravan to Ciudad Juárez in 2011. In April of 2013, they were recognized in El Paso, Texas, during the Annunciation House's annual Voice of the Voiceless event, where they received the Witness on the Border Award for their focused and continued struggle to shed light on the problem of women's disappearances in Ciudad Juárez and elsewhere in Mexico.

As with Marisela Escobedo, who collaborated occasionally with Olga Esparza and Ricardo Alanís, no record of a Facebook account for them existed until 2012. Their "late arrival" to Facebook (see Comité de Madres on Facebook.com), however, did not mean that they did not make use of technology to make their cause known in the early years after their daughter's disappearance. Through their networks "on the ground," their announcements and invitations were made public on Facebook. In addition, through his personal e-mail account, Ricardo Alanís often provided information regarding the upcoming activities of their committee. For instance, early in 2012, in chain e-mails and via their allies on Facebook that included a wide spectrum of activists, from anti-militarization organizations to Trotskyite groups and feminist organizations like Red Mesa de Mujeres, they sent a flyer inviting people to a day-long event called Jornada de Solidaridad y Exigencia de Justicia (A Day of Solidarity and Demand for Justice) at UACJ. The day of solidarity events marked the third anniversary since Mónica Janeth's disappearance (see flyer: https://www.facebook.com/photo.php?fbid= 2977550081690&set=a.1629798308738.2080326.1350018779&type=1#! /photo.php?fbid=2977550081690&set=a.1629798308738.2080326.1350 018779&type=1&theater).

Mindful of the importance of coalitions, Olga Esparza and Ricardo Alanís have established their presence with a wide spectrum of organizations, including the local anti-militarization activist groups and leftist groups based at the university, where Mónica was a student. This alliance building has been critical in bringing awareness (at least to anti-militarization groups) of the often-overlooked nexus between militarization and the resultant exacerbation of women's vulnerability, as manifested in their disappearance and femicide. Whereas anti-militarization movements and the traditional left have often neglected to elaborate a discourse about gendered violence in contexts of war and militarism, in Juárez, this recent alliance might provide an aperture for a needed and much more elaborate and inclusive praxis.

A young woman with her face covered to protect her identity demonstrates for one of the disappeared, Mónica Janeth Alanís Esparza. Photo by Renato Díaz.

Promising examples of this nascent alliance have developed gradually but visibly during the demonstrations after the assassinations of Marisela Escobedo in 2010 and Susana Chávez in 2011. In both cases, members of anti-militarist groups such as Frente Plural Ciudadano were seen actively participating in marches to demand justice. In addition, they joined their voices with those of feminist groups such as Red Mesa de Mujeres in public pronouncements to denounce violence against human rights activists and authorities' negligence regarding femicide.

At the beginning of 2013, former members of the now-defunct or inactive Frente Plural Ciudadano became highly visible in their protest against femicide and gender violence, including women's disappearances in Ciudad Juárez. As members of the Juárez chapter of Yo Soy 132,[3] they walked in the winter days of January on a week-long journey with several mothers to the city of Chihuahua. Once in the city, mothers, but not members of Yo Soy 132, met with some of the state's high-ranking government officials. Governor César Duarte, they were told, could not meet with them as he was traveling that day to tend to other commitments, though they had announced in advance the day of their arrival. At the meeting, the mothers asked that several sets of skeletal remains, in the public prosecutor's possession and presumably belonging to females who could be their daughters, be identified and returned to their families. They also demanded a meeting with the governor. The mothers insisted that the governor provide a briefing on the status of the investigations regarding their murdered and/or disappeared daughters.

On March 8, 2013, the Juárez chapter of Yo Soy 132 and the Comité de Madres y Familiares con Hijas Desaparecidas, as well as Norma Andrade's Nuestras Hijas de Regreso a Casa, coalesced in a march to Mexico City. The march, according to participants and as recorded on their own social-media publications, was intended to "initiate a national movement against femicide" (see http://www.jzmov.com/yosoy 132juarez/?p=1174). The national movement that resulted in the march included mothers from other states, not just from Chihuahua, reflecting the widespread concern regarding femicide.

EL MIMBRE AND THE SOCIAL-NETWORK BACKLASH

Although social networks have proven to be important tools for activists—valuable resources for information dissemination and solidarity formation—they have jeopardized activists' safety, as proved to be the case for members of the Reyes Salazar family, whose history is traced to a former agricultural community known as Valle de Juárez, an area that is partially in the municipality of Ciudad Juárez. The family's history in the area is characterized by many as one of struggle and tragedy.

A family of bakers, the Reyes Salazar family is an important referent to other inhabitants of Valle de Juárez. Affiliated with the left-centrist Partido de la Revolución Democrática (PRD), several members of the family participated in various social movements including binational activism. In the 1990s, for instance, they participated in an environmental movement with groups from both sides of the U.S.–Mexico border that demanded and succeeded in preventing a nuclear-waste site from being built in Sierra Blanca on the U.S. side of the border. The planned site's proximity to Valle de Juárez made it an environmental hazard for the Reyes Salazars' community.

In 2009, the son of one of the most visible and politically active members of the family, Josefina Reyes Salazar, was killed. Conducting her own investigation, Josefina formally accused military personnel—who controlled surveillance activities as part of the so-called war on drugs—of killing her son Julio César. A few months later, her son Miguel Angel was detained and accused, without evidence, of drug trafficking. To this, Josefina responded with a hunger strike that resulted in her son's release three days after his arrest. Soon after, however, Miguel Angel was apprehended and imprisoned once again, so Josefina launched her own campaign for his release. This resulted in various threats that forced her to temporarily leave her beloved Valle de Juárez. Then, in the early days of January 2010, a few weeks before the

Villas de Salvárcar massacre, Josefina was shot and killed as she tended a small food-stall business.

Seven months had passed since the homicide of Josefina when Rubén Reyes Salazar, her sibling and a baker, was also shot to death. Rubén's homicide was followed by those of two other siblings, Elias and Magdalena, who were kidnapped and subsequently murdered. Thus in imminent danger, two of Josefina's three surviving siblings, Marisela and Saúl, their respective families including spouses and children, and their mother, Doña Sara Salazar, had to flee from their community.

Prior to leaving the border region of Valle de Juárez, the family was in the media spotlight. Marisela and Olga, the third surviving sibling, had lived in the United States prior to the killings but came to Juárez in solidarity for a two-week hunger strike outside of the state's attorney general's office—where they camped out—as a way to force state authorities into an exhaustive search for Elias Reyes Salazar, his wife, Luisa Ornelas, and Magdalena Reyes Salazar. It was in the difficult context of the hunger strike by Marisela and Olga that Méndez first met them and observed the support the family received from various local organizations that included anti-militarist groups, organizations traditionally linked to the left, anti-femicide groups, and human rights activists and organizations. In a matter of days, their case became known in the national and international arenas. Facebook and other social networks such as Twitter played an important role in the dissemination of information about the Reyes Salazar case. Sadly, and despite the national and international pressure involving Amnesty International and later the United Nations, Elias, Luisa, and Magdalena were found dead on a dirt road in the highly militarized Valle de Juárez.

Without many options, the surviving family members fled, and each of them has continued in their search for justice. From afar, they continue to denounce the situation in Valle de Juárez and to claim that the violence increased with the arrival of the military into their community.

However, the fear in Valle de Juárez did not end there. On the morning of December 27, 2011, a disturbing message from a well-known activist member of the anti-militarization coalition Frente Plural Ciudadano in Ciudad Juárez appeared on his Facebook wall. It alerted his contacts of an attack in El Mimbre, an *ejido* (communal land) in Valle de Juárez:

> I have just received a call from Marisela Reyes. She tells me that she has information about the presence of a command of paramilitary-armed men who are opening fire and targeting the people of El Mimbre

at Valle de Juárez, as well as setting ranches on fire. She tells me that she has tried to report this to authorities, but they don't want to take her report as she is not in Juárez. It is urgent that we mobilize to help those who are being massacred. (Méndez translation) (http://www .sinembargo.mx/27-12-2011/105860)

The message was indeed alarming. Within minutes this activist's Facebook contacts shared his message on their respective Facebook walls, others pasted it into e-mail messages, others tweeted it, and those with blogs published the information there.

In response, some activists called their close contacts for an urgent meeting, a few began to organize via Facebook a trip to El Mimbre, and others more cautiously waited for more information. However, as the hours progressed, information—aside from the original message posted—ceased and confusion increased about ways to respond.

The confusion stemmed from the fact that within a few hours the local newspapers, including *Diario de Juárez* and *Norte de Ciudad Juárez* digital versions, had also reported the Facebook information that the Frente activist had posted, but no one had confirmed its veracity. As Facebook and Twitter users insisted on the version that a massacre had occurred or was occurring, the news made it to the national newspapers, which finally began to work on confirmation of the story.

Contacted by reporters regarding the uproar in activists' circles and on social media, the state attorney general and the office of the governor had to issue a public statement. In it, they claimed that a massacre at El Mimbre had never occurred. Furthermore, they stated that no reports of shootings, arson, or homicides had been made by local authorities.

Yet, despite the official announcement, the idea that violent activity had occurred at El Mimbre continued even when some Facebook users conveyed the information that had been provided by state authorities. In the minds of certain activists, the government was trying to hide the massacre they insisted had occurred.

At the end of the day, the confusion finally faded away. A note titled "No se hallan grupos armados ni casas quemadas en El Mimbre" on the digital version of *Diario de Juárez* on December 27, 2011 (no longer available on the website), signed by Sandra Rodríguez, a well-known journalist, reported having visited the *ejido*. Through her story on *Diario* and her Facebook account, she confirmed that El Mimbre had had an uneventful day.

That same night, via e-mail and Facebook, the activist of the Frente Plural Ciudadano who had originally posted on the situation at El Mimbre admitted having stretched Marisela Reyes's version. As he explained the situation, he said that he had (wrongly) assumed that a massacre was occurring given the reported presence of armed men by Marisela Reyes. However, though he admitted having overreacted and misinterpreted the situation, he was still insisting, like a few other activists, that human rights groups, joined by the international Red Cross or another trustworthy entity, be granted protection to go inspect the area and verify once and for all that nothing had happened. The inspection never occurred. These events revealed the power of social networking and demonstrated that during turbulent times in Juárez, it can cause a backlash on well-meaning people.

Though the incident exposed Marisela Reyes, as her contact information and location could have been identified, human rights groups were able to take the necessary steps to prevent the incident from further compromising her safety. She is now in asylum in the United States and has movingly and valiantly offered her public testimony on the tragedy inflicted on her family and the inhabitants of Valle de Juárez.

THE U.S. SIDE OF THE BORDER: MURDER COUNTS, DENIERS, AND OTHER EVENTS

Meanwhile, on the other side of the border, U.S. cyber networking rose amid the violence of the drug war and militarism in Mexico under President Calderón. In more personal and direct-action ways, loose networks of people organized events, conferences, and solidarity rallies with various aims: to criticize Mexican and U.S. policies, to provide more accurate figures on murder counts beyond those that the various Mexican government agencies and public relations offices released (and that the media repeated), and to support the courageous activists in Ciudad Juárez. U.S. media coverage was sporadic, but in the cyber activism, which contained distant journalists on lists, journalists occasionally responded to challenges and framed or reframed their stories with different angles because of information they received.

GENDERED BODY COUNTS

Based in Las Cruces, New Mexico State University librarian Molly Molloy moderates the Frontera List, the Google group listserv frontera -list@googlegroups.com, which distributes multiple messages each day, mainly about the number of murders in Ciudad Juárez. In so doing, she keeps the horrific statistics on the screens of the more than one thousand persons who receive the messages, most of whom are English and/or bilingual speakers located on the U.S. side of the border (Staudt has been on the list since its inception in 2008). Molloy provides excellent coverage to *listeros* by forwarding messages with links from news sources in Mexico and the United States, both print and online, focusing especially on stories from *Diario de Juárez*. Some formal media in Mexico have been threatened and intimidated in their coverage, giving rise to what Guadalupe Correa-Cabrera and José Nava call the "gagging" of the press, which is especially relevant in northeastern Mexico, and the consequent rise of informal media coverage through websites, Facebook, and Twitter (2013). *Diario de Juárez* and *Norte de Ciudad Juárez* continue to cover murders, but without bylines in order to protect journalists as per their policy adopted in 2008. Of course, readers are wary of journalistic coverage because there is the perception that the media also manipulate or respond to extortion. Molloy received a Witness on the Border Award from Annunciation House at its annual Voice of the Voiceless event in 2011.

The Frontera List has become a source of information about murder counts in a setting wherein few trust either the statistics or the murder categorizations that emanate from the president's office and other government security agencies in Mexico. Molloy's numbers have stimulated mainstream U.S. journalist-*listeros* to reconsider using the cut-and-paste murder figure cited in other media, long given at 60,000 drug war–related murders in Mexico during the Calderón administration. Some of them, such as *Le Monde* and alternative media like Truthout, used Molloy's estimate of 120,000 in late 2012. Molloy has been cited in official sources including a U.S. Congressional Research Service report (Beittel 2011) and others.

Molloy has created an online source with primary attention to the total number of murders, rather than to civil-society activism and/or stories of personal tragedy, except to the extent that she forwards links to such stories as other media report them. Readers send comments to the Frontera List that Molloy, as moderator, may or may not disseminate. The University of San Diego's Trans-Border Institute, the closest U.S.-based equivalent listserv on crime in Mexico, produces a more academic and policy-oriented monthly newsletter with many articles; it uses the credible Mexico newspaper *Reforma* for its murder counts, but it is not a moderated list like Frontera. USD political scientist David

Shirk, himself well published in the areas of Mexican crime and law enforcement, is on the Frontera List and occasionally sends messages.

In contrast to the U.S.-based list, we also highlight another social-media news-dissemination network, a website administered by Spanish journalist Lolita Bosch and Mexican journalist Alejandro Vélez Salas since 2010. Called Nuestra Aparente Rendición (NAR) (Our Apparent Surrender), this site publishes articles (journalistic and academic) but also keeps a list and a count of the murdered in Mexico in an effort to "name and count." The names (provided when they have become publicly known) and counts of people who have been killed are accessible under a tab labeled "Menos días aquí" (Fewer days here). Users can also learn about the circumstances of people's deaths in that section. The information NAR presents is obtained by volunteers who take turns on a periodic basis feeding their database. Drawing their information from newspapers all over Mexico, they maintain statistics and a narrative of the dead by state. NAR is also found on Facebook and has thousands of friends. NAR's website, www.nuestraaparenterendicion.com, has already had more than 500,000 visits (by August 2013), not counting Fewer Days Here and Special Projects and Links.

Thus, there is no "monopoly" on counting bodies. Rather, variations in emphasis and purpose exist. NAR, for instance, proclaims a civic responsibility to count and to name as a way of memorializing the dead. But also, in offering descriptions of the circumstances of people's deaths, they attempt to produce a narrative of the violence.

As scholar-activists and *fronterizas*, we are attentive to ideological and personal agendas, not to mention the space/length and investigative time constraints, in all news sources, from newspapers to social-networking sites and lists. In the following paragraphs, we provide the recent historical context for the puzzling juxtapositioning of strategies to minimize and marginalize the problem of femicide and women's murders from both elite- and justice-oriented disseminators of news—even as the organizing, social networking, and resistance activities among courageous anti-militarization and justice Juarense activists have recognized femicide and included that agenda in their efforts. For U.S. activists, the listserv conjuncture—despite realities in Ciudad Juárez—situates anti-femicide activists as walking a fine line to navigate a treacherous pathway in maintaining visibility and awareness of the still-unaddressed violence against women among the horrific overall murder rates in the city.

No comparable social movement had existed that focused exclusively on men, whose deaths are frequently dismissed by official attributions of presumed guilt without investigation or prosecution, as we discussed earlier. That is, there is no separate antihomicide or *antihomicidio* movement, but rather, general challenges to militarization. Moreover, gendered perceptions of innocence and guilt appear to occur among members of the wider public and media: women and children were once presumed innocent of the drug and corruption business, although they were presumed "guilty" based on their presence on public streets and/or their clothing choices in the early blame game associated with femicide; men were always presumed guilty. Recently, however, in the years of the drug war, more and more authorities have attempted to attribute femicide to drug trafficking. Until anti-femicide activists began organizing in Juárez during the 1990s, women's murders (whether domestic violence murders or sexualized killings) and domestic violence were virtually invisible, as were gender-disaggregated breakdowns. Yet all too frequently, attention to women even now tends to become less visible without persistent feminist organizing work, whether separately or inside peace and justice organizations in the wider society.

The city's largest newspaper, *Diario de Juárez*, provided extensive coverage of the femicide in the 1990s and early 2000s, but not as extensive as its competitor press, *Norte de Ciudad Juárez*. In earlier decades, *Diario* was viewed as leaning toward the PRI, and *Norte*, more toward the Partido Acción Nacional (PAN), two major parties in Mexico. (No Juárez newspaper leans toward the left-leaning PRD.) However, we bring some skepticism to all the media reports, as do many activists, not only concerned about the threats and assassinations that inhibit/warp coverage, but also about negotiations that may be struck with officials or organized crime. Competition also exists between the *El Paso Times*, published in English, and the *Diario*; *Diario* owner and publisher Osvaldo Rodríguez Borunda began a daily El Paso edition (*Diario de El Paso*) in 2005. Competitive tension is also evident surrounding particular journalists. *El Paso Times* reporter Diana Washington Valdez developed expertise and wrote numerous stories on the murders of women, including an eight-page insert with names and pictures in 2002. After that, she published a book in Spanish and English, *The Killing Fields: Harvest of Women* (2006). Her coverage and persistence make her a magnet for threats and criticism.

Resentment had long existed about the widespread, international coverage of femicide in Ciudad Juárez and those who act and write publicly about it. Coverage ranges from reasoned analysis to occasional sensational titles or stories lacking context (see the spate of murder mysteries, films, and fund-raising efforts that were spawned by the femicide tragedies in Staudt 2008: chap. 4). Amnesty International produced and sold Spanish- and English-language posters in 2003 that contained a picture of a highway sign pointing to Juárez and a sign pointing to women directed at a cemetery (seemingly universalizing female death). After the first-stage anti-femicide binational organizing peaked in 2003–2004, producing the largest-ever cross-border solidarity march and supporting the production of Eve Ensler's *Vagina Monologues* (complete with a new monologue on a woman maquiladora worker's murder) in Spanish and English on both sides of the border, a well-funded backlash occurred among influential city elites to cleanse the "image" of Juárez (see early details in Staudt 2008: chap. 4 and contemporary embellishments described throughout this book).

No doubt, Juárez became a center point and inspiration for social movements in Mexico, Latin America, the United States, and parts of Europe denouncing violence against women. In earlier decades, women under brutal dictatorships in Chile and Argentina (Winn 2006: chap. 7) also inspired antiviolence activists worldwide. In Mexico, awareness led to a thorough study of nationwide domestic violence (2003–2004) and femicide (2007), with the latter generating a new law in 2007 directing Mexico's states to act on women's right to live "lives free from violence." That law ultimately became an unfunded mandate overwhelmed by Calderón's drug war, even after the Inter-American Court of Human Rights decision in 2009 that held the state responsible for inaction on three of the 2001 Campo Algodonero femicides and mandated a series of changes in law enforcement (see chapter 3). Clearly, a movement focused on ending violence against women through prioritizing the problem was long overdue and deserves continuity.

IS FEMICIDE A "MYTH"? (OR IS SEXUALIZED MURDER "NORMAL"?)

The elite, of which *Diario de Juárez* publisher Osvaldo Rodríguez Borunda is a part, sought to minimize the image of Juárez as the capital city of femicide worldwide through articles about excessive coverage, editorials, and communication outside the region from 2005 onward. Given the "maquiladora model" of development, industry and business elites depend on foreign investment in the export-processing industry, so they are leery of the bad press from murder coverage and possible reluctance to invest capital (though see chapter 2 on how violence does not deter foreign business investments). Femicide was the preview for what was to come—skyrocketing murder rates, especially of men; it expanded to men and women undergoing gruesome murders and executions in the city. After 2007, when there were approximately 400 murders in Ciudad Juárez, the city's murder rate jumped to about 1,600 in 2008, about 2,600 in 2009, and the all-time high of about 3,100 in 2010, as we noted earlier, with a nearly fivefold increase in women's murders and an almost tenfold increase in men's murders (drawing on frequently cited figures from the Frontera List).

In December 2010, at the American Society of News Editors conference held at the University of Texas at El Paso, which focused on journalists' risks in covering the violence in Mexico, *Diario* publisher Rodríguez Borunda maneuvered his way onto an already-published conference program without his name, delivering a plenary, six-page, single-spaced speech (complete with English translation distributed simultaneously by his staff) on the violence in Juárez with extensive coverage of what he called the "femicide myth" and criticism of its coverage in the *El Paso Times* (Staudt observation), without time granted for challenge, despite the *El Paso Times* editor Diana Washington Valdez's presence in the audience. Rodríguez Borunda mirrored former governor Patricio Martínez, who also called femicide a "myth," just as the murders were acquiring greater visibility.

In recent years, some media, including the Frontera List, joined Rodríguez Borunda's, Martínez's, and other elites' assault on anti-femicide activism, despite the origins of coverage in U.S. news, which piqued mainstream curiosity. Charles Bowden's 1996 article in *Harper's* magazine put women's murders on U.S. readers' maps with pictures of mummified female bodies that had been dumped in the desert surrounding Juárez; the article probably did more to shock and perhaps titillate U.S. audiences, long hooked on women's murders and sexualized violence in television and movie productions on the topic.

Bowden, a writer who has widely published books and articles, including magazine articles and the 2011 book coauthored with Molly Molloy titled *El Sicario: The Autobiography of a Mexican Assassin*, as well as the film based on it coauthored with Gianfranco Rosi, *El Sicario, Room 164*, has chronicled the violence with gritty, first-person, poetic, stylized narratives of conversations and observations in Ciudad Juárez. He frequently weaves sexualized violence into his books and public presentations, such as the stories about "Miss Sinaloa," a beauty queen with that title who was kidnapped, raped for days, and institutionalized in a mental facility thereafter. He rightly calls attention to the extreme brutality of murders in Mexico, and he examines how the dead are victims of U.S. and Mexican policies and sadistic organized criminals who kill mostly with guns smuggled from the United States. Bowden's work is a fine antidote to the neglect of Mexico in the U.S. mainstream press and to the official U.S. discourse, which absolves itself of responsibility for the deaths caused by the drug wars.

In *Murder City: Ciudad Juárez and the Global Economy's New Killing Fields* (2010), Bowden begins with graphic material, written for a wide audience without footnotes or sources. (One might note the sensationalist use of the "killing fields" phrase, birthed in the context of genocide in Cambodia, by both Washington Valdez and Bowden and commonly by other authors as well.) Bowden's prologue begins, "Miss Sinaloa . . . special, so fine," who "took the ride, my God, what a ride"; he parallels Miss Sinaloa's story with that of an unnamed woman victim. The first chapter's opening paragraphs describe other men and women murder victims, with sexualizing or eroticizing language on a dead woman's nakedness. The second chapter is titled "Miss Sinaloa." Bowden narrates how the caretaker, Elvira, interviewed at a mental institution at the Juárez periphery, described the twenty-four-year-old beauty queen to him, though readers might wonder about the linguistic embellishments, such as "her beautiful hair that hung down to her ass" (2010: 12). Miss Sinaloa hovers through the next chapter as well, a theme that connects the grim analysis of the normalization of torture, rape, and murder. Bowden emphasizes overall murder rates, and rightly includes men and women, but he also perpetuates the sexualization of women's murders in readers' minds. In an appendix, he abstracts media accounts of murders in Juárez, mostly from his primary media source, *Diario de Juárez*.

Although Bowden's books probably collectively have larger print runs than academic books on femicide and a larger audience than the tiny readership of specialized academic journals with articles on women, his close collaborator, coauthor, and moderator of the large Frontera List, Molly Molloy, editorializes her Frontera List posts with questions that are critical of the over-visibility of women's murders compared to men's murders, given the total body counts. At least several times per month, Molloy disseminates messages with gender-disaggregated murder counts by year, based on media coverage, reporting between 10 and 20 percent of victims as females. Activists use total numbers and Molloy uses gender-categorized percentages to illustrate the differences between men and women victims. She notes that a good portion of the women's murders come from intimate-partner violence, a point that does not contradict antiviolence activists' agendas and that has long been established in academic work on the topic.

Feminist activists have emphasized the way that women's murders in the 1990s, amid police impunity, previewed the 2008-onward violence that officials have never addressed. Molloy's conception of femicide as a "myth," given that the percentage of female murder victims is 10 to 20 percent of the total, which is below the U.S. norm, is based on what she portrays as "facts" to her 1,000-plus readers. A possible effect is the marginalization of women's murders or the criticism of activists who call attention to women's murders. When Molloy argues that in the United States, the murders of women comprise about 30 percent of the total, the comparative figures contribute to a "normalizing" of the murders of women that intentionally or unintentionally presents Mexico as a relatively safe place, using percentages alone, since a smaller percentage of women are murdered there. Perhaps the larger issue to raise about the daily murder count and/or this singular approach to understanding Ciudad Juárez is how it depersonalizes the deaths, deflects attention from the ways in which Juarenses deal with the issues, and provides a rationale for the continuing ascendant militarization approach to border "security." Of course, as border people, we know that the border rarely occupies mainstream media space without coverage of brutality and chaos.

OTHER MEDIA, BINATIONAL, AND U.S.-BASED SOLIDARITY EVENTS

Nonborder media covering Mexico and Ciudad Juárez—such as the *Los Angeles Times*, the *New York Times*, the *Houston Chronicle*, the *Dallas Morning News*, and the *San Antonio Express News*—also usually focus on violence and mayhem, including violence against women. It is always a "victory" for justice activists in Mexico to see the spread of coverage, plus it is a partial vindication of the international relations human rights boomerang theory (Risse, Ropp, and Sikkink 1999). Yet despite the media victories, militarized drug-war policies in both the United States and Mexico persist. Alternative policy strategies, such as regulating (i.e., legalizing) the drug trade, as advocated by several organizations, such as the Drug Policy Alliance and Law Enforcement against Prohibition, are rarely articulated in political settings, in which politicians usually sustain criminalization approaches to drugs. Bowden, however, never misses the opportunity to criticize the futile drug war in various books, interviews, and comments.

Moreover, the narrative of the border as a chaotic and violent place continues amid the absence of media and listserv attention to the sort of civil-society activism we document and analyze in this book. Media frequently ignore or give little attention to notable binational/transnational activist events. Although the large Global Public Policy Forum on the War on Drugs of 2009 received widespread coverage in the Southwest and in the *Economist*, its follow-up activities in 2010 went uncovered, though see the militarization versus trade debates of the U.S. congressional race in 2011, discussed in the next chapter. Yet other events became visible in the regional presses of El Paso and Ciudad Juárez and in the valiant coverage of Kent Paterson in the Frontera North-South News at New Mexico State University (fnsnews@nmsu.edu): the solidarity events at the border fence to remember the Villas de Salvárcar massacre of January 30, 2010; the ¡BASTA! Border Activism Summit for Teaching and Action conference at the University of Texas at El Paso in 2011; and periodic press conferences and fund-raising efforts associated with refugees, threatened journalists and activists, and others seeking U.S. asylum—a grueling and time-consuming process involving detention and all-too-few U.S. lawyers willing to work pro bono (though we would recognize the efforts of Carlos Spector, Las Americas Immigrant Advocacy Center, the University of Texas at Austin's Human Rights Clinic, and human rights activist Rubén García [see chapter 5]). Molloy's Frontera List also posts Paterson's articles, as does Laura Carlsen's Americas Program (www.cipamericas.org).

Planning and preparation for events rely on a combination of face-to-face meetings and social networking through electronic means. Normally, the process is speedy and efficient, but on occasion ignorance, lack of foresight, and the inclusion or addition of unchecked e-mail addresses complicate, undermine, or ruin efforts. Following are just a few brief examples of complications.

1. In planning a solidarity event, one English-only-speaking Hispanic activist posted a message to a large group saying, "Don't send me anything in Spanish," giving rise to snide remarks about linguistic racism and some tense interactions via e-mail, not to mention diminished trust for U.S. activists.

2. In public protests and press conferences, people sometimes hi-

jack dissemination with their own personal agendas and use social networking to badmouth others. If or when this "goes viral," the messaging is confusing to readers and can disarm activism. In one instance, without checking for *Diario de Juárez* journalists on the e-mail list, the Chihuahua governor's appearance in El Paso was canceled when the counterprotest plans became known in *Diario*. Perhaps the journalist and/or his boss, Osvaldo Rodríguez Borunda, had a connection with the PRI governor, who was thus able to avoid public embarrassment.

3. Occasionally, a listserv participant or Facebook friend in activist organizing will suggest reckless tactics through electronic communication. In one such incident, a reckless suggestion was made in a large listserv of university students from both sides of the border to burn the Mexican flag—a tactic that would surely have backfired. The role of agent provocateur has a long history, but one that can be sped up with devastating consequences through electronic means. It is unknown whether the technology will subject all of those on a list to surveillance by anonymous/unaccountable hackers or by the government "security" apparatus, in 2013 made ever so obvious in whistleblower disclosures and Freedom of Information Act revelations about Department of Homeland Security keywords that trigger further investigation (including words like "border," "El Paso," and "Ciudad Juárez"). Event officials may seek to test the waters and then frame groups or include individuals on mailing lists who respond positively.

People may bring material self-interest to their interventions in social movements. During the first stage of anti-femicide activism, mothers of murdered women asked the question publicly and privately: who profits from our pain? (Staudt 2008: chap. 4). In 2010, Estee Lauder, a New York clothing (Rodarte) and cosmetic (MAC) manufacturer, developed product lines focused on femicide and maquiladora workers, with pictures in their marketing materials of thin, pale, ghostly models that looked like zombies. The MAC lipstick line had shades with names like "Ghost Town" (see http://www.nbcdfw.com/the-scene/fashion /MAC-Kisses-Off-Juarez-Inspired-Product-Names-98799069.html). The manufacturer approached Staudt and other U.S. border activists about donating a part of the profits to women's nongovernmental organizations in Ciudad Juárez. These women's organizations' leaders deemed the "profits" to be dirty money that commercialized death and thus could not be accepted. Meanwhile, thanks to an article and video on the feminist website jezebel.com, a website for responses developed; in Staudt's perusal of nearly 1,200 posts at the time, approximately 80 percent challenged the clothing and makeup lines as essentially "profiting from pain." The manufacturer withdrew its initiative.

CONCLUDING REFLECTIONS

This chapter examined civil-society resistance to U.S. and Mexican militarization strategies, the anti-femicide organizing confluence with it, and its enhancement (though not without problems) by technology and social networking. Furthermore, because technology and social-networking media are employed in a volatile context of fear and intimidation that limits willingness to participate, their use has allowed expanded numbers of experienced and inexperienced activists to connect, organize, and resist the militarization and impunity, albeit still at great risk.

Drawing from our fieldwork in the trenches of activism, we described and analyzed several instances that we rendered as vignettes about Juarense activists, beginning with the story of a Facebook user who intentionally or unintentionally "friended" thousands who, like him, were fed up with the violence. We moved on to a vignette about Marisela Escobedo, whose courageous and tireless activism for justice for her murdered daughter, Rubí, led to her assassination in what her son and other observers have called a state crime. The parents of disappeared daughters, such as of Mónica Janeth Alanís Esparza, networked with people who increasingly, through a collective process of sharing their stories, learned to recognize the nexus between militarization and the exacerbation of women's vulnerability to femicide and disappearance. The vignette about a suspected, but ultimately "false-alarm," massacre in El Mimbre shows the speed of networking and how it induced widespread media coverage and response from the governor's office.

On the U.S. side of the border—where fear and intimidation are not operative except perhaps the unease of having official security apparatuses pursuing unknown levels of surveillance—cyber-speech and free-speech activists engage in spreading information and planning binational solidarity events and press conferences with colleagues from Ciudad Juárez. Contrasts between murder-count listservs are evident, depending on whether their base is in Mexico or the United States. Perplexingly, some have used listserv dissemination to challenge attention to and focus on women's murders. In so doing, they might be marginalizing and normalizing the deaths, perhaps with the intention to raise the visibility of men's murders. Influential voices like the publisher of *Diario de Juárez* continue to perpetuate their myth that femicide was a myth. We find such discourse mystifying because in the first stage of anti-femicide activism, people on both sides of the border were horrified but wary about believing the grisly details of sexualized torture murders. Now, with equally torturous (though not sexualized) men's murders—given not only execution-style killings, but also beheadings and mutilation murders—people or at least activists in Juárez recognize and understand the *preview* that anti-femicide activists attempted to sound in their early organizing efforts against a law enforcement and military apparatus operating with absolute impunity. So, while a conjuncture between anti-femicide and anti-militarization forces has occurred in Mexico—effectively communicated with social networking via Facebook, Twitter, and YouTube—U.S. mainstream and alternative media and listservs remain fixated on separatist movements and the narrative of Juárez as a chaotic, violent "other" and leave civil-society activists' work out of their analysis, as if it did not exist. Mistrust about agendas, nationalist and otherwise, emerges among activists, especially when they do not know or see each other in person. Civil society's relative invisibility is inextricably related to media focus rather than the reality of *la Resistencia Juarense*, as we analyze in this book. We find that disheartening, and we believe it is important to respect the voices and actions at ground zero, in Ciudad Juárez, where the political opportunity structure has shifted and where activists have established what promise to be long-term connections between anti-femicide and anti-militarization activist groups.

Is there a post-conflict future in Ciudad Juárez? In the following chapters, we tentatively answer affirmatively because of the work of visionary, courageous, hard-working activists and because of some changes occurring in the political opportunity structure and its occupants—the cast of characters who govern the political economy of the border region. Though official voices from capital cities make border policies or instigate drug wars, border voices will have to be heard in those spaces of power because, as Laura Arriaza and Naomi Roht-Arriaza recognize, social reconstruction must be a local process, and "in transitional justice, as elsewhere, all politics is local" (2008: 153). Todos Somos Juárez, the social-welfare program discussed in chapter 3, is proof of the failure to which policies that do not situate citizens and their dignity at the center are destined.

We are encouraged by the way technology and social networks offer some protection, expand media coverage, and even induce some government accountability, albeit a minimal level in the Mexican and U.S. contexts. Furthermore, we are heartened by the critical ways in which technology has facilitated and spread justice and peace-oriented activism. However, we strongly believe, as activism at the borderlands illustrates, that those connections must be grounded in personal relationships of trust.

Lastly, while body counts are important reminders of the destruction wreaked on Mexico, two key issues must not be overlooked in the quest for a post-conflict future and reconstruction: (1) that privileging body counts of dead people without a systematic effort to find out who they were, that is, without naming and properly honoring them, might create a sense of "victimization, injustice, discrimination, and the desire for revenge" (Barsalou and Baxter 2007: 1) and (2) that while keeping a record of the dead is vital for future legal action and demands for justice, emphasizing the deaths at the cost of shedding light on those who resisted and worked toward peace and justice obscures truth and the determination of people to reclaim their dignity. Our vignettes aim toward the process of documenting—that is, documenting for justice and reconstruction. We hope that U.S. activists work to change their government's policies on drugs, guns, and trade—policies that produce violence and mayhem in Mexico.

TOWARD TRANSNATIONAL SOLIDARITY: CONTESTING THE BORDER NARRATIVE IN A U.S. CONGRESSIONAL RACE, TRIBUNALS, AND FAITH-BASED ACTIVISM

What's important is to maintain the hope:
una vida de esperanza.
JAVIER SICILIA, VOICE OF THE VOICELESS AWARD ACCEPTANCE
SPEECH, APRIL 28, 2012, EL PASO

IN THE PREVIOUS two chapters, we analyzed courageous activists who have changed the narratives of public and formerly hidden discourses in Ciudad Juárez. Their game-changing events have roused new public discourses and new coalitions and alliances within and across borderlines in what has become known as *la Resistencia Juarense.* Besides vibrant social-movement activism, augmented with social-networking technology, border citizens have also sought new kinds of elected leaders. In one election on the U.S. side of the border, citizens grew weary of the dominant border-security agenda that militarizes the border and the drug war, and voters ousted a longtime incumbent U.S. congressman in a primary election.

In this chapter, we examine three major sets of events of key significance for the changing border narrative. Together, they reflect an expansion of civil-society strength on each side of the border and in cross-border solidarity. We have been immersed in planning, preparing for, participating in, and/or observing all three of these sets of events. The events, which were not very hidden as they were being organized and performed, exhibited cracks in the official transcript—a transcript that many, besides human rights activists in Cuidad Juárez, had contested, thus representing a broader base of resistance than the one represented by activists alone. The resistance included people in the business and faith-based communities and epitomized shifts on the U.S. side of the border as well. In two of the three cases we examine in this chapter, our analysis shifts to north of the border, El Paso.

Our outline for the chapter follows. First, we analyze how voters in the El Paso area's 2012 primary election ousted eight-term congressional incumbent Democrat Silvestre Reyes, a former U.S. Border Patrol sector chief, partial architect of the border-security agenda, and former chair of the House Intelligence Committee, in favor of Beto O'Rourke, a former El Paso City Council representative whose leadership struck a national nerve when he was the only local government leader in the United States at the time to call for a policy debate on the drug war in 2009 and 2010 with a specific rationale linked to its effects on Mexico. El Paso's border argument with the drug war, and rationale for alternatives, enriched the domestic focus that U.S. drug-war critics had already attempted. Second, we examine the four-decade-old international Permanent Peoples' Tribunal, historically linked to the World Social Forum, and its national-local manifestation, with Ciudad Juárez chosen as the site for its introductory court session with transnational moral authorities sitting in judgment of the government of Mexico in 2012. The tribunal in Mexico, called the Tribunal Permanente de los Pueblos, Capítulo México, not only connected the anti-femicide agenda with peace and justice, but also integrated a total of seven key issues, including a challenge to the neoliberal market economy and support for global democracy, justice, and accountability. International jurists from Europe and South America gave a qualified opinion on Mexico *in* Ciudad Juárez, with all that it symbolizes. Third, we analyze faith-based human rights activists who sensitively incorporated new narratives linking militarization and violence against women to the drug war in events that exhibited cross-border solidarity. With these three sets of events, the stage has been set for possible transformation of the binational border region. Yet variations of the official discourses remain entrenched, albeit in a wall that is cracked and crumbling in places.

CONGRESSIONAL ELECTION: CONTESTING THE BORDER POLICY NARRATIVE

The Sixteenth Congressional District of Texas is one of only three genuinely *border* districts in the U.S. Congress.[1] El Paso's surprising Democratic Party primary election outcomes in May 2012 acquired significance and visibility well beyond the border, and mainstream-media national coverage (in the Associated Press, the *Washington Post*, and *Time* magazine), international coverage (in the *Economist* magazine), and coverage in alternative, social-media outlets. We analyze the election for its contrasting discourses about the border and the border's narrative future: militarization versus binational/global trade, each problematic in its own ways, as we cover in the closing chapter.

At the Texas border with Mexico, people vote predominantly Democratic, albeit with lower voter turnout rates than in other parts of the country (almost 50 percent of registered voters turn out in presidential elections). However, the 2012 primary drew El Paso's second-highest turnout ever in a primary election (Roberts 2012c).

Five candidates ran in the Democratic primary election for the Sixteenth District seat, but the major competition occurred between just two: eight-term incumbent Silvestre Reyes and former two-term representative on the nonpartisan El Paso City Council Beto O'Rourke. While each of the two main candidates listed mainstream issues as his top priorities, not surprisingly, border themes hovered in the historical background, with the two men having divergent visions of the region. We therefore view the election as a struggle for the soul of the border region and for how the border would be characterized in this one of three U.S. congressional border districts, strengthened with the additional number of members from the Congressional Border Caucus. Staudt participates in, teaches about, and observes local politics; she served as one of several "questioners" in debates among candidates in the 2012 primary, including the Central Business Association debate in February 2012, with approximately three hundred attendees, but this section also refers to published sources for corroborative documentation.

INCUMBENT SILVESTRE REYES

Silvestre Reyes, sixty-seven years old and a former U.S. Border Patrol chief and architect of the 1993 operation called Border Blockade and then renamed Operation Hold the Line,[2] identified three priorities in the 2012 election: jobs and the economy, health care, and defense and border security. After Reyes won his first congressional election in 1996, he faced no serious challengers for reelection until this race, in which he campaigned under a banner shown on many billboards around the city reading "Reyes works/Reyes *trabaja*." While he was serving in Congress, he claimed many achievements over the years, including the expansion of the Fort Bliss army base (a claim that many politicians made)—the biggest military base at the border, built in the mid-nineteenth century to strengthen control over the border. Reyes was a past and present player in the government's border-security apparatus, responding to the "chaotic" border narrative and the "immigrant invasion." The Department of Homeland Security, created in 2003, doubled and tripled the professionals in its many agencies, such as Immigration and Customs Enforcement and Customs and Border Protection, and augmented other federal agencies' presence at the border, such as the U.S. Department of Justice Drug Enforcement Administration, the Department of Defense North Joint Task Force North Command, Biggs Army Air Field, and the El Paso Intelligence Center, among others. Reyes made bold comments as a congressman about Mexican drug cartels: to paraphrase, that he was seeking to deal with them like the United States did with terrorists in Pakistan, not ruling out drone missile strikes, and that he would openly involve U.S. law enforcement and military forces in Mexico (Crowder 2011). He also supported the use of unarmed predator drones that reportedly were flying into Mexico, in response to which border scholar David Shirk stated, "The border will never be secure enough" for some legislators, and border scholar Timothy Dunn guessed, "There is no limit on what they will spend on border enforcement for political ends. . . . As long as it's framed as a security issue, it's bullet-proof" (both cited in Paterson 2010c).

As chair of the House Intelligence Committee, Reyes acquired high visibility and access to power brokers in Congress, the ability to influence political appointments to federal agencies, and support from business contractors with stakes in "securing" the border. He frequently said publicly that he personally knew Speaker of the House Nancy Pelosi and Secretary of Defense Leon Panetta and could bring them to the border (which he did). Although Reyes supported the construction of a border fence/wall in Sunland Park, New Mexico (next to El Paso) (Dunn 2009: chap. 4), he voted against the Secure Fence Act of 2006. For many years, he and his staff organized border-security conferences at the University of Texas at El Paso, which drew major political appointees such as border and drug czars and the secretaries of the U.S. Department of Homeland Security, Michael Chertoff and Janet Napolitano, as well as corporate and industrial contractors such as Raytheon, Lockheed Martin, and Boeing, among many others who secured tables at the conferences to showcase their equipment and software. Staudt attended the annual border-security conferences from 2007 to 2011 and spoke on panels at the last two; her speech there in 2010 was disseminated on the Americas Program website (Staudt 2010).

Tom Barry produced a three-part analysis drawing connections between Reyes and border-security corporation campaign contributors, using federal election data, and detailed El Paso's "defense/security contracting boom" (2009). Barry documented Reyes's position in the top third of congressional earmark activity for various contractors, bringing in $24 million in earmarks. Barry also showed Reyes to be among the top twenty recipients of contributions from defense-industry contractors in the 2008 and 2010 election cycles (ironically, next to Libertarian-Republican Ron Paul). Inspired by former president Eisenhower's parting words on the military-industrial complex in 1960, the politician-agency-corporate relationships have been called the "Border Security Industrial Complex" (Staudt, Payan, and Dunn 2009).

CAMPAIGN CONTRIBUTIONS

Given Reyes's prominence, he acquired a vast lead in campaign contributions compared to Beto O'Rourke. Both President Obama and former president Clinton endorsed Reyes. According to the Federal Election Commission's filings, donations to Reyes for the 2012 primary election amounted to $936,178, while O'Rourke's donations totaled $379,296. The local versus national sources of these contributions offer insights as well: 24 percent of Reyes's donations came from local sources, compared with 74 percent of O'Rourke's donations (Roberts 2012a). However, O'Rourke also benefited from a Super PAC (political action committee), named the Campaign for Primary Accountability, which targeted incumbents in a political system that favors incumbents (Macedo 2005). Bill Sanders, a business developer who is part of the transnational Paso del Norte Group (now the Borderplex Alliance) and O'Rourke's father-in-law, contributed to the Super PAC. However, of the various incumbents that this Super PAC targeted, both Democrat and Republican, only incumbent Reyes lost his primary election, while the others were reelected, as is common in incumbent-favored U.S. politics.

CHALLENGER BETO O'ROURKE

Beto O'Rourke, founder of Stanton Street Technology, successfully ran for two terms as representative in one of eight El Paso City Council seats in nonpartisan elections, which are typical of U.S. cities. He was associated with several young newcomers in El Paso politics like Verónica Escobar, Susie Byrd, and Steve Ortega, who, while Democrats, do not identify with the old guard of the El Paso Democratic Party

(Crowder 2012a). O'Rourke, aligned with so-called progressives on the city council, made several controversial decisions, including those supportive of "smart growth" development (as opposed to the typical sprawl pattern found in many cities) and civil rights issues, such as partner benefits for gay and lesbian city employees. The progressives also passed resolutions against the border fence/wall.

Perhaps the most controversial principled stand that O'Rourke and fellow councilperson Steve Ortega took was to call for a debate on the effectiveness of the drug war, given the extreme violence in Mexico—particularly in Ciudad Juárez, with its interdependent economic relationship with El Paso. The Paso del Norte metropolitan region of El Paso–Ciudad Juárez is a major gateway—a "drug war zone"— through which Mexican traffickers ship marijuana and other drugs to the United States (Campbell 2009), a profitable but illegal trade with a large drug-consuming population. U.S. Customs and Border Protection figures for drugs confiscated in the El Paso Sector (West Texas and New Mexico) show that marijuana constitutes 98 percent of the illegal drugs confiscated there, measured in pounds (U.S. Customs and Border Protection 2008, 2011), but experts estimate that only 10 percent of drugs are interdicted at the border. O'Rourke and Ortega took a recommendation from the City Border Relations Committee to express solidarity with Juarenses by calling for "supporting an honest open national debate on ending the prohibition on narcotics" on January 6, 2009 (Staudt attended and testified at these city council meetings), inspiring backlash and threats. Moreover, the local media later headlined O'Rourke with the discourse of pot and legalizing pot, once even parodying him in a political cartoon, showing him smoking a pipe.

The resolution, supported by all eight city councilpersons, was vetoed by Mayor John Cook. Congressman Reyes and other state representatives began putting pressure, in verbal and written form, on the councilpersons to retreat from this resolution, threatening that government money would be withheld from El Paso and its "laughing-stock" position on drugs. In another vote, O'Rourke and Councilpersons Ortega, Byrd, and Anne Morgan Lilly reaffirmed their stand in favor of the resolution, but the other four backed down and voted with Mayor Cook. Instead of getting buried in local media coverage, national visibility resulted from this pioneering, unusually risky move by a city council in a political system wherein politicians seek to show their "toughness on crime" and avoid stigmatizing, controversial issue positions like questioning the prohibition of and war on drugs.

Ciudad Juárez and El Paso mayors José Reyes Ferriz and John Cook during the opening session of the Global Public Policy Forum on the War on Drugs at the University of Texas at El Paso in 2009. Photo by Laura Trejo. Courtesy of UTEP News Service.

After the vote, with a team from on and off campus, including Councilman O'Rourke, Staudt coordinated a binational campus-community forum, the Global Public Policy Forum on the War on Drugs, with a balanced set of scholars, advocates, and officials (see the program, speakers, and summary at http://warondrugsconference.utep .edu). O'Rourke said publicly in various follow-up activities and conferences in other parts of the United States that normally local councils do not weigh in on national public policies, but that the border is disproportionately burdened with policies on the war on drugs, immigration, and the border wall (Staudt and O'Rourke 2013).

Rather than focus on the effectiveness of the drug war, O'Rourke adopted several priority campaign issues: generating high-skill, high-paying jobs, and especially reducing long waits at the international port-of-entry bridges and potential job losses in the interdependent border economies; and improving the local Veterans Affairs medical facility for El Paso's many veterans, given the VA's 2008 study that determined that El Paso's VA center was the worst in the nation. O'Rourke's campaign flyers emphasized the phrase "Time for Change," meaning not only in the representative, but in the way Congress does its business in what some view as unethical ways. Both Reyes and O'Rourke had an interest in obtaining more Homeland Security staff, but for different agendas.

Besides traditional mailers and endless debates, the thirty-nine-year-old O'Rourke relied on social-networking technology, with online videos, Facebook postings, online donations, and tweets—all cost-effective methods that connected with younger voters, who normally vote at lower rates than middle-aged and older voters. As the campaign heated up and lengthened from the usual March primary date to late May due to Texas-wide redistricting court challenges, O'Rourke also focused on Reyes's absenteeism in Congress (which fueled popular jokes about the "Reyes Works" slogan with slogans like "Reyes Works—NOT!").

Meanwhile, a series of media investigative reports about corruption, hinting at connections to Reyes, bothered many El Pasoans (fatigued with years of accusations about representatives). In yet another report, Citizens for Responsibility and Ethics in Washington completed an

El Paso City Council representative Beto O'Rourke speaks, *right*, with Mayor John Cook and UTEP President Diana Natalicio seated at the table and Kathleen Staudt moderating in the background at the Global Public Policy Forum on the War on Drugs at the University of Texas at El Paso in 2009. Photo by Laura Trejo. Courtesy of UTEP News Service.

extensive report, titled "Family Affair," on members of Congress who hired family members (Citizens for Responsibility and Ethics in Washington 2011), and Congressman Reyes was number one on the nepotism list. Finally, when El Paso County Commissioner Willie Gándara Jr. was indicted by the FBI as a drug trafficker, Congressman Reyes's campaign was tainted, given the $9,000 campaign contribution it had received from Gándara that was not returned (Roberts 2012c).

As the campaign dragged on, angry charges flew back and forth. We focus here on those relating to the drug war and O'Rourke's questions about its cost and ineffectiveness that reemerged in the publication of his book coauthored with Councilperson Susie Byrd, titled *Dealing Death and Drugs: The Big Business of Dope in the U.S. and Mexico* (2011). The Reyes campaign took out expensive TV ads, including during the Super Bowl, and Reyes continuously and inaccurately referred to O'Rourke as a candidate who pushes "drug *use*" (our emphasis), even with children, and gave quotes to the media about "O'Rourke and his drug-use legalization activists" (Aguilar 2012). When journalists asked about the billions spent on the drug war, the ease of obtaining drugs in the United States, and the thousands who had died in Ciudad Juárez, Reyes's response was, "Some fights are worth fighting. Some things are worth continuing to invest in. Waving the white flag of surrender I don't think is an option" (quoted in Crowder 2012b).

PRIMARY OUTCOMES

With the announcement of early returns on election day, May 29, 2012, Beto O'Rourke was ahead with 51 percent of the votes. As the evening progressed, he maintained and finished with a majority among the five candidates, at just 50.5 percent, thus avoiding a runoff election. Reyes won 44 percent of the vote, with the rest split among the other three candidates. O'Rourke won big on the west and east sides of El Paso, the west being his former district on the city council and home to more independent and Republican voters, some of whom crossed over to vote in the Democratic primary (Moore 2012). As civility began to diminish by the time the two weeks of early voting that Texas allows began in mid-May, O'Rourke was articulating an eloquent optimism, Reyes, an angry posture. In a Q&A article entitled "Beto vs. Silver" (Silvestre's nickname) in *What's Up*, a paper and online weekly that appeals to younger voters, O'Rourke answered the first question with, "I'm excited about El Paso," while Reyes answered his first question with, "I think these next few weeks it's going to turn into the dirtiest race El

Paso has ever seen" (Lambert 2012). National observers and media noted that O'Rourke's support for alternative drug policies did not undermine his victory. It is uncertain whether O'Rourke will be able to address this issue effectively in the polarized U.S. Congress.

The election and its campaign discourse, as we have analyzed, shows the contrasting views of the border, with one side leaning toward the militarized border-security model and the other toward questioning existing policy models and focusing more on binational trade, cooperation, and peace in El Paso's neighbor city, Ciudad Juárez. Heretofore, border trade has been extensive, with U.S. Customs and Border Protection processing $2.3 trillion in trade at the border in 2011, an increase from 2010, and 340 million travelers (U.S. Customs and Border Protection 2011). But the interdependence is asymmetrical, given the low wages paid to the majority of export-processing workers in the some three hundred maquiladoras in Ciudad Juárez and Mexico's artificially low legal minimum wage of US$4–5 per day. Both the militarized and trade models exhibit flaws, and neither addresses the underlying economic inequalities.

TRANSNATIONAL JUSTICE? MEXICO ON TRIAL, IN JUÁREZ

Though Ciudad Juárez has a long tradition of organizing and mobilization around labor, environmental, land, and electoral issues as well as femicide and anti-militarization, its history, actors, and ways of struggle and resistance have scarcely been documented. Though activists and organizers acknowledge the importance of *recuperar la historia*, or "recuperating history," and the need to *sistematizar la experiencia*, or "systematize experience," most organizations and activists have been able to maintain only a limited record of their struggles and organizing efforts.

That is why the Permanent Peoples' Tribunal (PPT) formed a critical next step in Juárez's history of organizing and resistance. Through unique collective actions that brought the Mexican state before an international jury, the PPT afforded an important number of veteran and not-so-veteran groups—including grassroots and nongovernmental organizations—the possibility of consolidating various long-held aspirations into an all-encompassing project. The aspirations included (1) the articulation among groups of a common agenda, (2) the individual and collective recuperation of their history and struggles as organizations and collectives, and (3) the systematic documentation of cases and aggravations. Thus, as longtime Movimiento Pacto por la Cultura activist and organizer Verónica Corchado stated at the end of the inaugural hearing of the PPT that Mexico held in Ciudad Juárez in June 2012, the tribunal became "un paso hacia la dignidad" (a step further toward dignity). Méndez documented this history as she participated, with fellow members of Grupo de Articulación Justicia en Juárez, in the planning, documenting, and organizing of the tribunal in Juárez.

A BRIEF HISTORY OF THE PERMANENT PEOPLES' TRIBUNAL

The Permanent Peoples' Tribunal (PPT) emanates from the Russell Tribunal, which was founded in 1966 by British philosopher Bertrand Russell. The Russell Tribunal was initially constituted to bring the United States government and its allies to trial on charges of violating humanitarian law and crimes against human rights during the Vietnam War. However, in 1974 and 1976, it convened a second time to indict the various Latin American military dictatorships, most prominently those in Chile and Brazil.

With the conclusion of the trial against military dictatorships in Latin America, Lelio Basso, a close associate of Bertrand Russell's and a key collaborator in the establishment of the Russell Tribunal, sought to continue the struggle for peoples' rights through the Leilo e Lisli Basso Issoco Foundation's petitioning of the Permanent Peoples' Tribunal. Thus established to provide visibility to communities and peoples whose individual and collective rights have been systematically violated, the tribunal affords a public space to denounce the failure of institutions at the national and international levels to respond to allegations of crimes against humanity and to do so with the aura, discourse, and symbolic tools of the rule of law, still so lacking in many countries around the world.

Yet, like the Russell Tribunal, the PPT is a "tribunal of opinion." Its authority as an instrument for the procurement of justice is related to the ways in which it is organized and constituted. And though the indictments it issues are not linked to the legal system of any particular country, its statements, recommendations, and reports have influenced national and international public opinion and have effectively pushed the use and enforcement of various instruments of international law on behalf of individuals and entire communities. Equally important, on numerous occasions, the tribunal has identified the gaps and limitations of those international judicial tools that they have employed, insisting on and working toward the achievement of more efficacious means for procuring justice.

The legitimacy of the PPT, as an expression of ethical conscience, emanates from the moral character of its members with distinguished trajectories and from diverse countries and its thirty-five-year record of commitment in support of people's struggles against the innumerable transgressions of their most basic rights. The PPT's current sixty members are scholars, artists, writers, politicians, and experts in international law, human rights, and international humanitarian law. At various times, these members have acted as jurors in the more than thirty-five sessions dealing with violations of the self-determination of communities and nations.

MEXICO'S PERMANENT PEOPLES' TRIBUNAL: MORAL
AUTHORITIES TAKE THE STATE TO TRIAL IN JUÁREZ

The establishment of the Permanent Peoples' Tribunal in Mexico was the result of a lengthy process. It involved the collective effort of a number of intellectuals and social organizations with affinities to leftist popular movements. Collectively, the organizations sought to call attention to the "alarming situation" in Mexico. Moreover, advancing that the state and various transnational companies—as in the case of Colombia—were responsible for violations against human, economic, social, and environmental laws that derived from the state's misuse of economic and political power, the promoters of a PPT in Mexico sought to justify the need to convene one in their country.

On the second and successful attempt, in 2010, a Mexican chapter of the PPT was proposed. Guided by the feedback from the general secretary of the PPT, Gianni Tognoni, the revised justification pointed to the specific ways in which some of the allegations presented were of particular relevance to the tribunal as those had already been the object of a lawsuit and trial in Mexico and had not been resolved by the corresponding institutions or by other international entities. In addition, the new petition articulated the relationship between the neoliberal policies of recent decades and the political, economic, cultural, and social crises that Mexicans were then witnessing and experiencing, including the most recent human rights catastrophe resulting from former president Felipe Calderón's drug war, where thousands had been killed and thousands were said to be disappeared.

In October 2011, it was officially announced that a chapter of the Permanent Peoples' Tribunal would be established in Mexico and would

A poster for the Tribunal Permanente de los Pueblos, Ciudad Juárez, Chihuahua, May 2012. Photo by Kathleen Staudt.

take the state to trial for crimes against humanity. The announcement was received with great enthusiasm and hope by the influential group of promoters that had petitioned the PPT's presence in Mexico. From their perspective, the work it would involve could effectively serve as a tool to bring the country's heterogeneous resistance movements together, and to create and employ a *new tool* in the struggle to denounce the Mexican state. In addition, the PPT in Mexico represented an opportunity to be heard by moral authorities from around the globe and to break the gates of censorship and the encircling system of institutional recognition that the Mexican state, transnational corporations, international financial organizations, and global institutions had created around Mexico's democracy.

In the northern state of Chihuahua, word of the PPT came via the various human rights groups and organizations that have always maintained a strong network with social organizations in Mexico City, where most of the promoters of the PPT were based. Subsequently, during a regional meeting of human rights groups from Juárez and other parts of the state in the city of Chihuahua, a formal presentation on the establishment of the PPT was made by one of the promoters from Mexico City. To the mostly veteran human rights groups with ties to the left and popular movements as well as the progressive sectors of the Catholic Church in Chihuahua, the PPT seemed to be an important and promising new attempt in their search for justice and truth (Méndez observation).

In particular, groups and activists were attracted to the ways in which the promoters of the PPT had conceptualized the case against the Mexican state. The promoters had seven themes or issues deriving from the neoliberal state agenda, and they included the most heterogeneous agendas and concerns in the accusation. Those themes were:

1. Dirty war as a form of violence, impunity, and lack of access to justice
2. Femicide and gender violence
3. Migration, refuge, and forced displacement
4. Violence against workers
5. Violence against corn and food sovereignty
6. Environmental devastation and people's rights
7. Misinformation, censorship, and violence against journalists (Tribunal Permanente de los Pueblos, Capítulo México 2011–2014) (Méndez translation)

We note that femicide and gender violence are integral to the list and positioned early on the list, rather than being absent or an afterthought. This integration illustrates the conjunction of issues from local to national in Mexico.

Initially, promoters of the PPT suggested that the tribunal's first hearing could be held in Ciudad Juárez. The city, after all, synthesized the consequences of neoliberalism, and what had happened there foretold a possible future for the rest of Mexico. Thus, the installation of the Tribunal Permanente de los Pueblos, Capítulo México in Ciudad Juárez served as a symbolic and political statement. But in addition, promoters of the PPT recognized and trusted the capacity of organizers and activists—especially those in the Juárez coalition known as Grupo de Articulación Justicia en Juárez—to embark on the political and logistical work that such a project involved.

The organizational aspects of the tribunal were elaborate, and, with no prior experience of participation in a tribunal such as the PPT, some-times organizers were unclear about how best to proceed. But also, the last three years in which the city had witnessed the bloodshed and vio-lence that had resulted from President Calderón's war against drug cartels had taken a toll on organizations' willingness to participate in efforts that were identified as solely making an impact in the national sphere and with a more oblique relation to local agendas and emergen-cies of the current political and social moment. Nonetheless, as the process of organizing the tribunal unfolded, members of Grupo de Ar-ticulación, as well as other invited activists, human rights defenders, and a number of scholars from local universities, began to appreciate the strategic importance of the tribunal in advancing an agenda of so-cial justice that did have direct connections to their own local agendas and concerns.

Any lingering concern about the national agenda eclipsing the local agendas was dissipated when the PPT proposed that Chihuahua present its own case. That is, where others in the country would present and articulate their cases and locate each of them under one of the seven themes, Chihuahua would become a theme unto itself, as verbally agreed by organizers. In it, Juárez would have a prominent place since its organizers, activists, and scholars had documented—over the years—many of the cases they intended to present. Locating the PPT in Ciudad Juárez verified the centrality of the city and its state as the iconic place of violence and injustice, but also of resistance and mobi-lizing, in Mexico.

THE TRIBUNAL IN JUÁREZ

In the subsequent two and a half months, from the first conversation in the city of Chihuahua to the first hearing, a number of organiza-tions and individuals coalescing in the Grupo de Articulación Justicia en Juárez, as well as their networks and allies in El Paso, Texas, worked on the various political alliances, documentation, and practical chores that organizing the tribunal required. Two meetings were held at the local universities of both border cities. At the Universidad Autónoma de Ciudad Juárez (UACJ), a number of academics, community orga-nizers, and activists met to discuss the details of the tribunal and to in-vite others to participate. In El Paso, scholars, activists, and organizers met at the University of Texas at El Paso (UTEP). In these two meetings, people raised important questions, brought up key issues, and made commitments to work on the tribunal.

Tribunal Permanente de los Pueblos poster, May 2012. Photo by Kathleen Staudt.

Organizing for the PPT in Ciudad Juárez required enormous energy and resources. Many of those resources were out of reach to organizations, as economic funds are always scarce. However, with remarkable resourcefulness, organizers were able to secure—with the assistance of allied academic supporters—the UACJ's cultural complex, which contained a building that could seat, provide work space, and even feed the 500 people who were expected to attend and participate in what was called the PPT's General Introductory Hearing. In addition, they organized to host and feed the 200 to 250 *caravaneros* and *caravaneras* who would travel to the city to attend the hearing and some, to testify in it. But most importantly, they created a thirty-five-page document called the *Audiencia General Introductoria Documento Chihuahua*, or *Documento Chihuahua* (Grupo de Articulación Justicia en Juárez 2012), that detailed the case they would present on behalf of the citizens of the state.

The *Documento Chihuahua* described some emblematic cases that represented the many crimes against humanity in Chihuahua. For instance, under the theme "Dirty war as a form of violence, impunity, and lack of access to justice," the case of the disappearances, murders, and persecution experienced by the members of the Reyes Salazar family was carefully detailed; under "Femicide and gender violence," the femicide case of Rubí Marisol Frayre Escobedo was included, as well as the subsequent murder of her mother, Marisela Escobedo Ortiz, who was demanding justice for her daughter. The case of the "Mexilios," or Mexicans forced into exile in the United States during the previous four years due to the escalating violence, was discussed under "Migration, refuge, and forced displacement." Furthermore, the document detailed how "violence against corn and food sovereignty" had been occurring with the restructuring of the economy that produced a "destructuration of agriculture in the state of Chihuahua," leaving many without a means of subsistence. For evidence on "environmental devastation and people's rights," the document described the ways in which illegal extraction of pinewood was occurring in the Sierra Tarahumara. Under "Misinformation, censorship, and violence against journalists," journalists from Juárez testified on the precarious conditions under which they were carrying out their jobs and also the ways in which they had become targets of criminal organizations and the police when reporting. The 2008 assassination of *Diario de Juárez* journalist Armando Rodríguez, "El Choco," was described.

On May 26, 2012, two hundred participants in Juárez greeted a caravan of six buses from organizations in various Mexican states, such as Chiapas, Michoacán, Estado de México, Guerrero, Morelos, Zacatecas, and Coahuila. The jury and staff representatives of the Permanent Peoples' Tribunal arrived afterward, flying in from Mexico City, where all of them had congregated after traveling from their respective countries. Greeted by members of the local and national press, a few members of the jury made statements expressing their eagerness to hear and learn from the testimonies of organizations and individuals in Mexico.

The three-day General Introductory Hearing was installed by Gianni Tognoni and Simona Fraudatario, both of Italy, staff representatives of the Permanent Peoples' Tribunal. The following people were among the distinguished members who served on the jury:

- Mireille Fanon Mendes (France), president of the Frantz Fanon Foundation, member of the International Association of Democratic Lawyers, and UN expert to the Afro descendants Work Group
- Nora Cortiñas (Argentina), cofounder of the Madres de la Plaza de Mayo and human rights defender

- Antoni Pigrau Sole (Spain), professor of international law at the Universidad Rovira i Virgili (Tarragona)
- Alejandro Teitelbaum (Argentina), attorney and member of the Federación Internacional de Derechos Humanos y de la Asociación Americana de Juristas
- Graciela Daleo (Argentina), professor and affiliated faculty member of the Cátedra Libre de Derechos Humanos de la Facultad de Filosofía y Letras at the Universidad de Buenos Aires, and survivor of the concentration camp at the Escuela de Mecánica de la Armada in Buenos Aires during the military dictatorship (1976–1983)
- Gill Boheringer (Australia), former dean of the Macquarie Law School at Macquarie University in Sydney, Australia, and director of the Center for the Critical and Historical Study of the Common Law

During the hearing, participants presented testimony, provided material evidence, and shared a litany of grievances. The jury patiently listened, received the materials provided, and asked questions in two sessions that lasted ten hours each. Since it was transmitted via Internet by alternative media such as Radio Zapote from Mexico City, viewers in other cities and countries could follow the events at the General Introductory Hearing.

Grupo de Articulación's political work of convoking and engaging other groups in the city was arduous and broad in reach, even crossing the international border and spreading into El Paso, Texas, where Grupo identified and called upon collaborators and allies. But this participation also signaled the binational nature of the issues that affect the city of Juárez, internationalized through the PPT and its transnational activists and prominent jurists, who represented moral authorities in judgment of the state. While media coverage was extensive in Mexico and elsewhere, it was virtually nonexistent in the United States.

At the beginning of the General Introductory Hearing in Juárez, Tognoni announced to the press and those in attendance that at the end of the three-day hearing, the jurors would present a "qualified opinion" regarding the accusations and arguments presented. Furthermore, he explained that the qualified opinion would be further elaborated in writing in the subsequent weeks. True to the stated procedure, on the third and final day of the introductory hearing, a number of jurors spoke in recognition of people's systematic documentation regarding the accusations and their grave nature. In an opening statement, Tognoni said that what the jurors found on the evidence presented was a form of "terrorismo de estado" (state terrorism), that is, the use of a state's power against its citizens. The audience applauded Tognoni's statement, signaling approval of the jurors' assessment (Méndez observation).

Jurors offered more detailed and sometimes complex analysis at the end of the hearing. For instance, they made connections between Latin America's and Mexico's political economy and the human rights crises that were described in people's testimonies. In fact, mirroring people's accusations connecting the North American Free Trade Agreement (NAFTA) and its ensuing policies in Mexico to their precarious lives, they urged Mexican activists and civil-society organizations to investigate and identify legal mechanisms that they could employ to propose the withdrawal of Mexico from NAFTA. They also suggested various international treaties that could be used in such pursuit. Moreover, they underscored the importance of peoples' collective mobilizing and resistance as key in bringing states and governments into compliance with existing laws and international treaties to protect vulnerable groups such as indigenous populations, women, and children. The session ended with the audience chanting in unison "JUS-TI-CIA" and the jury standing to listen to the chant. Finally, everybody, jurors and audience, were standing up and clapping (Méndez observations).

Following through, on May 30, 2012, the jurors put out a *dictamen*, or "opinion" (Tribunal Permanente de los Pueblos 2012). The document underscored the importance of the testimony that was rendered and that works as a way of documenting. Mentioning that all testimony had been "verified" by the jurors, who considered it "an act of memory construction" (p. 24), the tribunal affirmed people's stories of transgression, which they referred to as "memories of pain, dispossession, impunity and injustice" (p. 24), in a way that no governmental entity in Mexico had done. Equally important, the document advanced that those memories are the fabric that makes up solidarity, struggle, the organizing that emerges daily, and the fellowship that is forged on such a path. Inspiringly, they affirmed that testimonies such as those offered in Juárez "made memories of what was suffered" but also "of the paths traveled and those ahead in the journey towards the construction of a life of dignity and justice" (p. 24) (Méndez translations).

Politically, the *dictamen* expanded on certain key points that had been enunciated by the jurors but not elaborated sufficiently, given time constraints during the hearing. It established people's testimony as evidence of the veritable and intricate nexus between free trade and state violence and identified a link between structural violence and violence directed to nonconformity and organizing. Such acts from the state were confirmed in the document as "state terrorism" (p. 22). The document also confirmed and elaborated on the urgency of reviewing Mexico's permanence in NAFTA, given the human rights violence that had been documented and was tied to the pernicious economic, political, and social effects on people and the environment: "lives and deaths, precarious and lost jobs, raped women and girls, disappeared and disposed in graves, forced abandonment of one's land, and homeland, identities destroyed as their corn has been destroyed" (p. 24) (Méndez translation).

FAITH-BASED CROSS-BORDER SOLIDARITY: ANNUNCIATION HOUSE

With isolated exceptions (Hondagneu-Sotelo 2008), local religious congregations across the United States have been reluctant participants in human rights movements, such as immigration reform. Yet national denominations of mainstream Protestant churches and particularly the Catholic bishops articulate strong social-justice positions, occasionally crossing borders in person and in faith solidarity. See, for example, the joint statement from Mexican and U.S. Catholic bishops, "Strangers No Longer: Together on the Journey of Hope" (2003).

El Paso is home to multiple faith organizations, including those that provide legal assistance, advocacy, and shelter to transnational sojourners. Annunciation House, established in El Paso in 1978 as Central American refugees fled wars in their homelands, provides hospitality to migrants and gives them a voice at its annual Voice of the Voiceless event. Each year at this fund-raising event, usually held in an El Paso Catholic church, up to a thousand people hear speakers, witness award presentations to courageous human rights leaders, and dine on a supper of rice, beans, and dry tortillas as a reminder of the everyday consumption of up to half the populations of many Central and South American countries, integrated into a global economy on disadvantageous terms. Rubén García founded the organization and continues to lead Annunciation House. Its mission statement is

In a Gospel spirit of service and solidarity, we accompany the migrant, homeless, and economically vulnerable peoples of the border region through hospitality, advocacy, and education. We place ourselves among these poor so as to live our faith and transform our understanding of what constitutes more just relationships between peoples, countries, and economies. (www.annunciationhouse.org/mission/)

The Voice of the Voiceless events of 2012 offer a moving, inspirational depiction of cross-border solidarity and an expansion of the voices and visibility of courageous activists on both sides of the border. We pluralize "voices" because the 2012 events began almost a week before the dinner, with numerous testimonies, picture displays, and speeches by activists and clergy leaders, both priests and nuns. Each evening, projectors flashed the names of the approximately 10,000 people murdered since 2007 in Ciudad Juárez onto the side of the downtown Annunciation House building. We both participated in these events.

A conference began at Cathedral High School on Friday evening, April 27, 2012, and continued on Saturday with an immigration forum, "Foro Sobre la Inmigración: The Right to be Human," featuring speakers who spoke mostly Spanish to a bilingual audience of over one hundred people, most of them in the binational social-justice community. At one of the largest annual dinners in the history of the Voice of the Voiceless event that Saturday night, Annunciation House honored Voice of the Voiceless Award recipient Javier Sicilia of the Movimiento por la Paz con Justicia y Dignidad in Mexico. Sicilia spoke about hope at length on Saturday morning at the conference and again briefly after the dinner.

The Voice of the Voiceless dinner in 2012 was exceptionally memorable for the way it bridged Catholicism and indigenous religious practices in syncretic ways. Vatican II in the early 1960s encouraged reconciliation of Catholic beliefs with indigenous practices (Martin 2009: 12). At the Annunciation House dinner, indigenous and Mexican symbols and practices infused the Catholic atmosphere in sight, sound, and even smell, with copal incense, a resin burnt in Catholic churches especially in Mexico and countries to the south, in the air.

Below, we analyze the conference and dinner discourses and performances for the way their practices respected and affirmed civil-society activists in northern Mexico in supportive ways. Annunciation House inclusively wrapped around and deepened loyalties from both the already committed and people newly committed to the cause (especially among the Catholic faithful), communicating a binational human rights narrative on the U.S. side of the border.

Projection of the names of the murdered in Ciudad Juárez during Annunciation House's Voice of the Voiceless events of April 2012. Photo by Renato Díaz.

Yet, measured by the yardsticks of international relations theorists of human rights (e.g., Risse, Ropp, and Sikkink 1999) introduced in earlier chapters, little media attention was given to the Annunciation House events of the week except in Catholic publications and on social media like YouTube and the Annunciation House website. Director García's powerful and moving speech went beyond his passionate speeches of previous years; he criticized the drug war and the havoc it wreaks on Mexico. Thus, El Pasoan and Juarense activists acquired limited linkage to transnational media coverage in the hope and intent of spreading awareness and putting pressure on the Mexican and U.S. governments and transnational religious institutions to act to end the bloodshed of what is increasingly called the "dirty war of militarization" (evoking transnational comparisons with the *guerra sucia* [dirty war] of Argentina in 1978). Although the *El Paso Times* provided pre-event coverage—an image of the projection of names memorializing those who have been killed during the drug war—it offered no post-event coverage. For Catholic and human rights activist messengers, the event no doubt deepened commitments and would cross over to Javier Sicilia's August 2012 cross-border caravan reaching from Mexico's mainstream across into the U.S. mainstream (see chapter 6).

ANNUNCIATION HOUSE: CONFERENCE
PRIOR TO THE DINNER

At the conference at the Cathedral High School Auditorium, the audience for Saturday morning's speakers and panelists began at about 60 people and swelled to a full house of about 125. While the event was grounded in the Paso del Norte metropolitan region of El Paso–Ciudad Juárez, speakers from distant places reinforced the global, transnational, and larger regional dimensions of militarization and its damage to human lives.

The first speaker, U.S. citizen Jennifer Harbury, whose husband was killed in Guatemala in 1992, spoke in both personal and abstract ways about military torture, U.S. interrogation and humiliation models from Abu Ghraib, and the follies of investing in militarism rather than education and health. Former Catholic priest Michael Seifert, an Industrial Areas Foundation–affiliated Valley Interfaith leader from South Texas, began his speech with the personal relational techniques that form IAF principles and practices: he asked people to introduce themselves to those who sat nearby. He spoke of a conflict that spread to northeastern Mexico, focusing on violence against migrant populations crossing through Tamaulipas, now called the "Valley of Sorrow," given its gateway location also used by organized criminals for their illicit activities including transporting illegal drugs (see Correa-Cabrera and Nava 2013). Speaking in poetic terms infused with Christian symbolism, Seifert addressed the well-developed "cultures of hate" for the "other" in the United States, found even in video games. Seifert set migration in a biblical context, with its many stories of migration and the "absence of borders to heaven." He compared the torture and suffering of migrants with the tortured Christ on the cross when asking, "My father, why have you abandoned me?" And he drew parallels of an apocalyptic border with the biblical book of Revelation. Horrified at official language, Seifert decried the way murder victims have been called "collateral damage," terminology also used by the Department of Homeland Security (DHS) in its sweeps for felons that resulted in record-setting deportations of 400,000 unauthorized immigrants in 2011, the vast majority of them nonfelons trapped in DHS "Secure Communities" local law enforcement checks (see María Hinojosa's PBS *Frontline* documentary "Lost in Detention," 2011). With props like a wooden bell, making eerie cathedral-like sounds for the ultra-quiet audience, Seifert personalized and humanized immigration and border militarism tragedies with religious discourse.

A group of mostly women activist panelists including Cipriana Jurado spoke about their work, spreading "witness" to the audience. These included Leticia Chavarría, cofounder of the Comité Médico Ciudadano de Ciudad Juárez; Betty Campbell, a Catholic nun; Silvia Méndez, affiliated with the Paso del Norte Human Rights Center; and Marisela Reyes Salazar, Valle de Juárez activist in exile (see chapter 4 for discussion of the assassinations of several of her family members). The activists personalized the anguish of mothers of disappeared girls and women by repeating the question "Dónde esta mi hija?" (Where is my daughter?). Noted peace and justice activist Javier Sicilia spoke for thirty minutes, without notes, with words of hope in this *fuerza ética* (ethical force). He spoke of horrors, but also of *la dignidad en el dolor* (dignity in pain) in religious language.

The conference reinforced the visibility of women's leadership in the struggle for peace and justice. The majority of the faces at the front were female, partially validating our analyses in this book. Women missed no opportunity to make visible their missing daughters and the sexualized violence, whatever the numbers or percentages the murder counts might show.

ANNUNCIATION HOUSE DINNER

The 2012 Annunciation House dinner, a three-hour, carefully choreographed and scripted event at Santa Lucia Church Hall, offered visual stimulation both inside and on the church grounds. Outside the hall, attendees passed by *altares*, altars and tables set up to remember and mourn the dead (usually constructed on the Day of the Dead at the border in late October and early November). Youth from El Paso's St. Pius X Catholic Church[3] sang pre-event songs, and the church's young *matachín* dancers, dressed in church colors, moved to their own drumbeats, thereby infusing indigenous rituals into this quasi-religious event.

Perhaps the most dramatic moment at the dinner involved a slow, somber parade of individuals carrying, in baskets on their heads, symbolic offerings to the more publicly known murder and assassination victims—activists and journalists—through the room, naming each one and then announcing in Spanish followed by the audience responding, in the style of litany, "Están con nosotros" (They are with us).

The parade to *dar voz y cara a los muertos* (give voice and face to the dead ones) personalized their existence in ways more compelling than the impersonal body counts do. Announcers at the dinner repeated the shocking figure of scores of thousands murdered in Mexico and over 10,000 murdered in the border region alone, for what was repeatedly called the "absurd" drug war. In a moving speech, Rubén García gave a critique of the absurdities of the drug war, making a rousing call to action to all those present.

CONCLUDING REFLECTIONS: TRANSNATIONAL SOLIDARITY?

In this chapter, we have analyzed the ways that ideas and solidarity efforts crossed borders in three key events: a U.S. congressional election; an international tribunal where jurists joined forces to take the entire government of Mexico to a moral trial, yet situated in Juárez; and a religiously inspired event to remember those who died, those who struggle, and those responsible for murders. The events occurred in the Juárez–El Paso region because it had become the emblematic space that symbolized connections between the global and the local about a futile war on drugs, state impunity, and the havoc wreaked on human beings, especially those in northern Mexico, with its tragically high murder rates of women and men. The three events analyzed illustrate how leaders threaded together critiques of violence against women with critiques of militarization in the borderlands. The movements, no longer separate in the display of unique and powerful symbolism of two of these three events (the tribunal and the Annunciation House dinner), conjoined and gained visibility in upward and outward ways. These events show agendas that are no longer hidden, but not yet mainstreamed in official agendas, either. The openness of the conjuncture of critiques against violence demonstrates the broader base of support that challenged the old separatist and one-sided narratives. While the media covered the tribunal in Mexico, in the United States, there was much media coverage of the Democratic primary election for Texas's Sixteenth Congressional District: Reyes versus O'Rourke and the framing of the future borderlands, reaching the mainstream in ways the other two events did not.

Beto O'Rourke's challenge to long-term congressional incumbent Silvestre Reyes illustrated an idea-based struggle over which would be the ascendant border paradigm: militarization or trade. A former

border patrol chief turned congressman, Reyes helped create the archi-
tecture for the Border Security Industrial Complex and its consequent
militarization. In so doing, he helped generate jobs in the various federal agencies that controlled the border and made border crossing more
challenging, not only for people crossing but also for people bringing
goods for business. Thus, the influential business community, or at
least parts of it, had stakes in pushing for new leadership that would
make trade more efficient and that would reduce polarization and in-
efficiency among business trading partners on both sides of the border.

O'Rourke, with others on the El Paso City Council, had already
pushed for hidden discourses to become public while he served on the
council, over his two four-year terms—discourses that challenged the
lengthy war on drugs and the violence it was engendering in Mexico.
The challenge gave rise to a broadened base of support among those
who questioned the impact of militarization on trade relations. These
hidden discourses not only became public, but helped to make cracks
in the official discourse and cause it to crumble in places.

The international Permanent Peoples' Tribunal has a long track
record of following injustices and bringing distinguished jurists and
experts to hold officials to account in a public, moral setting using the
symbols and players of a legalistic drama. We view the choice to in-
augurate the sessions of the Mexico chapter in Ciudad Juárez as enor-
mously significant: it invoked the city as ground zero for the seven
issues, threaded together, about which to take on the state. The choice
also demonstrated the way violence against women had been connected with key injustices in a setting now more integrated than separate. Finally, Grupo de Articulación Justicia en Juárez took responsibility for organizing the complex events, validating its leadership role
in the civil-society activism of the region.

The tribunal spread outward and upward a transnational solidarity
that would continue to strengthen the connections to issues in the
Americas (i.e., the Western Hemisphere) and the world, such as the
neoliberal, deregulated agenda, the dirty war, and the imposition of
authoritarian rule. A distinguished group of jurists with multiple af-
filiations in Europe and Asia participated in the multi-day events. That
Nora Cortiñas, cofounder of Argentina's Madres de la Plaza de Mayo,
would participate symbolized the ways in which disappearances in
northern Mexico resembled those during the "dirty wars" in nations
to the south (Winn 2006: chap. 9). Caravans of buses brought leaders,
activists, and experts from other parts of Mexico to the tribunal, re-

affirming the place of Juárez as a magnetic site and model for effective civil-society activism.

The conference and syncretic dinner of Annunciation House in 2012 also crossed the lines of the territorial border with its criticism of the drug wars in both Mexico and the United States and the resulting murders of scores of thousands of people, including activists and journalists. It also crossed the lines of Catholicism, Mexican and indigenous symbolism, and secular social-justice philosophy and laid the groundwork to include more people of faith in activism. The culminating supper closed a week of activity focusing on the approximately 10,000 people murdered in Ciudad Juárez from 2007 to 2011 and the murders' connection to the struggles of immigrants and ineffective policies, including U.S. foreign policies in Central America and Mexico. That the event took place in a sacred space, a church, signaled a significant venue for moral judgments to be passed on unjust policies and murders. Although media coverage of the event was minimal in the United States, it was coupled with a deep emotional engagement for those who participated personally and communicated to their friends and relatives using faith-based language.

However, a week of faith-based challenges to official discourse does not necessarily spread or sink into people's minds. Only months later, as activists on both sides of the border prepared for Javier Sicilia's caravan throughout the southwestern United States, caravaneros and caravaneras encountered difficulty getting mainstream faith congregations and synagogues to endorse the visit with its platform questioning the drug war and easy availability of assault weapons at gun dealerships along the border (see chapter 6), though a resolution supporting it passed in the El Paso City Council. Unlike national religious denominations, local institutions have a mix of congregants, some of whom may "talk the talk" of human solidarity across borders, but remain reluctant to "walk the walk," some being gun owners, veterans, and border patrol professionals. Churches are sensitive to possible dissent among congregants of differing opinions and those who may be hostile to the idea of questioning public policy, even in a democracy.

While the U.S. media hardly cover social-justice events, such as that at Annunciation House, the Mexican media did cover the Permanent Peoples' Tribunal, with its potentially transformative messages. In the U.S. mainstream media, coverage of murder and mayhem generates headlines in ways that democracy, calls for justice, and accountability do not. The danger of murder-count coverage of blood and death is that it may result in a numbing fatigue among some groups in the United States and it may normalize chaos among the "others" in Mexico for a mainstream audience all too ready to believe the worst about their neighbors to the south.

Unusual in studies of civil-society and social-movement activism, this chapter analyzed a case in which social-movement narratives have entered the mainstream of electoral politics, at least at the border. If social movements and organized interests seek to change policies like those involved in the drug war, some sort of engagement across the lines of civil society to government must eventually occur. The sparks of such occurrence took place in the El Paso area's 2012 Democratic primary election of Beto O'Rourke and his victory in the November congressional election. As difficult as this transition seemed to be, such connections in Mexico may face even more daunting challenges. In recent elections, Ciudad Juárez has been thoroughly entrapped in Partido Revolucionario Institucional–dominated victories at the municipal and state levels. Alignment with the PRI engulfs activists in history and saddles them with the baggage of a political party that has yet to fully adapt to or respond to the charges and claims made by peace and justice activists. Many activists avoid such taint, but in so doing they are opting to remain disconnected with the official political process.

In Washington, DC, one congressional representative can hardly make a dent, even with several border representatives, or the Border Caucus, in the House of Representatives that is relatively conservative in its focus on border "security" in the more militarized paradigmatic approach. Moreover, national engagement in a highly polarized U.S. Congress, where the base of support for questioning sacrosanct policies is barely visible, will be more difficult unless connected with mainstream, organized interests who use a variety of arguments and evidence to challenge the drug war, to call into question militarized border security, and to use the discourse of human rights in a country where such principles have little traction (Soohoo, Albira, and Davis 2007). If and when border trade overwhelms border security as the ascendant paradigm, civil-society and social-movement activists may focus once again on the economic injustices and wage inequalities that characterize border life on both sides—still part of the official discourse that advertises competitiveness and the comparative advantage of low-wage workers in Juárez. Their low salaries remain "hidden," unlike the murders that draw media coverage, however sensationalist, to the border.

SOUTH-TO-NORTH SOLIDARITY: SICILIA AND PEACE AND JUSTICE MOVEMENTS AT THE BORDER

*Together, we established an unprecedented bi-national agenda.
. . . In an act of civilian diplomacy, Mexican and American
citizens traveled across U.S. territory to focus the spotlight on
this national humanitarian crisis caused by a painfully misguided
bi-national policy based on the evils of war.*
JAVIER SICILIA, CARAVAN FOR PEACE, EL PASO, 2012

IN THE SUMMERS of 2011 and 2012, poet Javier Sicilia and a caravan of activists (*caravaneros* and *caravaneras*) and families of victims from Mexico's recent wave of violence toured the north of Mexico and the United States. This was not the first time that justice movements had performed at the border, in Mexico, or in the United States. During first-stage anti-femicide activism, the 1990s through 2004, the Mexico Solidarity Network (Mueller, Hansen, and Qualtire 2009) also moved through both countries, though perhaps not with the same level of attention; after all, it was a woman-focused, feminist movement and somewhat segregated from the mainstream. But by the time the murder rate began escalating in Ciudad Juárez in 2008, once-hidden discourses had become very public, not only through Sicilia's encouragement that people tell their stories and show their pictures at all stops of the caravan, but also by way of the broadening base of support that his movement, the Movimiento por la Paz con Justicia y Dignidad, was gaining in wider geographical spaces in Mexico and the United States.

On their tour, Sicilia and the *caravaneras* and *caravaneros* called for alternatives to existing policies in both countries. Anchoring his discourse on human rights and employing language that evinced his strong Catholic upbringing and faith to address the issue of justice, Sicilia and the movement questioned policies that "respond to violence with more violence." Sicilia said the movement was one of "two great social movements of the last 20 years in Mexico, the Zapatistas and the Movement for Peace," the Zapatistas drawing from Maya indigenous traditions, but both of them drawing on poets, writers, and artists. He called the Movimiento por la Paz one that "disrupts the one-sided political discourse," erupting a moral discourse into public life (all from Bleifuss 2012: 24).

The national Movimiento por la Paz con Justicia y Dignidad acquired wide media visibility in Mexico and surprisingly in the United States as well. After founding the movement following the tragedy of the murder of his son Juan Francisco, Sicilia became an emblematic figure: a father, with back slightly bent, wearing casual brown clothes and hat, with a gentle, near-religious air about him and a very deep voice speaking slow, measured words. Thus, in gender terms, his prominence parted ways with the Juarense women who had initially provided visibility to the impunity surrounding their murdered daughters. A poet and essayist, prior to the tragedy and the emergence of the national movement, Sicilia was widely known in Mexican cultural, academic, and political circles. His weekly editorial contribution to *Proceso* magazine provided him with certain national visibility and sympathies among the progressive readers who identified his column by its signature closing that called for—among various demands—governmental recognition of the San Andrés Accords signed with the Zapatistas in Chiapas, and with a demand that femicide cease in Juárez. Thus, he continues to acknowledge the gendered dimensions and consequences of the crisis. Sicilia's work and writing demonstrate a commitment to social causes; and in the case of Ciudad Juárez, they evince respect and admiration for their unrelenting mobilizations against violence toward women. As we discussed at the close of chapter 3, Sicilia was featured as one of the multiple "persons of the year" that *Time* magazine chose for that special issue in 2011, putting the spotlight on protesters for democracy, social justice, and freedom, from those in the so-called Arab Spring in North Africa to Sicilia in Mexico.

In this chapter, we describe and analyze two Sicilia-led caravans. The first one, known as the Caravana del Consuelo and/or Caravana al Norte, departed from Cuernavaca, Morelos, and arrived in Ciudad Juárez, Chihuahua, and El Paso, Texas, in the hot desert month of June 2011. The second one, touring the United States, occurred a little more than a year after the Caravana del Consuelo. This caravan, called the "Caravan for Peace," traveled from the U.S. West to East Coast, part-

Postcard for the Caravan for Peace, August–September 2012. Courtesy of
Ted Lewis, Global Exchange.

nering with Global Exchange, an international human rights organization. The coalition presented in public forums a verbal alternative
debate around the drug war in many speeches in multiple cities during
the August 12–September 12 caravan.

From the first caravan in Mexico to the second tour across the
United States, Sicilia modified his perspectives on several issues. As
we describe throughout this chapter, these revised perspectives might
be read as illustrative of the growth and maturity of Sicilia—the activist
and leader—and the movement that he inspired and contributed to
founding. For instance, his and the movement's stance against militarization became more definitive as he learned and witnessed during the
first caravan how in each state and city, Calderón's war against drugs
spurred varied forms of violence, thus also requiring differentiated demands and responses from citizens and activists. In addition, Sicilia's
point of view in favor of the legalization of certain drugs such as marijuana was prominent and publicly stated throughout his tour across
the United States. And finally, by the end of the first caravan, it became clear that the movement was decidedly what members would
call, during a national assembly in January 2012, a "victim's movement"
despite the hefty political document and lofty objectives made public at

Mexico City's Zócalo in May 2011, when the movement called for the refoundation of the nation, a political reform including citizens' candidacies, or *candidaturas independientes*, and the rejection of a recent labor reform that would reverse the gains of the 1930s labor movement in the constitution that was being discussed in Congress, among other important but seemingly disparate matters.

THE CARAVANA DEL CONSUELO, JUNE 2011

Initially baptized as the Caravana por la Paz con Justicia y Dignidad, based on the movement's name, the first caravan evolved into the Caravana del Consuelo. The change in name, as Javier Sicilia often explains, was related to the realities and "pains" he and other caravaneros and caravaneras were encountering in the various regions of Mexico's north. Hard hit with the violence, people from towns—tiny and large—would come out with handmade signs and relatives' pictures to welcome the caravan on its way to Juárez. *Caravaneras* and *caravaneros* often share that Sicilia, moved by the sight, would request that the drivers stop so that he and those bystanders at each stopping point could talk briefly.

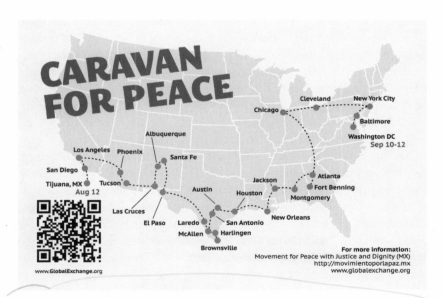

Postcard for the Caravan for Peace, showing the route. Courtesy of Ted Lewis, Global Exchange.

Those short conversations turned out to be about people's personal loss and grieving in the context of the drug war. In their brevity and honesty, they offered everyone an opportunity to console each other. Consolation, as Sicilia recognizes, is a collective act, and the first and most basic form of justice. Consolation, Sicilia wrote in a letter to Juarense activists, is a form of justice that does not depend on the political will of authoritarian and insensitive states and governments but is a form of justice that all victims of Calderón's war needed, were owed, and could provide to each other.

Comprising roughly six to seven hundred *caravaneros* and *caravaneras* traveling in fourteen buses, plus others in private cars and vans, the caravan included victims' families and activists of diverse causes from all over Mexico, including those from Atenco, Michoacán, Veracruz, Sonora, and Chiapas, among others. A robust presence of representatives from national and international media was visible; some traveled with the caravan and others traveled in their own media vehicles. A few activists from the United States met the caravan in Ciudad Juárez as well. Among them were representatives from the Fellowship of Reconciliation and Global Exchange. All *caravaneras* and *caravaneros* were hosted for two nights in Juárez, their room and board organized and provided by several Juarense nongovernmental organizations, *asociaciones civiles*, local Catholic groups, nuns, and the seminary. Despite the short notice of the caravan's arrival, the Juárez groups' successful handling of the required logistics and acquisition of the resources necessary to receive and host such a large number of people without asking them for compensation of the many costs, as well as the organization of multiple activities for three consecutive days, evinced the unparalleled degree of organization and built capacity of Juarense civil society.

The caravan was received at the Benito Juárez statue, a Juarense landmark that is often recognized as being located at the city limit coming from the south. To welcome Sicilia and the caravan, the Asamblea Juarense por la Paz con Justicia y Dignidad, the temporary coalition of coalitions that was created to host and plan the caravan's activities, asked Luz María Dávila—the mother of two young men killed at Villas de Salvárcar and the woman who had confronted Felipe Calderón publicly at the meeting announcing the creation of Todos Somos Juárez—to greet and welcome the caravan.

The *asambleístas*' invitation to Luz María—which she readily accepted—sent a strong message in various directions. That is, in Luz María's welcoming *abrazo* (embrace) of Javier Sicilia, *asambleístas* wished to signal their conviction that this would remain a citizens' movement from which a national pact for the pacification of the country would emerge. Thus, as Luz María had previously done, *asambleístas* were also sending a clear message of rejection of any form of dialogue or involvement with local, state, and federal governments.

Furthermore, in the Sicilia–Luz María embrace, *asambleístas* were showing unity—despite the fact that within the coalition of coalitions, people and organizations at times clashed over their diverse and divergent ideological perspectives and practices. Such divergences also existed between certain organizations in the *asamblea* and some in the Movimiento por la Paz con Justicia y Dignidad. Beyond the differences, however, in the context of war and tragedy, all recognized that Sicilia— an influential intellectual—and Luz María—a modest maquiladora worker—both represented part of the nation's "moral reserve" (Ameglio 2010). As Willivaldo Delgadillo (2011b) wrote in the days prior to the Sicilia and Luz María embrace, "When they embrace, their moral force will be fusing a nation's demand that can hardly continue to be ignored by the country and the international community: Mexico wants peace with justice and dignity and thousands are willing to mobilize to reach that objective" (Méndez translation). The embrace took place in June of 2011 amidst a crowd of international and national journalists, all of whom wanted the best spot to capture such a symbolic moment.

The caravan's and Javier Sicilia's stay in Juárez was memorable. Though the city had been recognized by Sicilia as "the epicenter of pain and tragedy," activists and organizers were showing, through carefully planned and executed activities, that they were also the epicenter of resistance. Notwithstanding the complexity of the logistics, which were exacerbated by differences of opinion and vision, Juarenses warmly received the *caravaneros* and *caravaneras*. Led by Luz María Dávila, the first activity upon the caravan's arrival took place at Villas de Salvárcar, where fifteen people were massacred at a party in 2010, including Luz María's two sons (see chapter 3). There, through *testimonios* and sharing of their stories, people gave and received consolation and the recognition that their pain was real, beyond official conceptions of their losses as "collateral damage" (Méndez observations).

The next morning, women's groups led the caravan to Campo Algodonero, where eight bodies of tortured and murdered young women were dumped in 2001. Mothers of femicide victims offered their testimony. Anti-femicide activists talked about the long journey toward justice. Visibly touched, Sicilia stood there listening attentively to the stories the women shared. Warmly, he hugged those who approached him and offered them words of comfort (Méndez observations).

As planned, but with some delay, after Campo Algodonero, the caravan made its way to the Universidad Autónoma de Ciudad Juárez, where the *caravaneras* and *caravaneros*, as well as the organization members and other Juarense participants, gathered in various work groups to discuss different topics for several hours. The ambitious expectation—which proved to be unachievable—was that a pact around the topics discussed would be agreed upon, drafted, signed, and publicly presented (Méndez observations).

The complexity of the topics, the limited amount of time to discuss them, and the diversity of positions—from those of victims' relatives and activists, to a varied constellation of political ideologies and doctrines—made discussions endless and polarizing. In some work groups people engaged in verbal attacks over differences in perspective. Families of victims and other groups, mainly from outside of Juárez, complained about the "radical" positions that certain participants wanted to take. And activists from Juárez saw with discomfort and suspicion that certain activists from other states sought to engage with their local, state, or federal government in their quest for justice. Mirroring that view, certain groups claimed that "justice would never come from criminals" and condemned that course of action. A few groups from Juárez, especially human rights activists and organizations, defended the right of people to decide whether or not to engage in dialogue with governmental representatives. From their perspective, families of victims could do so and should not be told not to demand justice from the state's legal system, however flawed it might be.

With time upon them, the plenary session was unable to reach consensus on a draft document of a pact. Minutes recorded listed numerous points that people had made, but they sometimes reflected participants' contradictory views. In the end, groups from Juárez—particularly those in the Frente Plural Ciudadano—along with others from Mexico City, such as the COMECOM (Coordinadora Metropolitana contra la Militarización), demanded that the minutes be recognized as the pact. Others, in the Movimiento por la Paz con Justicia y Dignidad, including Sicilia and his close associates, were not ready to recognize the minutes from the work groups as a pact. More time was necessary to resolve the long lists of inconsistencies and contradictions represented in the minutes (Méndez observation).

Without reaching an agreement on a pact, the caravan and activists left the university to travel downtown to the Monumento a Juárez, one of the city's plazas. (See Julián Cardona's photograph at the end of this book, page 171.) When they arrived, the plaza was full of people. There at the monument, Sicilia delivered a brief pronouncement that referred vaguely to the pact. This upset various organizations in the Asamblea Juarense and other groups that shared a common agenda with those organizations. The disagreement eventually led to fissures within the Movimiento por la Paz con Justicia y Dignidad and to the dissolution of the Asamblea Juarense (as described by Díaz [2012]).

While the debates were erupting in the work groups, not far away at the Santa Fé international bridge that connects the cities of Juárez and El Paso, a group of people was gathering to march from El Paso to the Monumento a Juárez, where they would witness the signing and public presentation of the pact. In her "Hacia una solidaridad verdadera" (Toward a true solidarity [Méndez translation]), Kerry Doyle (2011b) describes how a "binational group" constituted by *Juarenses and Paseños* (El Pasoans) marched together, and how, as they and she joined in this action, questions surfaced about solidarity and the meaning of walking side by side with people in Juárez. To those questions, Doyle seems to have found an answer the following day, when she narrated the ways in which organizations from El Paso welcomed and received Javier Sicilia and a number of *caravaneros* and *caravaneras*.

In particular, Doyle describes a document that was thought by its authors to be the U.S. version of the pact that was supposed to have been signed in Juárez. In it, organizers and activists begin to recognize, according to Doyle (2011b), the responsibility that they share with regard to the violence in Mexico. Thus, in the U.S. version of the pact, organizations ask the U.S. government to exhort the Mexican government to procure justice and protection for the victims of the war, as well as to expedite investigations that bring to justice all of those involved in crimes related to the so-called drug war. The pact also asks for immediate asylum in the United States and legal protection from the U.S. government for victims fleeing from the violence. Finally, it demands an end to the Mérida Initiative.

The fracture or rupture of groups coalescing in the Asamblea Juarense, though difficult, was not surprising to those who actively participated in the *asamblea*. In a highly volatile political and national context, groups in Juárez—like others in the nation—are not untouched by the complexity in which the Movimiento por la Paz is embedded. Willivaldo Delgadillo (2011b) explains to a Mexico-wide audience in *La Jor-*

nada that since the Zapatista insurrection in the first half of the 1990s, there had not emerged a social movement that had "awakened" people's "conscience, imagination, and willingness to debate" until Sicilia's Movimiento por la Paz con Justicia y Dignidad. As such, the expectations placed on it, he recognizes, were unrealistic. So much so that though it is true that the movement represents a more unique, genuine, and attractive space for political debate than that afforded by other political spheres, it is not reasonable, Delgadillo contends, to expect that all actions will stem from it.

Notwithstanding the ruptures and differences, the unrealistic expectations placed on the movement, and the often naïve calls for unity when in reality activism in Juárez as in the rest of Mexico has always exhibited heterogeneous ideologies, agendas, and ways of organizing, Sicilia's caravan made visible the problems with former president Calderón's war by dismantling an insidious official discourse that placed the blame on its victims. In dismantling the pervasive discourse that sought to legitimize violence and death, Javier Sicilia articulated and has afforded activists—old and young—a new political language. This new language is one that decenters the exaltation of militant ideologies and emphasizes a collective quest for truth and justice.

THE CARAVAN FOR PEACE, AUGUST–SEPTEMBER 2012

Sicilia's second caravan, the Caravan for Peace, traveled across the United States in several buses and a number of private vehicles. Some of the *caravaneras* and *caravaneros* had joined Sicilia's first caravan to Juárez, but many were traveling with the caravan for the first time. Among them were relatives of victims from across Mexico, as well as Mexican and U.S. activists and members of nonmainstream media.

As Global Exchange reported on its website after the caravan, seventeen national U.S. organizations partnered on the Caravan for Peace, ranging from the Drug Policy Alliance and National Latino Congress to the NAACP and the Veterans for Peace. The caravan traveled with two large, well-decorated buses and other vehicles with signs painted on them about corrupt governors in northeastern Mexico.

Part of the caravan's message involved the destruction that assault-type and automatic weapons wreak in Mexico's high murder rates. Considerable numbers of such weapons are smuggled from the many gun dealers in the southwestern United States into Mexico. It was hoped that the caravan would raise awareness and that various cities would

One of two Caravan for Peace buses that traveled across the United States, from the West Coast to the East Coast. Photo by Kathleen Staudt.

then adopt the Responsible Firearms Retailer Partnership voluntary code (see appendix 1). The voluntary code included ensuring that no sales would occur without background-check results, that employees would have background checks, and that firearms transactions at the point of sale would be videotaped. Although unaddressed in the code, another serious problem is that in various border cities, one can also purchase military-style uniforms and even Mexican State Judicial Police badge identifications, which are potentially useful to traffickers on either side of the border. We know of no government that adopted the code, with action components.

Caravan leaders took a five-point resolution to twenty-two major U.S. cities focusing on strategies to address the massive number of murders, the gun smuggling, the militarized drug war, and the money laundering that aggravate conflict in two friendly countries with interdependent economies, especially noticeable in the borderlands. The El Paso resolution is reprinted in full, adopted with one abstention by the El Paso City Council, in appendix 2, and a general acknowledgment by just five Spanish-surnamed council representatives in Los Angeles is in appendix 3. Since 2005, El Paso's city council has put forth a track record of resolutions showing its cognizance of the city's economic interdependence and cooperation with Ciudad Juárez (e.g., a symbolic resolution against the border fence/wall). Chapter 5 contains an extensive discussion of the unusual actions calling for debate on the drug war taken by the city council when Beto O'Rourke, now a congressman, was a city councilman.

Various U.S. regional human rights and social-justice groups endorsed the caravan's efforts, including the Border Network for Human Rights and Annunciation House in El Paso and Communities Organized for Public Service (affiliated with the statewide Industrial Areas Foundation) in San Antonio. Thus, Global Exchange and the *caravaneros* and *caravaneras* widened the constituency base of support around alternatives to the drug war and its consequent violence in Mexico. Yet, despite the national positions of mainstream religious institutions with antiwar, pro-immigration, and social-justice principles, none of the local El Paso churches or synagogues endorsed the caravan and its five resolutions, circulated to some ahead of time. Still, the El Paso City Council passed the resolution on August 21, 2012.

Local activists worked with receptive El Paso City Council representatives so that Javier Sicilia and the *caravaneras* and *caravaneros* would have a slot on the regular, Tuesday-morning city council meeting agenda. Of the eight-person city council, Councilperson Susie Byrd spearheaded these efforts. Staudt and Méndez attended the packed meeting, where hundreds of people sat and stood in the open council chambers, which are designed theatre style with video cameras to record meetings and video streaming to computer watchers anywhere and everywhere. One *caravanero* and Sicilia made persuasive remarks in Spanish (which were translated into English) to the council members, Mayor John Cook, and members of the overflow audience, many of whom were watching the meeting on monitors in the foyer (City of El Paso 2009, 2012). Sicilia spoke about the violence in Mexico and the need for changes to policies, and asked for support for the resolution. His comments integrated the murders of women with the extensive homicide, disappearances, police impunity, and militarized violence.

Rather than call for council dialogue immediately after Sicilia's eloquent speech, Mayor Cook allowed public comment. For some, this was initially disappointing, given the consensus that seemed to emerge after Sicilia's moving remarks, but the open-comment orientation ultimately resonated with the public organizational culture of

Javier Sicilia speaks to and dialogues with El Paso City Council representatives and the mayor at an August 2012 council meeting at City Hall, with video streaming, an overflow audience, and a media presence. Photo by Kathleen Staudt.

the city. Several local council watchers, retired and in attendance at most city council meetings, made extended public comments about the issues being Mexico's problem, rather than a U.S. responsibility. They focused on corruption in Mexico and disrespect for the rule of law there. One worried whether guns would be further controlled in the United States if action were taken to contribute to solving the problem in Mexico. Councilperson Byrd then read the resolution aloud, with strong conviction.

Then it came time for the council representatives to engage and ask questions. While they appeared receptive, two council members, Michael Noe and Eddie Holguin, took the opportunity to proclaim their support for the second amendment to the U.S. Constitution, no doubt to assure their constituents that the right to buy and use guns was not under threat in this decidedly public setting. A back-and-forth dialogue with Sicilia about guns ensued, somewhat tense and painful albeit with seemingly friendly gazes, involving posturing and attempts to corner Sicilia into taking a position he was not asking for (i.e., outlawing gun sales). Noe's and Holguin's questions about the drug war became hostile, with word games that sought to position Sicilia as an advocate of U.S. marijuana legalization, which he did not advocate at this meeting. This was not his intent with the resolution nor in his public presentation to the city council. Rather, he asked continuously for people to consider alternatives to the drug war, including treatment for addiction, without imposing a specific solution, thereby avoiding the manipulative intent to back him into a corner that would undermine council support for the resolution. With the momentum of the caravan and Sicilia's speech broken, some members of the audience stood up in silence and respectfully turned their backs to encourage commentators to complete their remarks. This symbolic pose was picked up and covered by the local media, and it was criticized by Frontera List moderator Molly Molloy at cyber distance. Mayor Cook and several members of the council restated, over and over, what the resolution did and did not say.

In the end, council members passed the resolution, becoming the only city that we know of among the twenty-two cities visited in the caravan's month-long trip across the United States to endorse the resolution in its entirety. For example, Huntington Park, California, mayor Andy Molina "acknowledged," with members of the council, the Movimiento por la Paz con Justicia y Dignidad and welcomed the caravan to their city, but did not approve the resolution. A group of five Los Angeles City Council representatives, rather than the whole council, signed a document "support[ing] and welcom[ing]" the caravan and recognizing its "concerns" to "end bloodshed and attain peace," but also did not approve the resolution.

After the city council meeting, the buses went to the large U.S. Drug Enforcement Administration (DEA) building in El Paso, which was totally fenced, locked, and without a representative to receive the hundred or so people. After *caravaneros* and *caravaneras* made short speeches to others standing in the driveway holding posters, a DEA sport-utility vehicle arrived with its lights flashing to deliver an urgent message to clear the driveway. Following that, several similar SUVs, driven by members of a Global Exchange partner organization, Law Enforcement against Prohibition, parked on the street, showing the LEAP insignia on the sides of the vehicles, proclaiming their support for ending drug-prohibition policies, which they deem to be as ineffective as the alcohol-prohibition policies of the 1920s and early 1930s (see www.leap.org for more information on LEAP's positions). All in all, the caravan's presence at the DEA headquarters was a symbolic public performance that strengthened activists' bonding with one another and provided photo opportunities, but the caravan failed to engage with the front-line agents or their representatives.

Ana Morales generated a list of U.S. media coverage of Sicilia's cross-country Caravan for Peace, city by city (Morales 2012). Patterns are immediately evident. Rather than mainstream press coverage in English, most of the coverage can be found in the alternative press, especially the Spanish-language press. The Global Exchange website contains blogs, city by city, discussing the caravan, but for El Paso, there is no coverage of the city council meeting and activists' engagement with public officials therein. Such engagement with the equivalent local council in Ciudad Juárez would have been impossible. Traditionally, it has been a closed rather than an open and transparent body, although it has been more public in recent years. More importantly, its occupants are affiliated with a layer of government much mistrusted and perceived to be partially complicit with the repression and surveillance of peace and justice activists. Before contrasts are drawn too sharply with the U.S. side, however, we acknowledge that without several progressive representatives on the El Paso City Council, the public event and surrounding dialogue at its meeting would not have been possible. Moreover, the resolution it approved did not and cannot change U.S. policy at the national level. Rather, it adds one more document to the critical, widening base of support for alternative policies.

In Mexico, far more media coverage occurred about Sicilia's U.S. Caravan for Peace, in print and video form. One video in particular stands out for us, and that is one that films Sicilia's personal, face-to-face meeting with Sheriff Joe Arpaio in Phoenix, Maricopa County, Arizona. The sheriff is well known for his anti-immigrant crusades that rounded up unauthorized workers, put them in tent jails, paraded them in emasculating pink underwear through public streets, and ultimately spent tax money on these public political performances in an electoral system where popularity is important and where sizeable numbers of conservative, anti-immigrant citizens vote. In a video that we viewed, Sicilia asks the sheriff, human being to human being, to consider the dignity of all people; and when Sicilia gently touches Arpaio's arm, viewers can see him apparently cringe in revulsion.[1]

Javier Sicilia speaking with Sheriff Joe Arpaio, Phoenix. Courtesy of
Ted Lewis, Global Exchange.

CONCLUDING REFLECTIONS

As we reflect on the month-long Sicilia visit with the caravan buses, after
the U.S. presidential nominating conventions, the campaign, and the
election, we see the caravan's impact of making people's once-hidden
stories more visible, of consoling people, and of increasing public solidarity around peace and justice movements for those who follow the
everyday lives of people at the border and in Mexico. However, we
notice little influence on the once-hidden, now-public discourse as it
affects U.S. policy and relations with Mexico. Indeed, during the U.S.
presidential debates, Mexico went unmentioned, even in the debate
focused on foreign policy. The absence of content on violence and injustice in one of the country's immediate neighbors calls into question
whether cross-border activism percolates upward and onward into the
capital city and major spaces of power in the United States. Mexico is

not only the second-largest trading partner of the United States, but also its collaborator in a flawed drug war. However, besides the twenty states in the United States that have legalized medical marijuana, voters in two states (Colorado and Washington) legalized marijuana for leisure use in the November 2012 elections. As states move more and more in this direction, if the federal system of government is respected (see Villalobos 2013), the government of Mexico will no doubt reconsider its own laws and drug strategy. In 2009, marijuana possession in small amounts was decriminalized in Mexico, but the drug prohibition laws still exist (Payan, Staudt, and Kruszewski 2013). Decriminalization versus legalization strategies pose very different questions for political strategies in both countries and for the drug war.

More important to both governments, with the 2012 election of President Enrique Peña Nieto and the reelection of President Barack Obama, is the prospect of opening Mexico further to increase trade relations and foreign investment, including the possibility of foreign funding for oil exploration and modernization of Mexico's national Petroleos Mexicanos (PEMEX). In late 2012, the *Economist* magazine published a sixteen-page supplement, "Special Report: Mexico," that celebrated the growth and economic expansion expected in Peña Nieto's presidential term. This neoliberal economic agenda coexists side by side with continuing economic inequalities, a problem hardly addressed in business discourse seemingly officialized with the movement from the once-publicized Juárez Competitiva to the now broadened border conferences focused on the U.S.-Mexico Competitiveness Agenda, with groups of government, business, and business consulting firms traveling to major border cities for summer 2013 conferences in San Diego, Laredo, and El Paso. (We both attended the conference in El Paso, where business consultant John Negroponte, former U.S. ambassador to Honduras, national security advisor under Nixon and Reagan, and director of national intelligence under President George W. Bush, was named an honorary Texan. His visible leadership shows the connections between business and government [as opposed to peace and justice activists and government].)

Set in the theoretical frameworks we pose in this book, Sicilia's visits to the Paso del Norte metropolitan region offer the opportunity to analyze the still-tenuous relationships among activists there and the counternarrative they have developed in the region. We can consider not only the relationships among activists in Ciudad Juárez, but also the cross-border solidarity relationships, when a media-savvy, external moral leader enters the political fray. Sicilia, from central Mexico and specifically the state of Morelos, did not, perhaps, completely comprehend the full havoc being wreaked on the northern border during his first visit. With his initial ambivalence about militarization, as expressed publicly in an improvised press conference in El Paso in June of 2011, his statements on the issue deepened the polarization among Juarense groups in the huge collaboration to receive him, known as the Asamblea Juarense por la Paz con Justicia y Dignidad, which ultimately disassembled. Considering the boomerang theory of human rights theorists (Risse, Ropp, and Sikkink 1999), his two visits show how media attention can backfire and undermine grassroots groups. By the second trip, criticism softened but left tensions remaining among activists.

Nevertheless, Sicilia was and is a game changer in the terms we have defined in this book. From his own personal experience, his writings, and his exposure to so many people on caravan trips, he drew on once-hidden, but now newly expanded public discourse that resonated with human rights, feminist, and anti-militarization activists. That discourse emerged from the deaths, destruction, and resistance among survivors, but was articulated with a vision of dignity, hope, and consolation. Yet, these discourses, in James Scott's terms, emerged with a linguistic twist. The discourse erupted more challenges in the Spanish language, except for unique but startling English-language exceptions like in the El Paso City Council and its cross-border solidarity activists. The border cities and their creative cross-border solidarity provided a model and pathway for transnational activism elsewhere in the world.

CHAPTER SEVEN

CONCLUSION: REFLECTIONS ON THE POSSIBILITIES OF POST-CONFLICT PEACE AND JUSTICE

[A]n active civil society on both sides of the border is the remedy.
TIMOTHY DUNN, ON THE DANGEROUS IMPLICATIONS OF
INCREASED BORDER MILITARIZATION (2009: 228)

IN THIS BOOK, we give witness to, document, and analyze the growing connections among those who oppose both violence against women and the militarization of the border. In this, our final chapter, we (1) summarize key findings and consider the debates about possible next steps of engagement with officials, (2) elaborate on and extend the ideas of the major theorists on whom we have drawn for their insights, herein grounded and gendered at the border and thus potentially enhancing border theories on civil-society relations, and (3) offer clues on what can be expected in future years under the presidency of Enrique Peña Nieto and beyond, as well as in U.S. policy toward Mexico, drugs, and trade, which heretofore seemed to merge, whether under Republican or Democratic leadership. Víctor Quintana Silveyra, state of Chihuahua director of Movimiento de Regeneración Nacional (MORENA), called Peña Nieto's cabinet choices dinosaurs and technocrats (quoted in Salmón 2012: 319A). Quintana holds mixed, but mostly dim, predictions for Mexico's near future, with the same political economy, "una política de relaciones exteriores sujeta a los intereses de Estados Unidos, y un trato 'jurásico' en la política interior" (a policy of external relations subject to U.S. interests and a "Jurassic" deal in internal policy) (quoted in Salmón 2012). Like Quintana, we remain skeptical about Peña Nieto's political will and ability to bring about substantial changes. However, we are guardedly optimistic about Mexico's future: we argue that civil society *is* growing and strengthening itself in Mexico, with a sophisticated ability to connect with transnational civil-society organizations and media in the larger North America and the world.

SUMMARY OF FINDINGS

Once a feminist and human rights movement against femicide and family violence, with few results despite its global and media visibility, an opportune political context of fear, militarization, and government impunity gave rise to new conjunctures among those in the movement who sought "no more deaths," peace, and justice, including gender justice. After pioneering activism and leadership from feminist and human rights groups in the 1990s, and with outlier levels of violence in Ciudad Juárez after 2007, both men and women activists understood and acted upon the linkages between violence against women, hyper-homicide rates, and militarization. They questioned the government's so-called security strategy—a strategy that induced high levels of insecurity instead and resulted in horrific numbers of murdered men and women.

Through militarization, which aggravated and increased the violence, the public lost confidence in official transcripts that claimed to provide security and solve problems from organized crime. And with their no-longer-hidden transcripts, Juarenses creatively and persistently resisted official discourses, frequently with game-changing women leaders and/or the organization of activists around the deaths of women and children.

Disparate networks and groups—at rallies and via social media—sounded once-hidden but increasingly public counternarratives. Those narratives emerged in a broadened base, moving upward and outward to include some faith communities, some politicians, and high-visibility caravan travelers across wide geographic spaces in Mexico and the United States. Not surprisingly, tensions sometimes erupted among activists in this large, complex metropolitan and cross-border region—tensions based on political styles, agenda priorities, and collaboration with external leaders (such as Javier Sicilia).

People's perspectives are rarely identical, so we wouldn't expect them to think and act alike, whether in Ciudad Juárez, El Paso, Mexico, or the United States. However, there is one generalizable difference in nongovernmental organization (NGO) relationships with the state between Mexico and the United States: activists in Mexico seem less trustful and more wary of engaging in electoral campaigns than U.S. activists. Yet Mexican activists display a collective vibrance and more courage than those in the United States, who tend to pursue more individualistic actions, such as voting, donating money and time, and posting and forwarding social media.

Movement activists face dilemmas over whether and how to move their counterhegemonic practices into engagement with government, where policies and laws are made and enforced. After all, awareness raising and counternarratives alone have their limitations. Thus far, the Mexican government problematically responded to nearly two decades of organizing with a variety of ineffectual commissions, unenforced laws (including all of the many requirements of the Inter-American Court of Human Rights' Campo Algodonero decision), and lip-service to Todos Somos Juárez patronage that seemed to benefit the wealthy as much as provide meager additions to social services (which were always provided in the country but were renamed in Juárez). These seriously flawed responses fed cynicism and worries about co-optation, in addition to serious questions about the extent to which the political system resembled anything like a democracy.

Will the malgoverned move toward the acquisition of voice, power, and roles in governance? The founding chairman of the United States–based La Raza Unida Party of the early 1970s, José Angel Gutiérrez, asked this question at the party's fortieth anniversary conference in El Paso in 2012 (Staudt observation). The party started as a short-term political party and now rests unevenly as part of the largest "minority" group (Hispanics, Latinos/as) in the United States, soon to be a majority group in five southwestern states and a reputedly solid voter bloc in most of the swing states that delivered their Electoral College votes to reelect President Obama in the 2012 election. We can only wonder whether the challenges to the drug war will take another forty years, raising questions here too about democracy in the United States—real, or in name only?

COMPLICATING THE BORDER NARRATIVE

Our analysis in this book provides a complementary, new narrative to the previous portrayals of the border as a place of violence and mayhem—a narrative that maintains attention to the often-forgotten region. Some networks are informational, such as listservs that count the dead and forward various media articles and links about the borderlands. For the hundreds of journalists, academics, and activists on such lists, the news paints grim pictures of the situation. While the grim narrative is part of reality, just as is the puzzling, new, economic-miracle narrative of "growth with violence" that the *Economist* put forth in its 2012 supplement called "Special Report: Mexico," reprinting in its "World in 2013" a speech by President Peña Nieto, the official narratives hardly include the dense, courageous, and rich civil-society activism that we analyze in this book. The activism analyzed in this book, nevertheless, comes with complications like those we discuss below.

ORGANIZING AT THE EPICENTER: CIUDAD JUÁREZ

In Mexico, the historic concern of citizens who network and organize in civil society has been to challenge policies freely and critically, often in public marches and rallies, but to maintain their independence and thus avoid co-optation by the state. When *asociaciones civiles* (A.C.'s), that is, nonprofit organizations, accept grants from government and private sources, potential economic dependency and political co-optation may develop, such as what exists in Todos Somos Juárez money—what some viewed as dirty or blood money, made available as the peaks of violence surged in Mexico's epicenter of violence, Ciudad Juárez. Yet many are guided by the operating principle *la justicia es primero* (justice is first), or *nada en Juárez sin justicia* (nothing in Juárez without justice), signaling a continuing Juarense wariness not only of engagement with the state until justice is first achieved, but also of engagement with national peace and justice activists like Javier Sicilia. Many were initially wary of working with Sicilia because he exhibited ambivalence about calling for an end to militarization in the beginning of his caravan journeys, but some warmed up to him in Juárez and in the rest of Mexico when he ultimately came to the conclusion to make that call.

TOWARD ACTIVISTS' ENGAGEMENT WITH GOVERNMENT . . . OR NOT?

The compelling principle of certain groups and organizations to avoid negotiation and engagement with officials until justice is achieved begs several questions: When will justice be achieved? Who signals its achievement? Might feminist, peace, and justice activists work in or during a transitional period toward justice? If so, how? As is the case in many civil-society organizations, especially those in contexts of authoritarian states, extensive distrust and fear, and societies with questionable respect for the rule of law, divisions exist among activists in Ciudad Juárez over both the content and style of their practices.

Beginning in the 1990s, women activists laid a good foundation for collaborative work and alliance-building, albeit with tensions over goals, strategies, and decisions to engage with government or not. While it is true that anti-femicide marches and rallies have not been as visible in recent years as in the past, there is no doubt of the gains made in focused strategies tied to the Campo Algodonero case brought to the Inter-American Court of Human Rights, the court's ruling, and the new opportunities and strategies it has offered, especially with the visibility of the government's noncompliance with a respected, external international institution while fervently but ultimately demagogically claiming to respect human rights principles with various paper treaties. Feminist activists continue to resist the possibility of being swallowed by the state's official discourse, which aims to appease and silence voices under the pretense of responsiveness. Whatever the time period, personality differences and styles foster disagreement, exit strategies from groups, the birth of new groups, and groups taking recess.

Social movements, many short lived, expand awareness and alternatives. What role exists for them beyond resistance or countering narratives? Some turn into NGOs, *asociaciones civiles*, or nonprofit organizations that press government officials for change and to provide services or training for their constituents. The phrase "social work" has a broader meaning in Mexico than in the United States, but whatever the country, the organizations can suffer from staffing and funding reductions. In the late 1960s and the 1970s, the antiviolence U.S. feminist movement's agenda moved into the creation of publicly funded and subsidized shelters and new procedures in law enforcement (Staudt 2008: chap. 5). With few exceptions, analysts rarely considered both the strengths and the shortcomings of ex-movement NGOs' agendas once routinized in government or in the officially approved, tax-exempt nonprofit sector.

In Ciudad Juárez, some civil associations register with the government and seek funding, potentially muting their discourse and voice, given their dependency on generating revenue to maintain offices, pay staff, and pay for utilities. The same dependent relationship can exist in U.S. nonprofit organizations that qualify for a tax-exempt 501(c)(3) status from the Internal Revenue Service (IRS), and are therefore forbidden from overt political and partisan activities. Many other organizations operate with explicit political agendas, using other IRS designations or registering as political lobby organizations. In the field of international development, analysts have differentiated between "people's organizations" and "contractors" (Alvarez 1998; Korten 1990). Organizations like these become intermediaries that compete in the contexts of pluralist liberal democracies, however flawed and unequal the competition, given their different levels of control over monetary resources.

FROM SOCIAL WORK TO ENGAGEMENT IN ESTABLISHMENT POLITICS

Activists in social movements often view those in established organizations with some wariness, even disdain, given the potential for co-optation. And they are cynical about those in government who co-opt NGOs and claim to solve problems through symbolic means. Yet, for public officials to "hear" movement agendas, the textbook strategies of pluralist democracy suggest that some engagement must occur, especially when the media do not live up to their responsibility to provide full news. Organizations like the Washington Office on Latin America and think-tank experts at the Woodrow Wilson Institute's Center for Mexico, based in Washington, DC, offer expert, lengthy, and thorough discourse to public officials in addition to the media.

We view the 2012 Democratic-primary-election struggle in Texas's Sixteenth Congressional District, analyzed in chapter 5, as illustrative of the paradox brought forth in militarization versus neoliberal economic agendas. Entrée with critiques of militarization and the drug war opened the door to a strengthened neoliberal border economic agenda — an agenda that until now has sustained glaring inequalities trumped by the positioning of the transnational border business community as a "right-priced" competitive workforce for foreign investment.

In first-stage anti-femicide activism, activists invested tremendous time and energy into meetings with government officials. Politicians often relish the opportunity to make noise and to exploit self-serving agendas. Nevertheless, some representatives do engage with crises for the "right" reasons, such as responding to constituents or upholding principles like justice.

In 2003, former U.S. congresswoman Hilda Solís was one such representative, who led a congressional fact-finding delegation to the border, with the reluctant yet eventual acquiescence of then-congressman Silvestre Reyes in his home base at the border. The delegation visited with officials in Ciudad Juárez, ate dinner with local officials and activists at the University of Texas at El Paso, and passed a resolution in Congress condemning the femicide.

After that symbolic gesture, congressional attention was over and perhaps their responsibility for the problem met in their eyes, but the drug war continued, as did money laundering and gun smuggling from the United States into Mexico, all of which wreaks havoc on violence in Mexico. Given scenarios like these, activists rightly worry about having their energy wasted as a public relations exercise. Now, a new challenge to U.S. drug policies of questionable effectiveness provides what is perhaps a stronger counternarrative with more mainstream support than the one sidelined as a "women's issue." Anti-militarization forces broaden that agenda, whether from the left in Mexico or from the right in the United States, where Libertarian voices criticize cost-ineffectiveness in futile drug-war policies and advocate reduced government subsidies to security business contractors (the Border Security Industrial Complex).

CHANGING DRUG-WAR NARRATIVES?

Across the hemisphere, people challenge the official transcripts of the war on drugs, thereby transgressing some politicians' once-hidden fear of questioning sacrosanct policies that would allow critics to criticize them as "soft on crime" or, even worse, as "drug pushers." We saw from the Sixth Summit of the Americas in Cartagena, Colombia, in 2012 that high-level politicians were willing to push to alter the inertia of failed drug wars with new agendas (also see Global Commission on Drug Policy 2011; LACDD 2009). Juan Manuel Santos, Laura Chinchilla, and Otto Pérez Molina, the presidents of Colombia, Costa Rica, and Guatemala, respectively, voiced public concerns about the failures of the United States–style militarized drug war and the multiplication of drug-trafficking organizations, which often have far more money than governments to corrupt law enforcement. Women's groups from multiple countries issued a statement after the summit about the reforming drug policy as a priority to reduce violence against women (Articulación Regional Feminista por los Derechos Humanos y la Justicia de Género et al. 2012). Many countries in the Americas had already decriminalized marijuana possession, for health and harm-reduction reasons, including Argentina, Brazil, Colombia, Ecuador, Mexico, and Uruguay (Council on Hemispheric Affairs 2012); in fact, Uruguay legalized drugs in 2013. For the first time, leaders "openly debated—although behind closed doors—whether the best way to stop the rolling disaster was an end to the U.S.-sponsored and dictated war on drugs, and at least partial legalization, or regulation, of the drug trade" (Guillermoprieto

2012: 39). The summit occurred during a U.S. election year, so President Obama preempted the critique and reiterated his refusal to consider legalization or decriminalization, but presumably he and his staff listened during and after the summit. The U.S. media barely addressed the content of the summit, given their priority focus on the scandal of U.S. Secret Service officers who solicited sex workers in Cartagena and then refused to pay them (sex also offers eye-catching headlines for the media). In the November 2012 U.S. elections, the states of Colorado and Washington legalized the recreational use of marijuana, and the Obama administration did not foil their move in the federal system of government.

SOURCES OF SOCIAL TENSION, BUT POTENTIAL STRENGTH

As in so many aspects of social analysis, gender, age, class, and nationality became sources of tension. Activists sometimes resolved the tension with simple yet effective challenges consistent with their ideologies.

GENDER   Men who became involved in anti-militarization work seemed to come to an understanding of the connections between the ugly, performance-style murder associated with homicide and femicide and the militarized conflicts among organized criminals, citizens, and federal and municipal police or military troops. They worked in coalitions, collaboratives, and alliances in which strategies shifted with changing political opportunity contexts. They took cues from the elaborate networks and organizational strategies that women pioneered in the 1990s and thereafter around violence against women. Occasionally, gendered tensions emerged: what we have called hypermasculinity performances, but something short of what Padilla (2011) calls *machismo-autoritarianismo* (chapter 2). When feminists, women leaders, and women activists called them out on those behaviors, the men activists' commitment to causes superseded gendered performances in this political era.

We offer an example of this from the Primer Foro contra la Militarización y la Violencia (First Forum against Militarization and Violence), October 29–31, 2010, organized by the Frente Plural Ciudadano. In that context, seemingly small gestures at a post-protest meeting illustrated not-so-quiet struggles consistent with the alliances that had formed. One of the organizers, a teacher and veteran activist, offered

José Darío Alvarez, a student shot and nearly killed at the Primer Foro contra la Militarización y la Violencia, being honored with a sign reading "Darío estamos contigo" (Darío, we are with you) during a march that ended at the Francisco Villa roundabout. Photo by Renato Díaz.

and brought a number of *edecanes* (hostesses) in tight miniskirts to assist in serving water and guiding people to rooms and places during the event. (We have seen this kind of ritualized gender-subordination performance at various government meetings over the years as well, including Mexico's televised 2012 presidential debates.) A young feminist from the Red Mesa de Mujeres publicly, on video, called him out at the forum for employing the practice of bringing women to serve. After her intervention, at the beginning of a panel, to express indignation, the audience clapped. And importantly, the *edecanes* were removed so that the activists could continue with mutual respect during panel presentations. Ultimately, though, gender tensions were minimal among the like-minded men and women who understood the connections between the various forms of official, criminal, and everyday violence. Other socially constructed and meaningful differences emerged as more important.

AGE   Younger, often university-based activists in Frente Plural Ciudadano (FPC), dismayed over ethical and corruption problems in the 2012 presidential campaign, some of whom became affiliated with Mexico City's Yo Soy 132, created their own, local chapter of Yo Soy 132 in Ciudad Juárez. The Juarense chapter used a sometimes confrontational style in their work, occasionally referring to that as "direct action" and grassroots alliance-building. The state and local divisions of the Movimiento de Regeneración Nacional (MORENA) contain a mix of young and veteran activists who help broker relationships among diverse people, though the youth are vocal and prominent. Some overlap exists between MORENA and FPC, and ideological sympathy exists between them in their critique of traditional party politics. Still, candidates running under the Movimiento Progresista ticket, including Leticia Ruiz and Víctor Quintana, got support from both the FPC and MORENA. That MORENA supported these candidates was expected, but that some in FPC even promoted and helped in campaign activities was intriguing as they had been skeptical of the usefulness of voting.

Youth have been remarkable and important in the ways in which they mobilize in Mexico. Young feminist successors to the middle-aged and older feminists add strength and creativity to the movements. In the United States, a vacuum seems to exist around youth mobilization, which is tied into electoral campaigns or to still-unfocused movements like Occupy. Some youth energy in the United States is consumed by volunteerism and social services, what is known in Mexico as *asistencialismo*, plus educator-facilitated service learning and its offshoots, the muted and focused counterpart in Mexico being *servicio social*.

RISKS AND INEVITABLE DIVISIONS: CLASS AND OTHER HIERARCHIES

The kinds of alliances we have described in this book are often loose and subject to vulnerabilities that can lead to tension and division. They spread word through social media, easily surveilled by dedicated and efficient authoritarians in government (however inefficient their law enforcement institutions may be).

Subterfuge is not the only means by which vulnerability is exploited. Open meetings attract diverse activists from not-so-like-minded networks and organizations who are there primarily to listen and perhaps report to others. Protests attract picture-taking military and federal police agents, aiming to intimidate and to record the activities of those under surveillance. Several establishment-oriented *asociaciones civiles* participate in the various collaborative organizations we have analyzed, partly to listen but also to learn, and at times, to support the complex transnational conferences that convene in Ciudad Juárez, such as the

May 2012 Permanent Peoples' Tribunal (see chapter 5), which brought hundreds of participants from all over Mexico and the world and was loosely linked to World Social Forums and their articulation of "alternative economies." Examples come in small and large forms. ˙

Activists learn to manage such constants. As a micro example, when a leader from a well-endowed organization offered to supply to the tribunal a well-known brand of soda, emblematic of global corporate hegemony, activists who are conscious of large-scale consumption choices—who work toward alternative economies and understand the role of the particular brand in fostering paramilitarism and unfair labor conditions—said no. After some puzzlement, the organization donated cash and left the choice for liquid refreshments to organizers, who purchased *jamaica* flowers from a cooperative in Chiapas and served an infusion. Seemingly small, these everyday practices accumulate with ripple effects for person-to-person awareness that can change what and how people think about global commodities, their impacts, and connecting principles with decisions (Méndez observations).

Some youth and activists write off what they label *perfumados* or *burgueses*, i.e., the privileged, whether those privileged are establishment elites or academics with middle-class salaries. Yet strategic allies among intellectuals and artists as well as in the critical establishment have potential contacts and resources for more dramatic and transformative events. Thanks to an establishment representative, a perennial opposition presidential candidate was invited and welcomed to speak in the north, specifically in Ciudad Juárez, where the Partido de la Revolución Democrática rarely generates majority votes. In another example, for the 2009 Global Public Policy Forum on the War on Drugs at the University of Texas at El Paso and the downtowns of both border cities, Plan Estratégico de Juárez offered crucial financial support for bringing Colombian former mayor of Medellín Dr. Sergio Fajardo to critique militarized drug wars and to recommend the alternative, economic and social investment in cities, to an audience of at least 1,500 (but at Cibeles, the elegant conference center).

In the dynamic political landscape created by activists and what some call *la Resistencia Juarense*, lone rangers also emerge: individuals without networks or bases of support who, perhaps for reasons related to their own strong egos, seek to initiate efforts, spread stories, or destroy reputations for few other reasons than the negative power that seems to come from destruction. Border regions have their fair share of such individuals on both the U.S. and Mexico sides, and many of them remain isolated because others don't trust them. Ultimately, the most effective activists in the efforts we analyze participate less to make themselves visible and more to enable other leaders and activists to emerge for voice, challenge, and counternarrative scripts. In this, we observe hybridity in civil society, on both sides of the border.

ORGANIZING ACROSS BORDERS: SOLIDARITY FOREVER OR NEVER?

Most of the organized action around femicide, militarization, and escalating homicide rates occurred first in Ciudad Juárez. Because the Paso del Norte metropolitan region contains cities so close together, sitting side by side in a space through which the international territorial line runs, personal relationships of friends and relatives link people together across the border. Their face-to-face relationships of trust bear no resemblance to the superficiality of those who read and post on large list-servs. Once people know one another and acquire trust through mutual responsibility to follow through on common goals, the social media connections can then take hold.

Still, challenges remain with the militarized, heavily controlled border that has existed since 9/11. The traffic across the border continues to be enormous, whether automobile, truck, or pedestrian. Waits at the ports of entry both coming to the United States and going into Mexico have lengthened, but interaction still happens, whether face to face or, once trust is established, through social media: e-mail, Facebook, and cell phones. As analyzed shortly before 9/11 (Staudt and Coronado 2002), nongovernmental organization (NGO) environmental and human rights groups understand their common interests in the borderlands, albeit separated by sovereign governments and inequitable economies. Personal and ideological forces propel interaction among people in "their" common region. One can easily see this interaction among business groups whose members cement their common interests in profits, connections, and subsidies from both governments in transnational organizations and networks. Ultimately, though, national sovereignty, different political systems, and contrasting agendas produce simultaneous and contradictory patterns: solidarity on some faith-based and ideological grounds and alienation over the narratives painted of the border—narratives for which consequences might strengthen the militarization agenda in dealing with murders and mayhem.

A protester with a wrestler mask holds a "Globalilems resistencia" (Globalize resistance) sign during a march. Photo by Renato Díaz.

An "Encara la violencia" (Face the violence) poster at an El Paso Caravan for Peace rally. Photo by Renato Díaz.

ADVANCING THEORIES WITH BORDER REALITIES

Our analysis calls attention to the ongoing tension between social theories that focus on human agency versus those that focus on social structures that may overwhelm individual and collective agency. In this book, we emphasize the human agency found in civil-society activists, from local to transnational, and the leaders who courageously countered official narratives and formed new narratives, of resistance, that took hold among many in an ever-broadening base of support. Leaders who changed the political and perceptual game reacted to a horrible massacre of teens, continuing and worsening insecurity in a militarized city of official pretenses of control, and long-term police impunity and complicity with organized crime.

Thus, we acknowledge that official discourses shaped society, but did not doom civil society to inaction. Rather, hegemonic discourses generated backlash and fervor in courageous activism. We interpret through vignettes and cases how people sought to construct their own versions of reality and possibly freer and more democratic futures, albeit under extremely adverse circumstances, including assassinations and threats of death. In these circumstances, the political parties seemed bankrupt, and the two largest of these have been tainted with corruption and militarization.

BRINGING GENDER AND THE BORDER TO SCOTT

In this book, we have drawn on political anthropologist James Scott's analyses of resistance. While few if any analyses apply Scott to the border, we found in his work a rich array of concepts and practices observable at the border, as women initially made the hidden public and joined with other men and women who challenged militarization with principles like peace, justice, and a changed culture. Once the hidden became public, activists used creative performances, at some risk to their lives. They practiced linguistic creativity as well. We showed the cracks in official walls, whether from activists, criminals, or even WikiLeaks. Such cracks created a space into which discourses might enter and spread, perhaps causing some of those official walls to crumble. Yet our analysis parted ways with Scott.

Unlike Scott, we analyzed the *gendered* challenges and expressions that began with women's moral outrage and personal agony over lost loved ones. In what started as a predominantly women's movement of feminists, mothers, and women human rights activists, a holistic movement of women and men emerged with creative deployment of strategies and tactics and public, high-profile actions. Linguistic creativity drew on gendered insights that crossed class and hierarchical lines. Most activists in this holistic movement understand the connections between violence against women and militarization. The militarization took a hypermasculine form, as Padilla (2011) and others observed.

Moreover, a methodological nationalism pervades many studies, including the work of Scott and those who followed him. While they avoid "seeing like a state," they tend to view societies as entrapped within nation-states rather than existing in borderlands that cross state lines. In the Paso del Norte metropolitan region, we observed mutual learning from sensitive cross-border organizing, but also aggravating and deepening distrust from those with agendas that emphasize epithets and violence alone. Border hybridity and all its simultaneous contradictions can be seen in these practices, the special focus of chapters 3 through 6. Both the Permanent Peoples' Tribunal and the

Inter-American Court of Human Rights decision show the possibilities of transnational activism and support that provide leverage to local and regional activists. Together they challenge corrupted states and the state-sanctioned structural violence they impose upon people.

Beginning with Scott's array of concepts on official and hidden transcripts, the former public and the latter made public by courageous activists, we extended his work with gendered analysis. We highlighted the role of women leaders, women's discourses, and women's pioneering activism from the 1990s, which laid the groundwork for the collaboratives and networks of current anti-militarization activism. We noted gendered discourses and insults.

Unlike Scott, we also insist, however, on asking what happens and when, beyond the resistance, including *la Resistencia Juarense* or the cross-border solidarity narratives that have emerged. Do resistance activists, including feminists and human rights activists, have a place in transitional processes? Can they sustain their open and creative practices with winnable candidates (usually from the nonmainstream parties)? Once the obscene state-sanctioned violence diminishes, will civil-society activists retreat, as individualism takes hold and migrants use this escape valve?

Inequalities may persist, along with the structural violence they impose, but the consequences of inequalities may be more hidden and individualized. Our work displays the ethical challenges posed to activists who seek to engage with officials, especially in the overarching neoliberal transnational global economic agenda. We live in a world with nation-states that pretend to govern with consent of the governed, but who among the governed speak, and who in government listens, especially on issues relating to business, wage rates, commerce, and trade?

BRINGING SOCIAL MEDIA, ALTERNATIVE MEDIA, AND THE LANGUAGE OF MEDIA TO INTERNATIONAL RELATIONS THEORISTS

We have also found insights in the terms of international relations theorists (Risse, Ropp, and Sikkink 1999) who pose a boomerang connection among local, national, and international organizations and networks that make abuse visible in the media and put pressure on abusive governments. To advance their approach with border counternarratives, we identified several patterns. First, anti-femicide activists drew on their established links with international NGOs, but more on their own terms than on the terms of the external organizations. Occasionally these links offered life-saving and survival assistance in the militarized atmosphere of fear, stigma, and mistrust. Second, we found irregular and singular, often more localized, media coverage of activism. While governments' official narratives aim to portray a region on the road to security, safety, and recovery, the dominant media narrate a region of chaos and violence. Media coverage on civil-society activism gets the short shrift, as we have noted several times. And occasionally, as with Javier Sicilia, media visibility backfires and creates dissension. Sicilia took almost a year to come around to a fuller critique of militarization, as understood and acted upon by on-the-ground activists in Ciudad Juárez.

In looking for the boomerang effects that challenge abusive governments, the problem is binational: one must address policies from both Mexico and the United States, linked in border-militarization strategies in ideological and budgetary ways. In other words, the United States is a serious part of the problem, yet few international NGOs concentrate as much attention there as they do on Mexico. U.S. policies promote wars on drugs, immigrants, and terrorists with a militarized-security strategy and official rhetoric that conceptualizes and justifies official policies. Grupo de Articulación Justicia en Juárez has insistently pointed out this issue and integrated it with the policies of groups in Juárez who didn't see the connection with the Mérida Initiative and on-the-ground crises there. Sicilia, at the least, brought the issue to the front and center in his Mexico caravan as well as in his second caravan, to the United States, even though its activities never got the media attention they deserved (discussed in chapter 6).

When Thomas Risse, Stephen Ropp, and Kathryn Sikkink wrote their book in 1999, social media and electronic alternative news barely existed, and not in the momentous forms available now. In this book, we have updated and advanced their perspectives with insights about the multiple alternative media that cover civil-society activism better than the establishment or mainstream press. Yet the carryover between media forms seems limited, as does the translation of Spanish to English and vice versa. It remains to be seen whether the clever, creative, and well-orchestrated movement activists primarily bond and reinforce themselves (what in movement, perhaps clichéd, terms is sometimes referred to as "preaching to the choir") or whether their messaging reaches wider publics and the decision makers that represent them, either perpetuating or changing laws and public policies.

Certainly, the efforts to reach new publics via faith-based principles and electoral strategies moved the discourse of femicide, demilitarization, and justice to wider segments of the population in both countries, but not to as many people as the existing border narratives on violence and mayhem, reinforced by government bureaucracies, reach. As journalists say, "If it bleeds, it leads," and phenomenally successful movement feats may never spark the same media attention as ten murders a day, sexualized killings, beheadings, and other horrendous tragedies in the drug war. Threaded into that analysis, we considered the effects of the 2012 Caravan for Peace that made its way from Mexico, across the border, and from the West to the East Coast of the United States, with the inspiring *fuerza moral* (moral force) of poet-turned-pacifist Javier Sicilia, whose twenty-four-year-old son was one of many sons and daughters murdered in what he routinely calls the "absurd" drug war.

The media coverage of Sicilia's caravan across the United States was minimal in the English-language mainstream press across the country. Its visibility was primarily in Spanish and alternative outlets. The obvious and clear patterns in the list generated by Morales (2012) show that media coverage of Sicilia's creative and dedicated *caravaneras* and *caravaneros* can be traced primarily to alternative press, especially social media and Spanish-language media. Widespread coverage is important, but we can only wonder if and doubt whether mainstream U.S. decision makers read the alternative press, especially the Spanish-language press. Moreover, we wonder if alternative-press readers are willing to "translate" from alternative media, plus organize and engage so that mainstream media and decision makers become aware of the messaging. Alternative-media readers perhaps share similar sentiments with cynical movement activists, as we analyze. Of course, Sicilia's visit was *not* one of "bleeding and leading." Rather, it was courageous civil-society activism that performed creative and artistic resistance worth covering. Do media decision makers view this as boring and not newsworthy?

POST-CONFLICT FUTURES

Is a post-conflict future possible in Ciudad Juárez and the mainstreams of both countries, a future that is peaceful, just, and with better wages for workers? We focus on peace. We close with tentative optimism in response to this question.

ON DECLINING MURDER RATES IN CIUDAD JUÁREZ

As we close this book, it seems appropriate to think ahead in political ways: about Ciudad Juárez, about the borderlands, and about Mexico and the United States. After presidential elections, many speculate about the next four (in the United States) or six (in Mexico) years, but even chief executives cannot predict future policies, given the changing political opportunity structure, the vagaries of the neoliberal global economy, and opposition forces, whether they are members of opposing parties in the national congresses or civil-society organizations and networks—those that support the existing dominant hegemony and its official public narratives or those that counter the narratives, like those on whom we have focused in the greater Paso del Norte metropolitan region.

The murder rate declined in Ciudad Juárez, both for homicide and for femicide, during 2012 to well under 1,000, and according to Father Oscar Enríquez from Centro de Derechos Humanos Paso del Norte, in 2013 the number declined to less than 500 (personal communication). Crime rates have allegedly gone down, according to the Mesa de Seguridad's September 2012 report, although its numbers are suspicious and contestable, given that many crimes go unreported to still-untrusted law enforcement institutions. One can never be sure of the total numbers—whether from the government or the media—and no doubt, contestation will soon begin over these figures, too. Yet disappearances continue, and no one has ever provided credible figures on the numbers of disappeared people. Why have murder rates gone down?

POLITICAL AND POLICE CONTROL Perhaps the iron-fist rule of the police chief, Lt. Col. Julián Leyzaola, made its mark on Juárez. Politicians' speeches and press releases from official agencies make such claims. Governor César Duarte recently claimed an exact reversal of impunity figures. Rather than the long-term, historic failure to investigate and prosecute over 95 percent of criminal cases, now he claims that the law enforcement machinery at the state level purportedly investigates and prosecutes 95 percent of cases successfully. We find that hard to believe, even ludicrous, given the lack of evidence to support his claims and also the improbable chance that in such a short period of time (less than a year) police and law enforcement cultures have changed completely.

In a series of documentaries about the city, beginning with *8 Mur-*

ders a Day (2011), the young New Yorker Charlie Minn compiled on-camera interviews and news clips from both Juárez and El Paso to portray Juárez as a murderous city, out of control and waging a war on the poor. Minn's second documentary, *Murder Capital of the World*, expanded his portrayal of the violence in Juárez by including Leyzaola's and Municipal President Héctor "Teto" Murguía Lardizábal's (2010–2013) perspectives and assurances of control being established in the city. In Minn's third and last documentary, *The New Juárez*, released in 2012, he painted a more balanced picture, with critical and noncritical comments about the police and public officials. One of the more fascinating parts of the film is its "insider" look at the Police Training Academy, its graduation exercises, and its seeming increase in professionalism—one that might be easily contested given its public record. Minn also did "drive-alongs" with police officers who are fearful, distrusting, and seemingly brave. But just as in the previous two documentaries about Juárez, Minn spent very little film time (minutes only), as is common among journalists, in the third documentary on civil-society activism and counternarratives, the focus of our book.

Murguía's political journey is intriguing. In Mexico's constitution, the no-immediate-succession principle (to avoid dictatorships like the pre-1910 revolution times under Porfirio Díaz) also applies to government elections at the state and municipal levels, where the latter political executives serve three-year terms. Murguía, who served as municipal president (mayor) from 2004 to 2007, was reelected for the 2010–2013 term after sitting out a term. He is a career politician with the Partido Revolucionario Institucional (PRI). Many people say that in his first term he was aligned with the Juárez cartel, the drug-trafficking operation that once controlled the *plaza* of the central gateway region into the United States drug market with affiliated gangs on both sides of the border, an accusation he denies (see Campbell 2009 on the "drug war zone" on both sides of the border). In the 2013 municipal elections, he was replaced with yet another PRIísta.

An anecdote in local political circles was brought up separately to both of us regarding a U.S. local official invited to Murguía's first inauguration party. He was told to board a bus that would take him to the ranch outside the city for the large gathering. Little did he know that the cartel owned the ranch and was hosting the party, so upon his return to the United States, he informed the local office of the Drug Enforcement Administration, whose officials told him that they had already heard the news.

THE SINALOA CARTEL'S RAPPROCHEMENT WITH MUNICIPAL OFFICIALS
When the Sinaloa cartel began expanding to other parts of Mexico in 2007, competition occurred with the existing Juárez cartel. President Calderón, under Joint Operation Chihuahua, sent in the military and federal police, adding to the warring among factions, not only among officials and residents, but also within criminal groups and among criminals and residents. During the last *sexenio* (six-year presidential term), the Sinaloa cartel allegedly gained the upper hand in many areas, with complicity of municipal, state, and some federal officials. Periodically, reports would show fewer Sinaloa affiliates jailed than those from other cartels (see selections in Payan, Staudt, and Kruszewski 2013).

Locally, informal conversations are full of speculations regarding the triumph of the Sinaloa cartel over La Línea, i.e., the Juárez cartel. Many speculate that the Sinaloa cartel now controls the Juárez *plaza*, since murder rates declined in 2012, and that current officials have made new arrangements with them to keep a relative peace and to avoid making murder rates so visible. Yet, over the *sexenio*, the warring cartels, mixed with problematic actions by law enforcement agencies, unleashed other organized criminals to include gangs that specialize in theft, extortion, kidnapping, human trafficking, and carjacking. Thus crime continues in Juárez, not necessarily reported to law enforcement agencies lacking public trust, so at apparently lower rates than those scandalous statistics documented in previous years.

Once the Sinaloa cartel established control over the central gateway, the brutality of organized crime and cartel competition appears to have moved east of Chihuahua to northeastern Mexico, especially the border states of Tamaulipas and Coahuila, where the Gulf Cartel and its breakaway group of well-trained former military and police agents, Los Zetas, compete over *plazas* in the multiple north-side highways to ship goods, legal and illegal, through the nearby ports of entry that channel traffic to Interstate 35 (Correa-Cabrera and Nava 2013). There, ruthless, performance-oriented displays of bodies are aimed at advertising hypermasculine bravado and generating fear among residents. With this proposition, one could argue that political and law enforcement agents have little impact on where organized criminals do their dirty work: the criminals decide.

CIVIL SOCIETY BEGINS TO MAKE A DIFFERENCE IN GOVERNANCE   Civil-society networks and organizations come in all types, from those that support the official transcripts and narratives in the business and nonprofit sector to organized networks that counter the narratives through formerly hidden discourse that becomes public. Earlier in this chapter, we summarized the accomplishments, hopes, and still-remaining tasks again. Occasionally, those now-public counternarratives enter and/ or match with the discourses of the transnational and Juarense elite, still coherent but somewhat fractured, with leaders willing to listen to and adopt or co-opt some of the counternarratives since it is in many people's self-interest to live in societies with peace and justice.

It has been encouraging to witness efforts at government oversight that have been initiated by Plan Estratégico and Red Mesa de Mujeres, among other Juarense organizations. Accountability and demands that local government actions be transparent are key in strengthening democracy. The Consejo Ciudadano para el Desarrollo Social is another example of a civil-society organization that has recently been working in pushing for policies that strengthen citizens' participation in local government. What often drives the business community is the search for stable means to earn their profits and generate more foreign investment. In the local free-trade publication *Juarez–El Paso NOW* (www .juarezelpasonow.com), the albeit-hyped, public relations–oriented content advertises Juárez as a competitive environment of hard-working, right-priced employees with smiling faces alongside a growing manufacturing hub with right-priced transportation costs in North America. Despite the violence, even in the worst years for outlier and high murder rates (2010, 2011), investment increased and maquiladora employees increased by more than 20,000 annually to an already-high base of manufacturing workers at nearly 200,000 in the greater Paso del Norte metropolitan region, according to the data-gathering Asociación de Maquiladoras, A.C.—employee numbers for which are touted in most issues. The business elite has long sought a better image for the city, but there are those who understand that the image alone is not the answer. An image of better law enforcement must match the reality of professional law enforcement institutions. Corruption and complicity with criminals serve few interests except those of the people who collect the "rent" from these sordid alliances.

We wonder when or how long it will take that business elite, including the transnational elites that tout the "competitive labor costs" of the region, to recognize the obscene levels of inequality on both sides of the border and within border regions and then begin to act on that recognition with living wages and better opportunities for people. Business is part of civil society, and its more enlightened elements need to step up to the plate to build a more humane economy in the so-called new Juárez. We believe that fairer, more equitable wages, coupled with an informed, strong, and vigorous civil-society activism to make democracy real and deep, will be key to bearing fruit for the community and citizens of Ciudad Juárez.

AND WHEREFORE JUSTICE?

Many activists believe that the region cannot move forward without justice. What would justice mean in this context?

Over more than two decades, obscenely high numbers of Juarenses have died at the hands of both organized crime and the state. For what and to whom are those murderers accountable? Mexican law enforcement institutions have not distinguished themselves in investigation and prosecution. We abhor the idea of a bloodbath, like those in other countries in civil-war contexts. Yet we also recognize the shortcomings of the truth and reconciliation commission processes that have occurred in other countries. After South Africa finally became "free," its Truth and Reconciliation Commission traveled the country to hear the whole "truth" from the formerly state-sanctioned torturers (some of whom still served in police forces) in exchange for their grants of amnesty. Under cross-examination, with lawyers and judges, partial truths got told. While some citizens moved ahead and forgave the terrorists, others live still in anguish and pain.

We have no answers to these questions. However, the answers must emerge from open, democratic processes in which the voices of victims, survivors, and activists are heard.

Responsibility for the violence and injustice is a shared, North American phenomenon. United States policies; money from drug profits, guns, and other armaments; weapons; and training form part of the larger picture of the search for justice. National borderlines and state sovereignty complicate those processes, short of reparations. Financial reparations can hardly compensate for lives, and they are unlikely to gain traction in the early twenty-first-century U.S. political climate.

IMPLICATIONS FOR BORDER STUDIES

Our analysis speaks not only to readers at the border and the mainstreams, but also to border theorists. In the introduction to their encyclopedic, thirty-one-chapter *Companion to Border Studies*, Thomas Wilson and Hastings Donnan argue, "Border Studies can no longer just

A protester holds a "Justicia sin Fronteras" (Justice without Borders) sign at a Caravan for Peace rally in El Paso. Photo by Renato Díaz.

ask us to 'see like the state.' Now we must see beyond and within the state . . . to recognize the multiple forms of disciplining work done within and between states, or within and between other political, economic, social, and cultural entities" (2012: 21). Our analyses reinforce their remarks in this interdisciplinary work that sees from the bottom up in a two–sovereign country, three-state, and multi–local government region along the U.S.–Mexico border. Analysts should engage with civil-society activism and elections, from the vantage point of borders, then scale up the local to the regional and national.

Attention to public transcripts, whether activists' hidden-to-public transcripts or those in and behind the scenes in Cartagena at the Sixth Summit of the Americas in 2012, focuses on those within (or at the borders of) the nation, as representatives and counternarrative spokespersons, yet this book posits the overarching neoliberal global economic order that also deserves attention. Neoliberalism idealizes both "limited states" and "market mechanisms" for a healthy, functioning economic order. Ironically, the "war on drugs" strategy uses big, expensive government institutions to criminalize the supply and demand for highly profitable, untaxed goods that cross national borders—the antithesis of a regulated market–oriented strategy. Despite neoliberal-economics media outlets like the *Economist* and the *Wall Street Journal* and Libertarian think tanks like the Cato Institute, business lobbies have not yet begun to challenge the bureaucratized drug war in ways that would free government spending for more productive investment.

Until public transcripts from more forces than those analyzed in this book, to include economic forces, challenge U.S. drug policies to a regulated drug regime (like alcohol), violence and mayhem will continue in Mexico. We wonder if those forces will act, particularly as the election of President Peña Nieto has been welcomed with open economic arms in the U.S. business community, in U.S. media coverage, and by U.S. officials who seem willing to perpetuate previous binational policies (see O'Neill 2012 on economic potentials in her optimistic and cleverly titled book *Two Nations Indivisible*). But will progressive voices in the business community get organized around visible calls for greater equality on both sides of the border and for living wages within those communities? If they support and expand Juárez resistance activism, what was once hidden could be public and potentially official, to the extent that business pushes various levels of government to act in the long-term public interests of the majority in democratic society.

For these reasons, it is all the more important to continue challenge and counternarrative development in even broader-based civil-society activism in both countries, from the borders and the mainstream, with support from transnational activists, for an accountable and less destructive drug policy, for fairer, more equitable wages between the two countries, and for serious attention to human rights policies and their enforcement. In so doing, a post-conflict future with *justice* could be possible in Ciudad Juárez, at the border, and in both countries.

Luminarias spelling the word "Justicia" at the Monumento a Juárez in downtown Juárez. Photo by Julián Cardona.

IN CHAPTER 7, we end the book with the certainty that a post-conflict period with justice will create the conditions for the rebuilding of Juárez. That optimism stems from the inspiring, sustained, and committed work that activists in Juárez and their allies in other latitudes, especially across the border, do. But certainties and optimistic visions can be fragile. As fragile as life itself.

When we were in the final stages of this writing project, in November of 2013, Méndez received the news from Red Mesa de Mujeres in Juárez that the remains of Mónica Janeth Alanís Esparza (see chapter 4) had been found. After DNA testing, Olga Esparza and Ricardo Alanís verified that indeed the remains released by the Fiscalía General del Estado de Chihuahua belonged to their long-disappeared daughter. The hope that sustained Mónica Janeth's valiant parents as they searched for almost four years is now gone. It is buried under the soil where she now rests.

During searches in the vast Juárez desert, Mónica Janeth's parents often wore T-shirts with a legend on their backs that read "Hasta dónde estés, te encontraremos" (Wherever you are, we will find you). And they did. As we join her family and community in grieving the loss of Mónica Janeth, it is our hope that her parents' example of strength and perseverance will inspire and strengthen committed scholarship and activism as we search for truth and justice, wherever it leads us. *Ni una más!*

RESPONSIBLE FIREARMS RETAILER PARTNERSHIP:
A 10-POINT VOLUNTARY CODE

The 10 points of the Responsible Firearms Retailer Partnership are:

1.   **Videotaping the Point of Sale for All Firearms Transactions.** Participating retailers will videotape the point-of-sale of all firearms transactions and maintain videos for 6 months to deter illegal purchases and monitor employees.

2.   **Computerized Prime Gun Trace Log and Alert System.** Mayors Against Illegal Guns will develop a computerized system that participating retailers will implement over time to log crime gun traces relating to the retailer. Once the program is in place, if a customer who has a prior trace at that retailer attempts to purchase a firearm, the sale will be electronically flagged. The retailer would have discretion to proceed with the sale or stop the sale.

3.   **Purchaser Declaration.** For sales flagged by the trace alert system, participating retailers will ask purchasers to fill out a declaration indicating that they meet the legal requirement to purchase the firearm.

4.   **Deterring Fake IDs.** Participating retailers will only accept valid federal- or state-issued picture IDs as primary identification. Retailers will utilize additional ID checking mechanisms.

5.   **Consistent Visible Signage.** Participating retailers will post signage created by the Responsible Firearms Retailer Partnership to alert customers of their legal responsibilities at the point-of-sale.

6.   **Employee Background Checks.** Participating retailers will conduct criminal background checks for all employees selling or handling firearms.

7.   **Employee Responsibility Training.** Participating retailers will participate in an employee responsibility training program focused on deterring illegal purchasers. The Responsible Firearms Retailer Partnership will create an online training system based on Wal-Mart's training program.

8.   **Inventory Checking.** Participating retailers will conduct daily and quarterly audits. Guidelines will be based on Wal-Mart's existing audit procedures.

9.   **No Sales Without Background Check Results.** Participating retailers would prohibit sales based on "default proceeds," which are permitted by law when background check has not returned a result within 3 days.

10.   **Securing Firearms.** Participating retailers will maintain firearms kept in customer accessible areas in locked cases or locked racks.

RESOLUTION

WHEREAS, an estimated 80,000 men, women, and children have been killed in Mexico, almost 11,000 of them in our sister city of Ciudad Juárez, during the past five years; and

WHEREAS, the people of El Paso and the surrounding region recognize our personal, practical, and economic connections with Ciudad Juárez and the country of Mexico; and

WHEREAS, it is strongly in our interest to reduce death, violence, and human rights violations on both sides of the border; and

WHEREAS, trafficked arms and munitions from the United States to Mexico is deeply involved in killings; and

WHEREAS, the trade in illegalized drugs is a driver of criminal profits, corruption, impunity, and violence, with negative effects on the border region; and

WHEREAS, money is the lifeblood of the criminal system in both countries and causes corruption in our home region; and

WHEREAS, human rights and human security in Mexican law enforcement and the military are key to building and sustaining a peaceful and secure society in Mexico; and

WHEREAS, accountability, civil and human rights, and security from death, harm, and exploitation are fundamental U.S. values that provide an enduring basis for a safe and prosperous border region, in particular when applied to migration enforcement and immigration policy:

NOW, THEREFORE, BE IT RESOLVED BY THE MAYOR AND THE CITY COUNCIL OF THE CITY OF EL PASO:

That the City Council endorses the following five principles for members of the U.S. public and U.S. public policy:

(1) Adhere to existing U.S. laws regulating gun and munitions sales, particularly with respect to trafficking to Mexico, and endorse the attached Voluntary Code of Conduct for the Responsible Firearms Retailer Partnership;

(2) Spur discussion about current drug policy;

(3) Improve tools against money laundering;

(4) Prioritize human rights and human security in U.S. cooperation with and assistance to Mexican law enforcement and the military; and

(5) Prioritize accountability, civil and human rights, and security from death, harm, and exploitation in U.S. migration enforcement and immigration policy.

[SIGNATURES ON FOLLOWING PAGE]

CITY CLERK DEPT.
2012 AUG 22 AM 8:09

ADOPTED THIS _____ 21st _____ DAY OF _____ August _____, 2012.

THE CITY OF EL PASO

John F. Cook
Mayor

ATTEST:

Richarda Duffy Momsen
City Clerk

APPROVED AS TO FORM:

Sylvia Borunda Firth
City Attorney

CITY CLERK DEPT.
2012 AUG 22 AM 8:09

12-1019-032/124782_3 (Revised 8/21/12)
Reso/Justice & Dignity for Mexico

2

RESOLUTION

WHEREAS, this summer, victims of the drug war in Mexico will travel across the United States to promote peace with justice and dignity on both sides of the border; and

WHEREAS, the 60,000 deaths, the 10,000 disappearances, and the 160,000 internally displaced people in Mexico during the past six years is a tragedy caused directly by failed security policies; and

WHEREAS, the "Caravan for Peace with Justice and Dignity" is embarking on a month-long voyage traveling over 6,000-miles through 20 cities and communities including Los Angeles, Santa Fe, El Paso, Houston, Montgomery, New Orleans, Chicago and New York — before arriving in Washington, D.C., on September 10; and

WHEREAS, a broad bi-national coalition of more than 100 U.S. civil society organizations joined the Caravan for Peace; and

WHEREAS, the Caravan for Peace's purpose is to honor the victims of the drug war by traveling across the United States to raise awareness of U.S. civil society, demanding new policies that will foster peace, justice and human dignity on both sides of the border; and

WHEREAS, the City of Los Angeles and surrounding areas is home to the second largest Mexican-origin population in the world (after Mexico City), an overwhelming majority of whom have ties to Mexico; and are deeply affected by the onslaught of violence.

NOW, THEREFORE BE IT RESOLVED that by the adoption of this resolution, the City of Los Angeles recognizes the concerns shared by Angelenos and the people of Mexico and supports and welcomes to Los Angeles and the United States the "Caravan for Peace with Justice and Dignity" for the promotion of their movement to end bloodshed and attain peace.

PRESENTED BY: _____
JOSE HUIZAR
Councilmember, 14th District

SECONDED BY:

CHAPTER 1

1. The number of murder victims in Mexico since 2006 is a wildly contested figure. During the Calderón administration, 2006–2012, many media and governmental sources agreed on approximately 60,000 (see *Economist* 2012d, for example), though Mexican government sources frequently differentiate between those associated with drug crimes and other murders. By the end of 2012, cited figures shot up to as high as 120,000 from sources independent of the often-tainted, politically charged official agencies: both the alternative Internet media source Truthout and the Mexican think tank Mexico Evalua reported that 120,000 murders had occurred. Yet, as we document in this book, independent scholars and Mexican government agencies acknowledge that over 95 percent of crimes go uninvestigated or unprosecuted, thus making it difficult to determine the "perpetrators" or "cause" of murders except for making political or snap judgments at the scenes of crimes. The widely disseminated *frontera* listserv, or Frontera List, which circulates among many journalists from Molly Molloy, librarian and coauthor of *El Sicario* with Charles Bowden, counts the dead in Ciudad Juárez frequently (see chapter 4). Molloy tallies the national murder count at approximately 120,000, rather than 60,000. Major media have begun to use the larger figure; see, for example, Hernández 2012.

2. These figures, widely cited and accepted, come from the Frontera List, noted hundreds of times. (Staudt has been on the listserv since it began in 2008.) At the Annunciation House week-long events in late April 2012, the names of the 10,000 murdered were projected onto the building's outside walls at night (see chapter 5). Murder figures for 2012 number 751 and for 2013, 485. It is important to remember, always, that these are not just numbers, but *people*, lost forever.

3. Feminists' use of the word "femicide" (Radford and Russell 1992) began in the early 1990s. Feminist anthropologist and legislator Marcela Lagarde y de los Ríos coined the Spanish word *feminicidio* because the translation of "femicide" into *femicidio* "is homologous to homicide and solely means the homicide of women." Lagarde translated the English term as *feminicidio* in Spanish "in order to differentiate from *femicidio* and to name the ensemble of violations of women's human rights, which contains the crimes against and the disappearances of women" (2010: xv). Feminist sociologist Julia Monárrez Fragoso elaborated on Lagarde's concept and defined it as "the assassination of a woman committed by a man, where one finds all of the elements of the relationship of inequality between the sexes: the gender superiority of man over the gender subordination of woman, misogyny, control, and sexism. Not only is a woman's biological body assassinated, but what the cultural construction of her body has signified is also assassinated, with the passivity and tolerance of a masculine state" (2010b: 69n1). Monárrez maintains a database at El Colegio de la Frontera Norte (COLEF) in Ciudad Juárez, with three or four categorical counts under "Feminicides" ("Intimate feminicide," "Systemic sexual feminicide," and "Feminicide based on sexually stigmatized occupations") and under "Assassinations" ("Orga-

nized crime and narco-trafficking," "Community violence," "Negligence," and "Not Specified") (Monárrez Fragoso 1998–, cited in López, Caballero, and Rodríguez 2010: 164–165). Rosa-Linda Fregoso and Cynthia Bejarano coin *feminicidio* in English as "feminicide," using it in the title of their book (2010). In this book, we do not differentiate among all the types of women's murders, nor do most activists. Staudt has also noticed confusion in numerous public audiences about the multiple terms and their meanings. Moreover, as many scholars and officials have noted, over 95 percent of murders are not investigated by Mexican law enforcement, so it may be difficult to differentiate among murders. Finally, as Lagarde indicates, "the political construct defining feminicide as a crime," while approved by the Chamber of Deputies, was "subsequently rejected by the Senate" (2010: xxiii). It is therefore not a legal category separate from homicide in Mexico. We will use "femicide" (English) and *feminicidio* (Spanish) interchangeably throughout the book.

4. Fregoso says Bowden recounts "his fantasies about Adriana, a 'whore' and former maquila worker" (2003: 15, drawing from Bowden 1998).

5. We have benefited from conversations with Willivaldo Delgadillo on these meanings.

6. While the more appropriate term might be "cactus roots," as one of our reviewers suggested, we know that grass once grew and still grows in this semiarid region, albeit then and now, under adverse conditions. Therefore, we think it appropriate to use "grassroots" for these activists who operate in grounded ways.

7. *Candidatos*, or "candidates," if more like *gatos*, or "cats," might cleanse cities of the rats in government.

8. Drawing on the United Nations' *Human Development Report*, 2010, Jina Moore notes widespread mobile-phone network coverage in Mexico, but also a "digital divide" in Internet access, with 90 percent of Mexicans having mobile and fixed, landline coverage, but only 22 percent having Internet access (2011: 31).

9. The boundaries of only three U.S. congressional districts are drawn to represent border people (in California, Arizona, and West Texas). All the others that are located on the nearly 2,000-mile-long border have been drawn northward to represent both border and nonborder residents, including New Mexico's southern district, with its tiny towns at the border, such as Columbus. Some analysts view the border region as incorporating approximately 25 miles of territory north (or south) of the border, while others use the 1983 La Paz Agreement between the two countries that denotes 100 kilometers (62 miles) on either side as the border region (Staudt and Coronado 2002: chap. 1).

CHAPTER 3

1. The description of Luz María Dávila's interpellation as a "game-changer" act was coined by Juarense writer Willivaldo Delgadillo. Here, however, we extend Delgadillo's concept of the "game-changer" act as it allows us to analyze other acts of resistance, such as those displayed by Marisela Escobedo and the activists involved in the Campo Algodonero case.

2. The secretary of Interior is far more important in Mexico than in the United States. He (always male) is second in command, and former secretaries are often candidates for president. The secretary controls state security.

3. This idiom means "we've had it up to here," but the phrase translates literally to "we're up to the mother," which suggests an upward violation of private female body space, so some feminists view it as sexist. See Martínez 2011.

CHAPTER 4

1. Prior to the homicide of Dr. Manuel Arroyo Galván, Professor Geraldo González Guerrero, also from the Universidad Autónoma de Ciudad Juárez, had been killed on December 3, 2008, and a few mobilizations had occurred. Added to the list of faculty from UACJ who were killed in the context of the "drug war" is Professor José Alonso Martínez Luján (November 13, 2009).

2. As we wrote this book, we visited Harto de la Violencia's Facebook profile again and realized that his page had changed substantially since the early days of 2010. Most of his contacts had been removed, leaving around 200 from the approximately 2,000 people he "friended" around the time of the march. We did not observe Harto's involvement in any other marches or rallies after the Marcha del Coraje, Dolor, y Desagravio. In fact, after the march, a debriefing session was scheduled, but he did not attend. Harto might not have been ready to participate in the nascent Frente Plural Ciudadano, the coalition that emerged after the Villas de Salvárcar massacre.

3. Yo Soy 132 is the Juarense response to the national Yo Soy 132 movement that emerged during Mexico's presidential campaign of 2012 when a group of students at Universidad Iberoamericana, a private Jesuit college in Mexico City, openly questioned Enrique Peña Nieto's candidacy and the political groups backing it. Trying to downplay the strong opposition to Peña Nieto's presence on the campus, the president of the PRI said there were only "a few" people from the Andrés Manuel López Obrador campaign who were trying to cause trouble. So the next day, students who had attended Peña Nieto's campus visit videotaped themselves saying their name and number, ending at 131.

CHAPTER 5

1. The other genuinely border districts are California's Fifty-first and Arizona's Second. Most congressional districts that touch the border stretch northward, thus muting strong border voices.

2. See Dunn 2009 for analyses of border blockades, especially Operation Hold the Line, for its architect Silvestre Reyes.

3. See Bañuelas 2011 for another moving presentation. Monsignor Arturo Bañuelas, a human rights activist who serves as a priest at St. Pius X, was a speaker at the cross-border solidarity event in Anapra, Chihuahua/Sunland Park, NM.

CHAPTER 6

1. See the video and other pictures on these websites: https://www.youtube.com /watch?v=Aamd4IIANS8I and http://www.bing.com/videos/search?q=notimex+ vieo+of+Javier+Sicilia+and+Sheriff+Arpaio&qpvt+notimex+video+of+Javier+Sicilia+ and+Sheriff_Arpaio&FORM=VDRE.

Aguilar, Julián. 2010. "Despite Violence, Manufacturing in Juárez Climbing." *Texas Tribune*, December 12. http://www.texastribune.org/texas-mexico-border-news /texas-mexico-border/despite-viol. Same article printed in *New York Times*, December 11, as "Profit Outweighs Risk in Juárez Factories." http://www.nytimes .com/w010/12/12/us/12tttecma.html?_r=3&ref=global-home&page/wa.

———. 2012. "Obama Endorses U.S. Rep. Silvestre Reyes." *Texas Tribune*, April 16.

Aiken Araluce, Olga. 2009. "Transnational Advocacy Networks, International Norms, and Political Change in Mexico: The Murdered Women of Ciudad Juárez." In Staudt, Payan, and Kruszewski 2009: 150–167.

———. 2011. *Activismo social transnacional: Un análisis en torno a los feminicidios en Ciudad Juárez*. Guadalajara, Mexico: ITESO (Universidad Jesuita de Guadalajara).

Alvarez, Sonia E. 1998. "Latin American Feminisms 'Go Global': Trends of the 1990s and Challenges for the New Millennium." In *Cultures of Politics, Politics of Cultures: Re-Visioning Latin American Social Movements*, edited by Sonia E. Alvarez, Evelina Dagnino, and Arturo Escobar, 293–324. Boulder, CO: Westview Press.

Ameglio, Pietro. 2010. "Resistencia civil y no violencia." *La Idea*. November. http:// laidea.agriculturaecologica.eu/2010/03/resistencia-civil-y-noviolencia/.

Amnesty International. 2003. *Intolerable Killings: Report of Ten Years of Abductions and Murders of Women in Ciudad Juárez and Chihuahua*. New York: Amnesty International.

Anzaldúa, Gloria. 1987. *Borderlands/La Frontera: The New Mestiza*. San Francisco: Spinsters/Aunt Lute.

Arriaza, Laura, and Naomi Roht-Arriaza. 2008. "Social Reconstruction as a Local Process." *International Journal of Transitional Justice* 2: 152–172.

Arsenault, Chris. 2011. "Invest in 'The World's Most Violent City': As a Drug War Rages in Juárez, Mexico, Investment in the City's Low-Wage Factories Has Actually Increased." *Juárez–El Paso NOW*, March 31, 15, 19.

Articulación Regional Feminista por los Derechos Humanos y la Justicia de Género: ELA—Equipo Latinoamericano de Justicia y Género (Argentina), Coordinadora de la Mujer (Bolivia), Corporación Humanas (Colombia, Chile, and Ecuador), EQUIS—Justicia para las Mujeres (México) and DEMUS—Estudio para la Defensa de los Derechos de la Mujer (Perú), Centro de Derechos Humanos de las Mujeres de Chihuahua—Mexico. 2012. *Revisión de la actual política anti-drogas: Una prioridad para reducir la violencia contra las mujeres en las Américas*. Comunicado hacia la Sexta Cumbre de las Américas. April. Unpublished. On file in Staudt's office.

Atencio, Graciela. 2010. "Feminicidio-femicidio: Un paradigma para el análisis de la violencia de género." *Feminicidio.Net*. December. http://www.feminicidio.net /index.php?option=com_content&view=article&id=67&Itemid=8.

Ayres, Jeffrey, and Laura Macdonald, eds. 2009. *Contentious Politics in North*

America: National Protest and Transnational Collaboration under Continental Integration. New York: Palgrave.

Bañuelas, Arturo. 2011. "Afterward: Peace and Justice without Borders." In Lusk, Staudt, and Moya 2012: 271–273.

Barry, Tom. 2009. "Former Border Patrol Chief Silvestre Reyes Now a Major Player in New Military, Intelligence and Homeland Security Complex." Part I Americas Program. www.cipamericas.org/archives/1858.

Barsalou, Judy, and Victoria Baxter. 2007. "The Urge to Remember: The Role of Memorials in Social Construction and Transnational Justice." Stabilization and Reconstruction Series, no. 5. Washington, DC: U.S. Institute of Peace.

BBC. 2010. "Wikileaks Cables: US–Mexico drugs [sic] war fears revealed." December 3. http://www.bbc.co.uk/news/world-latin-america-11906758.

———. 2011. "Mexico Updates Four Years of Drug War Deaths." http://www.bbc .co.uk/news/world-latin-america-12177875.

Behar, Ruth. 1996. *The Vulnerable Observer: Anthropology That Breaks Your Heart.* Boston: Beacon.

Beittel, June. 2011. "Mexico's Drug Trafficking Organizations: Source and Scope of the Rising Violence." Washington, DC: Congressional Research Service, RA-1576.

Bhabha, Homi. 1994. *The Location of Culture.* London: Routledge.

Bleifuss, Joel. 2012. "Javier Sicilia: Leading His Caravan to Washington." *In These Times.* May 17. http://inthesetimes.com/article/13175/javier_sicilia_leading_his _caravan_to_washington.

Bolaño, Roberto. 2008. *2666* (English translation). New York: Farrar, Straus, and Giroux.

Bonilla, Rafael, and Patricio Ravelo Blancas. 2006. *La batalla de las cruces* (documentary). DVD. Encuentro Hispanoamericano de Video Documental Independiente.

Bowden, Charles. 1996. "While You Were Sleeping." *Harper's,* December. http://www .harpers.org/archives/1996/12/while-you-were-sleeping.

———. 1998. *Juárez: The Laboratory of Our Future.* New York: Aperture.

———. 2010. *Murder City: Ciudad Juárez and the Global Economy's New Killing Fields.* New York: Nation Books.

Bowden, Charles, and Molly Molloy. 2010. "Who Is Behind the 25,000 Deaths in Mexico?" *Nation,* July 23. http://www.thenation.com/article/37916/who-behind -25000-deaths-mexico.

Bowden, Charles, and Gianfranco Rosi. 2011. *El Sicario, Room 164.* DVD. Directed by Gianfranco Rosi. Les Films d'Ici, 21 One Productions, Robo Films.

Bustillos, Sandra, and Rodolfo Rincones, eds. 2011. *Mujeres en Chihuahua hoy.* Ciudad Juárez: Universidad Autónoma de Ciudad Juárez.

Camp, Roderic Ai. 2010. *The Metamorphosis of Leadership in a Democratic Mexico.* New York: Oxford University Press.

———. 2012. *The Oxford Handbook of Mexican Politics.* New York: Oxford University Press.

Campbell, Howard. 2009. *Drug War Zone: Frontline Dispatches from the Streets of El Paso and Juárez.* Austin: University of Texas Press.

Caputi, Jane, and Diana E. H. Russell. 1992. "Femicide: Sexist Terrorism against Women." In Radford and Russell 1992: 13–21.

Carmona López, Adriana, Alma Gómez Caballero, and Lucha Castro Rodríguez. 2010. "Feminicide in Latin America and the Movement for Human Rights." In Fregoso and Bejarano 2010: 157–176.

Castañeda Salgado, Martha P. 2005. "De feminismos, verdades y videos," comentarios al documental: *La batalla de las cruces*, in "Género, feminismo(s) y violencia desde la frontera norte," special issue, *Nóesis, Revista de Ciencias Sociales y Humanidades* 15 (28): 171–176.

Catholic Bishops, U.S. and Mexico. 2003. "Strangers No Longer: Together on the Journey of Hope." Washington, DC: U.S. Conference of Catholic Bishops.

CEDIMAC (Centro para el Desarrollo Integral de la Mujer, A.C.). 2011. Press release. November 7. Ciudad Juárez: Centro para el Desarrollo Integral de la Mujer, A.C.

Chávez Cano, Esther. 2002. "Murdered Women of Juárez." In *Puro Border: Dispatches, Snapshots, and Graffiti from La Frontera*, edited by Luis Humberto Crosthaite, John William Byrd, and Bobby Byrd, 153–158. El Paso, TX: Cinco Puntos.

———. 2010. *Construyendo caminos y esperanzas*. Ciudad Juárez: Casa Amiga Centro de Crisis.

Citizens for Responsibility and Ethics in Washington. 2011. "Family Affair." http://www.citizensforethics.org/pages/family-affair-report-reveals-nepotism-abuse-in-congress (updated in 2012).

CNN Mexico. 2012. "Militares abaten a presunto asesino de la hija de Marisela Escobedo." November 21. http://mexico.cnn.com/nacional/2012/11/21/militares-abaten-a-presunto-asesino-de-la-hija-de-marisela-escobedo.

Cornelius, Wayne, and David Shirk, eds. 2007. *Reforming the Administration of Justice in Mexico*. Notre Dame, IN: Notre Dame University Press.

Correa-Cabrera, Guadalupe, and José Nava. 2013. "Drug Wars, Social Networks, and the Right to Information: Informal Media as Freedom of Press in Northern Mexico." In Payan, Staudt, and Kruszewski 2013: 95–118.

Council on Hemispheric Affairs. 2012. Press release: "The Future of Mexico's Drug Strategy." May 9. Washington, DC: Council on Hemispheric Affairs.

CPJ (Committee to Protect Journalists). 2010. *Silence or Death in Mexico's Press: Crime, Violence, and Corruption Are Destroying the Country's Journalism*. New York: Committee to Protect Journalists.

Croteau, David. 2005. "Which Side Are You On? The Tension between Movement Scholarship and Activism." In Croteau, Hoynes, and Ryan 2005: 20–40.

Croteau, David, William Hoynes, and Charlotte Ryan, eds. 2005. *Rhyming Hope and History: Activists, Academics, and Social Movement Scholarship*. Minneapolis: University of Minnesota Press.

Crowder, David. 2011. "Reyes: Take out Cartel Heads. Rep Thinks Drone Missile Strikes Possible." *El Paso Inc.* http://www.elpasoinc.com/news/top_story/article_7b4b33a0-605f-11e0-94ec-0019bb30f31a.html.

———. 2012a. "El Paso's Democratic Divide: What Reyes-O'Rourke Race Is Really About." *El Paso Inc.* 17, no. 38 (May 20–26): 1A, 5A–6A.

———. 2012b. "Read the Q & As, Then Vote." *El Paso Inc.*, May 27. http://www.elpasoinc.com/news/top_story/article_a77b1d2a-a83c-11e1-8bcc-0019bb30f31.

———. 2012c. "Republicans Helped O'Rourke Win: Despite Pot and Domestic Partner Stands." *El Paso Inc.*, June 3–9, 3A.

Dávila, Luz María. 2010. "Madre coraje confronta a Calderón." YouTube video. Posted by "Demos Desarrollo de Medios SA." February 12, 2010. http://www.youtube .com/watch?v=n2JrmJ8_vbQ.

Dávila, Patricia. 2012. "Quien mató a mi madre no es el Wicked, es Andy Barraza." *Proceso.* October 23. http://www.proceso.com.mx/?p=323288.

De la O Martínez, María. 2008. "Las mujeres y los movimientos de defensa laboral entre México y Estados Unidos: Un análisis de su influencia en comunidades no fronterizas." *Estudios Políticos* (Instituto de Estudios Políticos, Universidad de Antioquia) 32 (January): 255–275.

Delgadillo, Willivaldo. 2011a. "Juárez y el largo camino a la justicia." Juárez Dialoga. June 7. http://juarezdialoga.org/lsarticulistas/juarez-y-el-largo-camino-a-la -justicia/.

Delgadillo, Willivaldo. 2011b. "El gran desafío de Sicilia." *La Jornada.* June 23. http:// ww.jornada.unam.mx/2011/06/23/politica/008alpol.

Díaz, Luis. 2012. "El Movimiento: A Brief Analysis of the Role of Core Activists in the Development of a Unified Social Movement in Ciudad Juárez." Master's thesis, University of Texas at El Paso.

Domínguez-Ruvalcaba, Héctor, and Ignacio Corona, eds. 2010. *Gender Violence at the U.S.–Mexico Border: Media Representation and Public Response.* Tucson: University of Arizona Press.

Doyle, Kerry. 2011a. *Pacto por la Cultura: The Power and Possibility of Cultural Activism in Ciudad Juárez.* Master's thesis, University of Texas at El Paso.

——. 2011b. "Hacia una solidaridad verdadera." Juárez Dialoga. June 21. http:// juarezdialoga.org/ls-articulistas/hacia-una-solidaridad-verdadera.

Dresser, Denise. 2012. "Mexico and Beyond." Speech on Mexico's presidential elections, University of San Diego Trans-Border Institute. April 25. Video. http:// www.sandiego.edu/peacestudies/tbi/.

Dunn, Timothy J. 1996. *The Militarization of the U.S.–Mexico Border, 1978–1992.* Austin: University of Texas, Center for Mexican American Studies.

——. 2009. *Blockading the Border and Human Rights: The El Paso Operation That Remade Immigration Enforcement.* Austin: University of Texas Press.

Economist. 2011. "Special Report: The Future of Jobs: Winners and Losers." September 10, 7–8.

——. 2012a. "The Texas Primary: Over the Top." June 2, 36.

——. 2012b. "Mexico's Presidential Election." June 23, 40.

——. 2012c. "The World in 2013." "Mexico's Moment." November 21. http://www .economist.com/news/21566314-enrique-pe%C3%B1a-nieto-mexicos-newly -elected-president-sets-out-his-priorities-mexicos-moment.

——. 2012d. "Special Report: Mexico," supplement. November 24.

El Paso, City of. 2009, 2012. "City Council Meetings." January 6, 2009; February 9, 2009; August 21, 2012. www.elpasotexas.gov/video/php.

Enríquez, Oscar. 2011. "Paz y derechos humanos." Presentation at ¡BASTA! Border Activism Summit for Teaching and Action. October. University of Texas at El Paso.

Erturk, Yakin. N.d. "Sobre violencia contra las mujeres, sus causas y consecuencias." Geneva: Office of the U.N. High Commissioner for Human Rights. http://www .ohchr.org/SP/Issues/SRWomenPages/SRWomenIndex.aspx.

Eschle, Catherine, and Bice Maiguashca, eds. 2005. *Critical Theories, World Politics and 'The Anti-Globalisation Movement.'* London: Routledge.

———. 2010. *Making Feminist Sense of the Global Justice Movement.* Lanham, MD: Rowman & Littlefield.

Fairris, David. 2006. "What Do Unions Do in Mexico?" Universidad Iberoamericano, Mexico City. http://www.via.mx/campus/publicaciones/IIDSES/pdf/investigacion/iidses14.pdf.

Fernández-Kelly, María Patricia. 1983. *For We Are Sold, I and My People: Women and Industry in Mexico's Frontier.* Albany, NY: State University of New York Press.

Finnegan, William. 2010. "In the Name of the Law." *New Yorker*, October 18.

Fiscalía General de Justicia de la Zona Norte del Estado de Chihuahua. 2010. "Comisión indicadores." Presentation at the meeting of the Mesa de Seguridad of Ciudad Juárez, Chihuahua. September.

Fregoso, Rosa Linda. 2003. *MeXicana Encounters: The Making of Social Identities on the Borderlands.* Berkeley: University of California Press.

Fregoso, Rosa-Linda, and Cynthia Bejarano, eds. 2010. *Terrorizing Women: Feminicide in the Americas.* Durham, NC: Duke University Press.

Fuentes, César, and Sergio Peña. 2010. "Globalization, Transborder Networks, and U.S.–Mexico Border Cities." In Staudt, Fuentes, and Monárrez Fragoso 2010: 1–19.

García-Canclini, Néstor. 1995. *Hybrid Cultures: Strategies for Entering and Leaving Modernity.* Notre Dame, IN: University of Notre Dame Press.

Gaspar de Alba, Alicia. 2005. *Desert Blood.* Houston: Arte Público.

Gaspar de Alba, Alicia, with Georgina Guzmán, eds. 2010. *Making a Killing: Femicide, Free Trade, and La Frontera.* Austin: University of Texas Press.

Gibler, John. 2009. *Mexico Unconquered: Chronicles of Power and Revolt.* San Francisco: City Lights Publishers.

Global Commission on Drug Policy. 2011. *War on Drugs: Report of the Global Commission on Drug Policy.* June. http://www.globalcommissionondrugs.org/wp-content/themes/gcdp_v1/pdf/Global_Commission_Report_English.pdf.

Godínez Leal, Lourdes. 2007. "Gobierno de Chihuahua quiere convertir el feminicidio en mito." *Cimacnoticias.* July 12. http://www.cimacnoticias.com.mx/node/49273.

———. 2012. "La ciudad devorando a sus hijas, documental sobre feminicidio en Chihuahua." *Cimacnoticias.* October 29. http://www.cimacnoticias.com.mx/node/58323.

Gómez Licon, Adriana. 2010. "More than 4,000 Doctors Go on Strike in Juárez: Seven Hospitals Affected." *El Paso Times*, December 13, A1.

González Rodríguez, Sergio. 2002. *Huesos en el desierto.* Barcelona: Anagrama.

Gray, Lorraine. 1986. *The Global Assembly Line.* DVD. Distributor: New Day Films.

Grayson, George. 2009. *Mexico: Narco-violence and a Failed State.* New Brunswick, NJ: Transaction.

Greenhouse, Carol J. 2005. "Hegemony and Hidden Transcripts: The Discursive Arts of Neoliberal Legitimation." *American Anthropologist* 107, no. 3: 356–368.

Grupo de Articulación Justicia en Juárez. 2012. *Audiencia General Introductoria Documento Chihuahua* (Tribunal Permanente de los Pueblos, Capitulo México). Ciudad Juárez, Chihuahua: Grupo de Articulación Justicia en Juárez.

Guillermoprieto, Alma. 2012. "Drugs: The Rebellion in Cartagena." *New York Re-*

view of Books. June 7. http://www.nybooks.com/articles/archives/2012/jun/07 /drugs-rebellion-cartagena/?insrc=toc.

Hammersley, Martyn, and Paul Atkinson. 1994. *Ethnography: Principles in Practice.* 2nd ed. London: Routledge.

Hernández, Daniel. 2012. "Calderón's War on Drug Cartels: A Legacy of Blood and Tragedy." *Los Angeles Times,* December 1. http://www.latimes.com/news/world /worldnow/la-fg-wn-mexico-calderon-cartels-20121130.

Heyman, Josiah. 2012. "Culture Theory and the US–Mexico Border." In *A Companion to Border Studies,* edited by Thomas M. Wilson and Hastings Donnan. London: Blackwell.

Hinojosa, María. 2011. "Lost in Detention." *Frontline.* October 18. http://www .pbs.org/wgbh/pages/frontline/lost-in-detention/?utm_source=twitter&utm _medium=&utm_campaign=.

Hobden, Stephen. 2011. "The Developing World in International Politics." In *Politics of the Developing World,* 3rd ed., edited by Peter Burnell, Vicky Randall, and Lise Rakner. New York and London: Oxford University Press.

Hondagneu-Sotelo, Pierrette. 2008. *God's Heart Has No Borders: Religious Activism for Immigrant Rights.* Berkeley: University of California Press.

Human Rights Watch. 2011. "Neither Rights nor Security: Killings, Torture, and Disappearances in Mexico's War on Drugs." www.hrw.org/reports/2011/11/09/neither _rights_nor_security_0.

IDMC (International Displacement Monitoring Centre). 2011. "Figures for Drug-cartel Violence Displacement." Last updated November 25. http://www.internal -displacement.org/8025708F004CE90B/%28httpEnvelopes%29/0C812CE4640B 7B31C125794400380367?OpenDocument.

INEGI (Instituto Nacional de Estadística y Geografía). 2010. "Información Nacional por Entidad Federativa y Municipios." www3.inegi.org.mx/sistemas/mexicocifras.

Informador. 2010. "La impunidad en México alcanza al 98.5 de los delitos." November 7. http://www.informador.com.mx/mexico/2010/247146/6/la-impunidad -en-mexico-alcanza-al-985-de-los-delitos.htm.

Jacobs, Susie, Ruth Jacobson, and Jen Marchbank. 2000. Introduction to *States of Conflict: Gender, Violence and Resistance.* London: Zed.

Jaquette, Jane, ed. 2009. *Feminist Agendas and Democracy in Latin America.* Durham, NC: Duke University Press.

Karpf, David. 2012. *The MoveOn Effect: The Unexpected Transformation of American Political Advocacy.* New York: Oxford University Press.

Keck, Margaret, and Kathryn Sikkink. 1998. *Activists beyond Borders: Advocacy Networks in International Politics.* Ithaca, NY: Cornell University Press.

Korten, David. 1990. *Getting to the 21st Century: Voluntary Action and the Global Agenda.* West Hartford, CT: Kumarian.

La Botz, Dan, ed. 2012. *Mexican Labor News and Analyses.* http://www.ueinter national.org/MLNA/index.php#about.

LACDD (Latin American Commission on Drugs and Democracy). 2009. "LACDD: Toward a Paradigm Shift." Council on Foreign Relations. February 11. http:// www.cfr.org/drug-trafficking-and-control/latin-american-commission-drugs -democracy-toward-paradigm-shift/p18803.

Lagarde y de los Ríos, Marcela. 2010. "Preface: Feminist Keys for Understanding Feminicide: Theoretical, Political, and Legal Construction." In Fregoso and Bejarano 2010: xi–xxv.

Lambert, Dan. 2012. "Beto vs. Silver: District 16's Top Dem Candidates on the Issues." *What's Up*, May 16–23, 17.

Lloyd, Marion. 2005. "Uncovering Mexico's Dirty War." *Chronicle of Higher Education*, September 23, A26–A28.

Lozano Ortega, Marisela. 2011. "Human Rights Committee Investigating Alleged Mistreatment of Journalists in Juárez." *El Paso Times*, June 1. http://www.elpaso times.com/newupdated/ci_18182885.

Lugo, Alejandro. 2008. *Fragmented Lives, Assembled Parts: Culture, Capitalism, and Conquest at the U.S.–Mexico Border*. Austin: University of Texas Press.

Lusk, Mark, Kathleen Staudt, and Eva Moya, eds. 2012. *Social Justice in the U.S.–Mexico Border Region*. Netherlands and New York: Springer.

Macedo, Stephen. 2005. *Democracy at Risk: How Political Choices Undermine Citizen Participation, and What We Can Do About It*. Washington, DC: Brookings Institution.

Marchand, Marianne, and Anne Runyan, eds. 2011. *Gender and Global Restructuring*. London and New York: Routledge.

Martin, Kathleen J., ed. 2009. *Indigenous Symbols and Practices in the Catholic Church*. London: Ashgate.

Martínez, Oscar. 1978. *Border Boom Town: Ciudad Juárez since 1848*. Austin: University of Texas Press.

———. 1994. *Border People*. Tucson: University of Arizona Press.

Martínez, Rubén. 2011. "Mexico's Drug War: Crossing Borders." *Los Angeles Times*. May 8. http://articles.latimes.com/2011/may/08/opinion/la-oe-0508-martinez -sicilia-20110508.

Martínez-Cabrera, Alejandro. 2011. "Mexican President Felipe Calderón Opens Juárez Competitiva." *El Paso Times*, October 14, A1.

———. 2012. "Juárez Competitiva Organizer Denies Mishandling Money." *El Paso Times*, August 14. http://www.elpasotimes.com/news/ci_21306457/juarez -competitiva-organizer-denies-mishandling-money.

Mattiace, Shannon. 2012. "Social and Indigenous Movements in Mexico's Transition to Democracy." In Camp 2012.

Mesa de Seguridad en Ciudad Juárez. 2012. Crime Statistics, September. http://www .mesadeseguridad.org.

México, Gobierno Federal. *Estratégia Todos Somos Juárez, reconstruyamos la ciudad*. 2010. http://www.sep.gob.mx/work/models/sep1/Resource/889/2/images /todossomosjuarezb(1).pdf.

Mexico CNN. 2012. "Militares abaten a presunto asesino de la hija de Marisela Escobedo." November 21. http://mexico.cnn.com/nacional/2012/11/21/militares -abaten-a-presunto-asesino-de-la-hija-de-marisela-escobedo.

Meyer, Maureen. 2010. "Abused and Afraid in Ciudad Juárez: An Analysis of Human Rights Violations by the Military in Mexico." September. Washington, DC: Washington Office on Latin America. http://www.wola.org/publications /abused_and_afraid_in_ciudad_juarez.

Middlebrook, Kevin J. 1995. *The Paradox of Revolution: Labor, the State, and Authoritarianism in Mexico*. Baltimore: Johns Hopkins University Press.

Mikker Palafox, Martha. 2010. "World-Class Automotive Harnesses and the Precariousness of Employment in Juárez." In Staudt, Fuentes, and Monárrez Fragoso 2010: 119–143.

Minn, Charlie. 2011. *Murder Capital of the World*. DVD. www.charlieminn.com.

———. 2012. *The New Juarez*. DVD. J&M Productions.

Minn, Charlie, and Yota Matsuo. 2011. *8 Murders a Day*. DVD. Directed by Charlie Minn. J&M Productions.

Miroff, Nick. 2010. "Mexico Hopes $270 Million in Social Spending Will Help End Juarez Drug Violence." *Washington Post*, August 12.

Molloy, Molly. 2010. "Juárez Murder: Impunity Regardless of Gender." *Grassroots Press*, May 12.

Molloy, Molly, and Charles Bowden. 2011. *El Sicario: The Autobiography of a Mexican Assassin*. New York: Nation Books.

Monárrez, Julia E. 2002. "Feminicidio sexual serial en Ciudad Juárez." *Debate Feminista* 25 (April).

Monárrez, Julia E., and Socorro Tabuenca Córdoba, eds. 2007. *Bordeando la violencia contra las mujeres en la frontera norte de México*. Tijuana: El Colegio de la Frontera Norte.

Monárrez Fragoso, Julia E. 1998–. Base de Datos Feminicidio (archivo particular de investigación). Departamento de Estudios Culturales, Dirección General Regional Noroeste, El Colegio de la Frontera Norte.

———. 2009. *Trama de una injusticia: Feminicidio sexual sistemático en Ciudad Juárez*. Tijuana: El Colegio de la Frontera Norte.

———. 2010a. "Death in a Transnational Metropolitan Region." In Staudt, Fuentes, and Monárrez Fragoso 2010: 23–42.

———. 2010b. "The Victims of Ciudad Juárez Feminicide: Sexually Fetishized Commodities." In Fregoso and Bejarano 2010: 59–69.

Monárrez Fragoso, Julia E., and César Fuentes. 2004. "Feminicidio y marginalidad urbana en Ciudad Juárez en la decada de los noventa." In *Violencia contra las mujeres en contextos urbanos y rurales*, comp. Marta Torres Falcón, 43–70. Mexico City: Colegio de México.

Moore, Jina. 2011. "The Revolution Will Be Blogged." *Christian Science Monitor*, July 4, 26–31.

Moore, Robert. 2012. "GOP Vote Boosted O'Rourke." *El Paso Times*, June 11, A1, A5.

Morales, Ana. 2012. List of U.S. Media Coverage of Javier Sicilia's Cross-Country Caravan for Peace. Unpublished, on file in Staudt's office.

Morfín, Guadalupe. 2004. *Informe de gestión: Noviembre 2003–abril 2004*. Ciudad Juárez: Comisión para Prevenir y Eradicar la Violenia contra las Mujeres en Ciudad Juárez, Secretaría de Gobernación.

Mueller, Carol, Michelle Hansen, and Karen Qualtire. 2009. "Femicide on the Border and New Forms of Protest: The International Caravan for Justice." In Staudt, Payan, and Kruszewski 2009: 125–149.

Murphy Aguilar, Moira, and Susan Tiano. 2011. "¿A dónde se fueron las mujeres? Tendencias en el empleo y el género en la industria de la maquiladora en Ciudad Juárez." In Payan et al. 2011: 115–134.

Murphy Aguilar, Moira, Jan-Phillip Last, and A. César Carmona. 2011. "Discriminación, participación en el mercado laboral y crimenes contra mujeres en el Estado de Chihuahua." In Payan et al. 2011: 183–202.

NBC. 2011. "Inside Mexico's Drug War." 6 pts. *Dateline.* April 17. http://insidedateline .nbcnews.com/_news/2011/04/17/6485039-apr-17-inside-mexicos-drug-war?lite.

Nobel Women's Initiative. 2012. "From Survivors to Defenders: Women Confronting Violence in Mexico, Honduras, and Guatemala." June 5. http://www.nobel womensinitiative.org/2012/06/from-survivors-to-defenders-women-confronting -violence-in-mexico-honduras-and-guatemala.

O'Brien, Robert, and Mark Williams. 2007. *Global Political Economy: Evolution and Dynamics.* Basingstoke, United Kingdom: Palgrave Macmillan.

O'Dowd, Liam, and Bohdana Dimitrovova. 2011. "Promoting Civil Society across the Borders of the EU Neighbourhood: Debates, Constraints and Opportunities." *Geopolitics* 16, no. 1: 176–192.

O'Neill, Shannon. 2012. *Two Nations Indivisible.* New York: Oxford University Press.

O'Rourke, Beto, and Susie Byrd. 2011. *Dealing Death and Drugs: The Big Business of Dope in the U.S. and Mexico.* El Paso, TX: Cinco Puntos.

Ortiz-Ortega, Adriana, and Mercedes Barquet. 2010. "Gendering Transition to Democracy in Mexico." *Latin American Research Review* 45, no. 4: 108–137.

Osorno, Diego E. 2011. *País de muertos.* Crónicas contra la impunidad. Mexico City: Debate Editorial.

Pacto por la Cultura en Juárez. 2004. "Pacto por la Cultura en Juárez." Universidad Autónoma de Ciudad Juárez. http://docentes2.uacj.mx/museodigital/PACTO /IMAC/pacto_cultura.htm.

Padilla Delgado, Héctor Antonio. 2011. "Violencia militarización y género en el nuevo desorden Juarense." In Payan et al. 2011: 305–322.

Paterson, Kent. 2006. "The Ciudad Juárez Border Social Forum: Cross-Border Move-ment Growing." October 26. Fnsnews listserv. Copy on file in Staudt's office.

———. 2010a. "The Ruins of Juárez." February 23. Fnsnews listserv. Copy on file in Staudt's office.

———. 2010b. "Tough Times Persist for Ciudad Juárez's Workers." March 31. Fnsnews listserv. Copy on file in Staudt's office.

———. 2010c. "Manufacturing a Border Crisis." Americas Program. June 8. http:// www.cipamericas.org/archives/2508.

———. 2010d. "Ciudad Juárez: Enough Is Enough." December 13. Fnsnews listserv. Copy on file in Staudt's office.

Payan, Tony. 2006. *The Three U.S.–Mexico Border Wars: Drugs, Immigration, and Homeland Security.* New York: Praeger.

Payan, Tony, Kathleen Staudt, and Z. Anthony Kruszewski, eds. 2013. *A War That Can't Be Won? Binational Perspectives on the Drug War.* Tucson: University of Arizona Press.

Payan Alvarado, Luis A., Sonia Bass Zavala, Martha E. Pérez, and García y Jesús A. Rodríguez Alonso, eds. 2011. *De soldaderas a activistas: La mujer chihuahuense en los albores del siglo XXII.* Mexico City: Ediciones Eón.

Peña, Devon G. 1997. *The Terror of the Machine: Technology, Work, Gender, and Ecology on the U.S.–Mexico Border.* Austin: University of Texas, Center for Mexican American Studies.

Peña, Milagros. 2008. *Latina Activists across Borders: Women's Grassroots Organizing in Mexico and Texas*. Durham, NC: Duke University Press.

Pequeño Rodríguez, Consuelo. 2005. "Consideraciones para el estudio del trabajo de las mujeres en la industria maquiladora." In "Género, feminismo(s) y violencia desde la frontera norte," special issue, *Nóesis, Revista de Ciencias Sociales y Humanidades* 15 (28): 33–55.

Pérez García, Martha Estela. 2005. "Las organizaciones no gubernamentales en Ciudad Juárez y su lucha contra la violencia de género." In "Género, feminismo(s) y violencia desde la frontera norte," special issue, *Nóesis, Revista de Ciencias Sociales y Humanidades* 15 (28): 147–167.

———. 2011. "Procesos de empoderamiento: Mujeres de las organizaciones de la sociedad civil en Chihuahua." In Payan et al. 2011: 223–239.

Petrich Moreno, Blanche. 2012. "WikiLeaks and the War on Drugs." *Nation*, July 25. http://www.thenation.com/article/169076/wikileaks-and-war-drugs.

Poppa, Terrence. 2010. *Drug Lord: The Life and Death of a Mexican Kingpin*. 3rd ed. El Paso, TX: Cinco Puntos.

Portillo, Lourdes. 1986. *Las Madres: The Mothers of the Plaza de Mayo*. Video. Distributor: Xochitl Productions, Women Make Movies.

———. 2001. *Señorita extraviada*. Video. Distributor: Xochitl Productions, Women Make Movies.

Quintana Silveyre, Víctor. 2011. Presentation at ¡BASTA! Border Activism Summit for Teaching and Action. October. University of Texas at El Paso.

———. 2012. "Chihuahua: De la integración a la devastación." Presentation at Foro hacía el Tribunal Permanente de los Pueblos, Ciudad Juárez. March.

Radford, Jill, and Diana E. H. Russell, eds. 1992. *Femicide: The Politics of Woman Killing*. New York: Twayne.

Red Mesa de Mujeres de Ciudad Juárez and CLADEM (Comité Latinoamericano y del Caribe para la defensa de los Derechos Humanos de las Mujeres). 2012. *Campo Algodonero: Análisis y propuestas para el seguimiento de la sentencia de la Corte Interamericana de Derechos Humanos en contra del estado mexicano*. Mexico City: CLADEM.

Riaño-Alcalá, Pilar. 2006. *Dwellers of Memory: Youth and Violence in Medellín, Colombia*. New Brunswick, NJ: Transaction.

Rippberger, Susan, and Kathleen Staudt. 2003. *Pledging Allegiance: Learning Nationalism in El Paso–Juárez*. New York: Falmer/Routledge.

Risse, Thomas, Stephen Ropp, and Kathryn Sikkink. 1999. *The Power of Human Rights: International Norms and Domestic Change*. Cambridge: Cambridge University Press.

Roberts, Chris. 2012a. "O'Rourke Cuts into Reyes' Cash Lead in Dist. 16 Race." *El Paso Times*, April 16, A1, A7.

———. 2012b. "Money Questions:" "Beto O'Rourke Pays His Company with Supporters' Donations" and "Rep. Silvestre Reyes Records Tie Expenses to Daughter's Home in D.C." *El Paso Times*, May 13, A1, A8.

———. 2012c. "16th Congressional District Race: Rep. Reyes Outspent O'Rourke." *El Paso Times*, August 17, A1. http://www.elpasotimes.com/ci_21089702/reyes-outspent-orourke.

Rodríguez, Mauricio. 2011. "Víctimas abuchean a autoridades por inauguración de monumento en Juárez." *Revista proceso.* November 7. http://www.proceso.com .mx/?p=287406.

Rodríguez, Sandra. 2012. *La fábrica del crimen.* Mexico City: Planeta.

Rodríguez, Victoria. 2003. *Women in Contemporary Mexican Politics.* Austin: University of Texas Press.

———, ed. 1998. *Women's Participation in Mexican Political Life.* Boulder, CO: Westview Press.

Rodríguez, Victoria, and Peter Ward. 1994. *Political Change in Baja California: Democracy in the Making?* La Jolla, CA: University of California at San Diego, Center for Mexican–U.S. Studies.

Ruiz, Vicki L., and Susan Tiano, eds. 1987. *Women on the U.S.–Mexico Border: Responses to Change.* Boston: Allen & Unwin.

Sabet, Daniel. 2013. "The Role of Citizens and Civil Society in Mexico's Security Crisis." In Payan, Staudt, and Kruszewski 2013: 239–257.

Salazar Gutíerrez, Salvador, and Martha Mónica Curiel García. 2012. *Ciudad abatida: Antropología de las fatalidades.* Ciudad Juárez: Universidad Autónoma de Ciudad Juárez.

Salmón, Alejandro. 2012. "Gabinete de Peña, entre 'dinosáurico y tecnócrata': Víctor Quintana." *Diario de Juárez*, December 1.

Schatz, Edward, ed. 2009. *Political Ethnography: What Immersion Contributes to the Study of Power.* Chicago: University of Chicago Press.

Scott, James C. 1976. *The Moral Economy of the Peasant.* New Haven, CT: Yale University Press.

———. 1977. *Weapons of the Weak: Everyday Forms of Peasant Resistance.* New Haven, CT: Yale University Press.

———. 1990. *Domination and the Arts of Resistance.* New Haven, CT: Yale University Press.

———. 1998. *Seeing Like a State: How Certain Schemes to Improve the Human Condition Have Failed.* Yale Agrarian Studies Series. New Haven, CT: Yale University Press.

———. 2005. Afterword to "In Focus: *Moral Economies, State Spaces, and Categorical Violence.*" In Sivaramakrishnan 2005: 395–402.

Seelke, Clare, and Kristin M. Finklea. 2013. *U.S.–Mexican Security Cooperation: The Mérida Initiative and Beyond.* Congressional Research Service. June 12. https://www.fas.org/sgp/crs/row/R41349.pdf.

Sicilia, Javier. 2011. "El consuelo y la justicia de Javier Sicilia." *Contracorriente.* May 25. http://www.educacioncontracorriente.org/index.php?option=com_content& view=article&id=24271%3Ael-consuelo-y-la-justicia-javier-sicilia&catid=14%3A maestros&Itemid=29.

———. 2012. *Estamos hasta la madre.* Mexico City: Ediciones Temas de Hoy.

Simmons, William Paul, and Rebecca Coplan. 2010. "Innovative Transnational Remedies for the Women of Ciudad Juárez." In Fregoso and Bejarano 2010: 197–224.

Sivaramakrishnan, Kalyanakrishnan, ed. 2005. "In Focus: *Moral Economies, State Spaces, and Categorical Violence: Anthropological Engagements with the Work of James Scott.*" *American Anthropologist* 107, no. 3 (September): 321–330.

Smith, Jackie. 2008. *Social Movements for Global Democracy.* Baltimore: Johns Hopkins University Press.

Soohoo, Cynthia, Catherine Albira, and Martha Davis. 2007. *Bringing Human Rights Home*. 3 vols. New York: Praeger.

Stabile, Urberto, ed. 2010. *Tan lejos de Dios: Poesía mexicana en la frontera norte*. Mexico City: Endora.

Staudt, Kathleen. 1987. "Programming Women's Empowerment: A Case from Northern Mexico." In Ruiz and Tiano 1987: 155–173.

———. 1998. *Free Trade? Informal Economies at the U.S.–Mexico Border*. Philadelphia: Temple University Press.

———. 2008. *Violence and Activism at the U.S.–Mexico Border: Gender, Fear, and Everyday Life in Ciudad Juárez*. Austin: University of Texas Press.

———. 2009. "Violence at the Border: Broadening the Discourse to Include Feminism, Human Security, and Deeper Democracy." In Staudt, Payan, and Kruszewski 2009: 1–27.

———. 2010. "Strengthening Law Enforcement, Democratic, and Economic Institutions to Confront the Crisis in Ciudad Juárez." Americas Program (English and Spanish) of the Center for International Policy. http://www.cipamericas.org /archives/3403.

———. 2011. "Rethinking National Security Policies and Practices in Transnational Contexts." In *Security and Everyday Life*, edited by Vida Bajc and Willem de Lint, 101–121. New York: Routledge, 2011.

———. 2014. "The Persistence of Femicide amid Transnational Activist Networks." In *Binational Human Rights: The U.S.-Mexico Experience*, 165–180, edited by William Simmons and Carol Mueller. Philadelphia: University of Pennsylvania Press.

Staudt, Kathleen, and Irasema Coronado. 2002. *Fronteras No Más: Toward Social Justice at the U.S.–Mexico Border*. New York: Palgrave.

Staudt, Kathleen, César Fuentes, and Julia Monárrez Fragoso, eds. 2010. *Cities and Citizenship at the U.S.–Mexico Border: The Paso del Norte Metropolitan Region*. New York: Palgrave.

Staudt, Kathleen, and Beto O'Rourke. 2013. "Challenging Foreign Policy from the Border: The Forty Year War on Drugs." In Payan, Staudt, and Kruszewsi 2013: 217–238.

Staudt, Kathleen, Tony Payan, and Timothy Dunn. 2009. "Closing Reflections: Bordering Human Rights, Social Democratic Feminism, and Broad-Based Security." In Staudt, Payan, and Kruszewski 2009: 185–202.

Staudt, Kathleen, Tony Payan, and Z. Anthony Kruszewski, eds. 2009. *Human Rights along the U.S.–Mexico Border: Gendered Violence and Insecurity*. Tucson: University of Arizona Press.

Tabuenca Córdova, María Socorro. 2010. "Ghost Dance in Ciudad Juárez at the End/ Beginning of the Millennium." In Gaspar de Alba 2005: 95–120.

———, ed. 2011. *Mi Vida en Juárez*.

Tarrow, Sidney. 1998. *Power in Movement: Social Movements and Contentious Politics*. Cambridge: Cambridge University Press.

Tiano, Susan. 1994. *Patriarchy on the Line: Labor, Gender, and Ideology in the Mexican Maquila Industry*. Philadelphia: Temple University Press.

Time. 2011. "Person of the Year 2011: The Protester." Special issue, *Time*. December 19. http://www.time.com/time/specials/packages/article/0,28804,2101745_21021 38_2102238,00.html #ixzz1gYSnZ2Ke.

Tribunal Permanente de los Pueblos, Capítulo México. 2011–2014. *Boletín No. 1.* Mexico City. http://www.tppmexico.org/documentos/.

Tribunal Permanente de los Pueblos. 2012. "Libre Comercio, violencia, impunidad y derechos de los pueblos en México, 2011–2014." Dictamen. Rome: Segretaría General: Fondazione Basso. http://www.internazionaleleliobasso.it/?p=2655.

Turati, Marcela. 2011. *Fuego cruzado: Las víctimas atrapadas en la guerra del narco.* Mexico City: Grijalvo.

———. 2012. "Y todos somos Juárez, gran negocio." *Proceso,* no. 1879 (November 4): 17–21.

Turati, Marcela, and Daniela Rea. 2012. *Entre las cenizas: Historias de vida en tiempos de muerte.* Mexico City: Sur+ Ediciones.

UNESCO. 2012. "The Safety of Journalists and the Danger of Impunity." Report by the Director-General. http://www.unesco.org/new/fileadmin/MULTIMEDIA /HQ/CI/CI/pdf/IPDC/ipdc_dg_safety_report_rev.pdf.

United Nations. 2011. *La libertad de expresión en México: Informes de las relatorias de la ONU y de la CIDH.* Mexico City: Oficina del Alto Comisionado de las Naciones Unidas para los Derechos Humanos.

United Nations High Commissioner for Human Rights. 2010. "Actualización 2010: Informe sobre la situación de las y los defensores de derechos humanos en México." November. http://www.hchr.org.mx/Documentos/Libros/2010/ L241110B.pdf.

United States Customs and Border Protection. 2008. Press release: "Significant Enforcement Activity Highlights Recently Completed Fiscal Year for CBP." December. Washington, DC: Department of Homeland Security Customs and Border Protection.

———. 2011. Press release: "Significant Enforcement Activity Highlights Recently Completed Fiscal Year for CBP." December 11. Washington, DC: Department of Homeland Security Customs and Border Protection.

United States Department of Justice. 2012. "Immigration Courts FY2011 Asylum Statistics." February. http://www.justice.gov/eoir/efoia/FY11AsyStats-Current.pdf.

———. 2013. "Immigration Courts FY2012 Asylum Statistics." February. http://www .justice.gov/eoir/efoia/FY12AsyStats-Current.pdf.

United States Department of State. "Mérida Initiative." http://www.state.gov/j/inl /merida/.

———. 2009. "Remarks by Secretary Clinton." March 26. http://www.state.gov /secretary/rm/2009a/03/120955/htm. (No longer on the website.)

Valencia, Nick. 2010. "Jobs Seen as Way to Quell Juarez Violence." CNN. May 6.

Vila, Pablo. 2000. *Crossing Borders, Reinforcing Borders: Social Categories, Metaphors, and Narrative Identities on the U.S.–Mexico Frontier.* Austin: University of Texas Press.

———. 2005. *Border Identifications: Narratives of Religion, Gender, and Class on the U.S.–Mexico Border.* Austin: University of Texas Press.

Villalobos, José. 2013. "A Federalist George W. Bush and an Anti-Federalist Barack Obama: The Irony behind the Republican and Democratic Administration Drug Policies." In Payan, Staudt, and Kruszewski 2013: 174–192.

Vulliamy, Ed. 2010. *Amexica: War along the Borderline.* New York: Farrar, Straus, & Giroux.

Washington Valdez, Diana. 2005. *Cosecha de mujeres: Safari en el desierto mexicano*. Mexico City: Oceano.

———. 2006. *The Killing Fields: Harvest of Women*. Los Angeles: Peace at the Border.

———. 2011. "Initiative Aids Juárez along Road to Recovery." *El Paso Times*, October 9, A1, A5.

Wilson, Thomas M., and Hastings Donnan. 2012. "Borders and Border Studies." In *A Companion to Border Studies*, edited by Thomas M. Wilson and Hastings Donnan. London: Blackwell.

Winn, Peter. 2006. *The Americas*. 3rd ed. Berkeley: University of California Press.

World Bank. 2011. "GINI Index." http://data.worldbank.org/indicator/SI.POV.GINI.

Wright, Melissa W. 2010. "Femicide, Mother-Activism, and the Geography of Protest in Northern Mexico." In Gaspar de Alba 2005: 211–252.

Young, Gay. 1987. "Gender Identification and Working-Class Solidarity among Maquila Workers in Ciudad Juárez: Stereotypes and Realities." In Ruiz and Tiano 1987: 105–128.

Zepeda Lecuona, Guillermo. 2002. "Inefficiencies at the Service of Impunity: Criminal Justice Organizations in Mexico." In *Transnational Crime and Public Security*, edited by John Bailey and Jorge Chabat, 71–107. La Jolla: University of California at San Diego, Center for U.S.–Mexican Studies.